Why Daydream Education?

Daydream Education, the UK's leading provider of educational posters, has developed a versatile range of colourful and engaging revision guides that break down barriers to learning and encourage independent study.

Small in size, huge in content!

Designed to engage learners, our revision guides are the perfect alternative to the larger text-heavy revision guides. The accessible revision guides simplify key GCSE content into bitesize chunks of information to improve students' understanding and boost confidence.

" Daydream's new Revision Guides are colourful, engaging, clear, concise and up-to-date for the new GCSE specifications. The books ensure that students have exactly the right information for their exams, and I cannot recommend them highly enough. **"**

Anna Woodward
Teacher

Daydream Education | Unit 1 | Central Park | Western Avenue | Bridgend | CF31 3RH
Tel: 0844 800 1660 | www.daydreameducation.co.uk
Chris Malcolm Ltd. t/a Daydream Education. Registered in England and Wales. Company No: 04216204

GCSE Biology

Contents

Microscopy

Microscopes create magnified images of objects, such as cells, so they can be seen in more detail.

Light Microscope

The light microscope uses light waves and lenses to magnify objects.

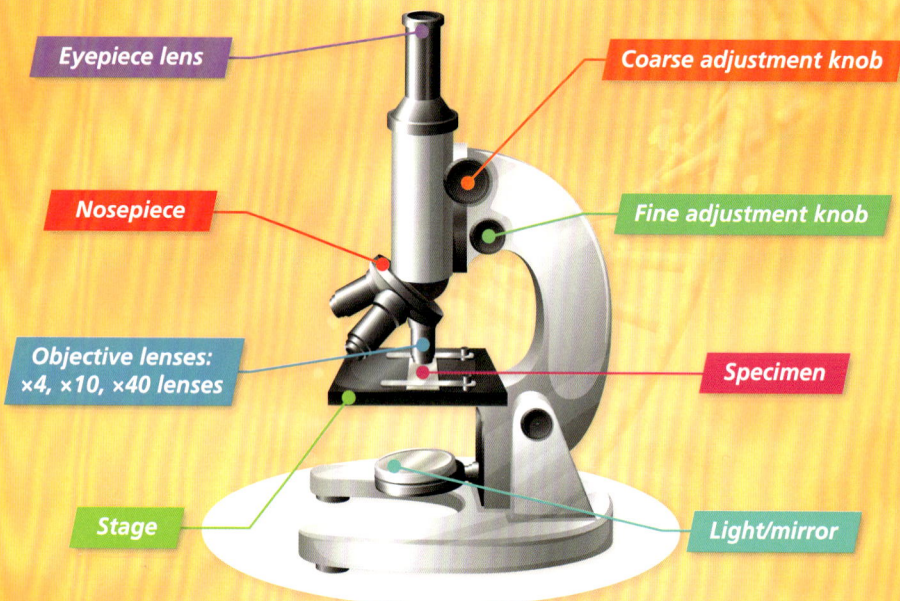

- Eyepiece lens
- Coarse adjustment knob
- Nosepiece
- Fine adjustment knob
- Objective lenses: ×4, ×10, ×40 lenses
- Specimen
- Stage
- Light/mirror

Onion cell biological drawing (Magnification × 100)

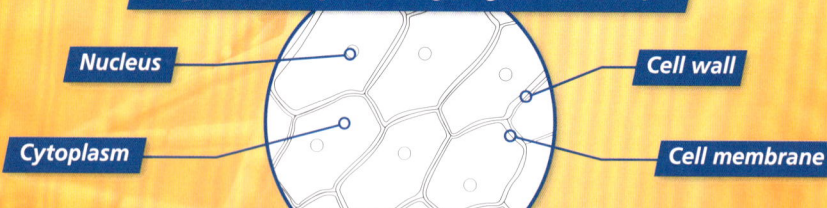

- Nucleus
- Cell wall
- Cytoplasm
- Cell membrane

$$\text{Total magnification} = \text{Magnification of eyepiece lens} \times \text{Magnification of objective lens}$$

Magnification is how much larger an image is compared to the real object.

$$\text{Actual Size} = \frac{\text{Image size}}{\text{Magnification}}$$

I
A | M

Microscopic objects are measured using these units:		
Millimetres	mm	$1 \times 10^{-3}\,m$
Micrometres	µm	$1 \times 10^{-6}\,m$
Nanometres	nm	$1 \times 10^{-9}\,m$
Picometres	pm	$1 \times 10^{-12}\,m$

daydream
EDUCATION

The image of a cell viewed at ×40 magnification has a diameter of 1 mm.
What is the cell's real diameter?

1	Substitute the numbers into the formula:	Actual size = $\dfrac{1}{40}$
2	Solve:	*Actual size = 0.025 mm or 25 µm*

Electron Microscope

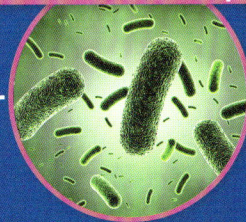

The electron microscope uses a beam of electrons to magnify objects.

The light microscope was invented in the 16th century, but a major advance in microscopy came in the 1930s with the invention of the electron microscope.

An electron microscope has a much higher magnification and resolution than a light microscope so smaller things can be seen in more detail.

Resolution is the ability to distinguish between two separate points.

A typical light microscope has a **resolving power** of 200 nm. This means it can distinguish between points 200 nm apart. The resolving power of an electron microscope is up to 0.2 nm.

The development of electron microscopes has enabled scientists to see structures more clearly and in more detail, which has increased our understanding of microscopic objects such as cells.

Light Microscope

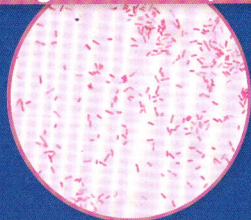

Electron Microscope

Bacteria viewed on a light microscope and an electron microscope

Microscope Practical Activity

Use a light microscope to observe, draw and label a selection of plant and animal cells.

1 To view a specimen under a light microscope, it must be mounted correctly on a slide, a strip of clear glass or plastic used with microscopes.

2 Follow these steps to mount a specimen.

— Cover slip

Place a drop of water on the centre of the slide.	**Position the specimen on the liquid.**	**At an angle, place a cover slip against the slide, and gently lower it to avoid air bubbles.**

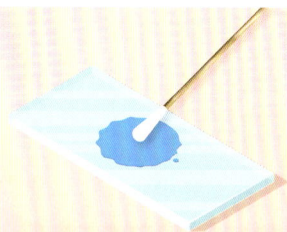

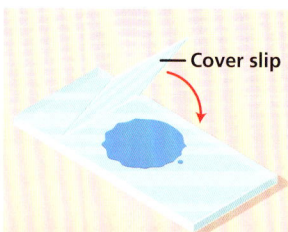

Remove excess water with a paper towel. You may also need to add a stain, such as iodine solution, to help highlight the different parts of the specimen.

3 Once the slide is prepared, clip it on the microscope stage.

4 Turn the nose piece to select the lowest power objective lens.

5 Turn the coarse adjustment knob to position the lens just above the slide.

6 Look through the eyepiece, and slowly turn the coarse adjustment knob to move the slide away from the lens until the cells come into focus.

7 Slightly turn the fine adjustment knob to bring the cells into clear focus.

8 When you have found some cells, turn the nose piece to switch to a higher power lens. Bring the cells back into focus by using the fine adjustment knob.

9 Using a pencil, make a labelled drawing of some of the cells. Do not add any colour or shading.

10 Write the magnification underneath your drawing. Remember to multiply the objective magnification by the eyepiece magnification.

Human cheek cell viewed at 400 × magnification

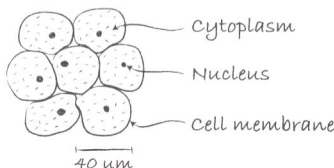

Cytoplasm
Nucleus
Cell membrane
40 um

daydream
EDUCATION

Cell Structure

All known living things are made up of one cell or more. Cells can be either prokaryotic or eukaryotic.

Prokaryotic

Prokaryotic cells, such as bacteria, are single celled organisms. They are a lot smaller than eukaryotic cells and their genetic material is not enclosed in a nucleus.

Plasmid
Small loops of DNA that are not part of the chromosomal DNA

Chromosomal DNA
A long loop of genetic material that is not enclosed in a nucleus

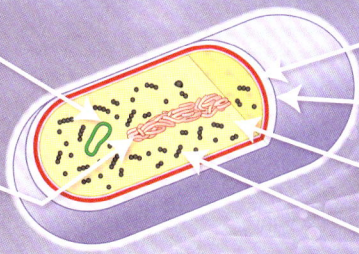

Cell Membrane

Cell Wall

Cytoplasm

Ribosomes

Eukaryotic

Eukaryotic cells are found in animals and plants, as well as in fungi and protists. They have a cell membrane, cytoplasm and genetic material that is enclosed in a nucleus.

Animal Cells
Most animal cells have the following subcellular structure:

Nucleus
Contains genetic material

Cytoplasm
Made up of a liquid gel that holds all cellular organelles; the place where chemical reactions occur

Ribosomes
The place where proteins are produced

Mitochondria
The place where aerobic respiration, which releases energy, occurs

Cell Membrane
A thin, selectively permeable membrane that controls which substances can enter and exit the cell

Plant Cells
Most plant cells have the same subcellular structure as animal cells, plus:

Cell Wall
Made of cellulose, which strengthens and protects the cell

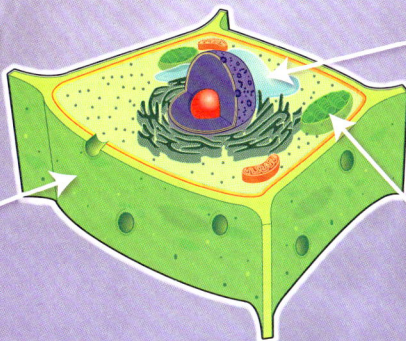

Large Central Vacuole
Filled with cell sap; stores materials and waste; and keeps the cell turgid (rigid)

Chloroplasts
Contains chlorophyll; the place where photosynthesis occurs

Cell Specialisation & Differentiation

Cell Specialisation
Cells may be specialised to carry out a specific function.

Animal Cells

Sperm Cells

The **acrosome** contains enzymes to help break down the egg membrane.

Mitochondria provide energy to power the tail.

The **haploid nucleus** contains half the number of chromosomes of a normal cell.

The **long tail** and streamlined shape enable the sperm to swim to the egg.

Nerve Cells

Nerve cells (neurons) are highly specialised for transmitting impulses around the body. They are long and have branched connections to join to other neurons and form networks.

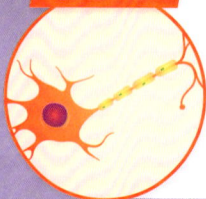

Muscle Cells

Muscle cells contain lots of mitochondria to provide energy. These cells can contract and relax, and they can also store glucose as glycogen.

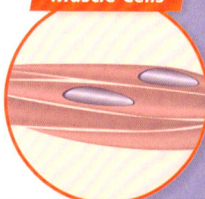

Plant Cells

Xylem Cells

Xylem vessels transport water and strengthen plant structures. They are made of dead cells that have lost their end walls and cytoplasm to become hollow tubes for transporting water. Their walls are thickened with lignin to provide strength.

Root Hair Cells

Root hair cells are found in the roots of plants and are specialised for absorbing water and mineral ions. They have hair-like projections that provide a large surface area for water absorption.

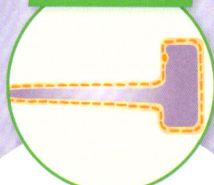

Phloem Cells

Phloem vessels transport sugars (sucrose) in plants. Phloem cells have perforated end walls and a very thin layer of cytoplasm to aid transport. Each cell has an attached companion cell, which supplies materials the cytoplasm normally makes.

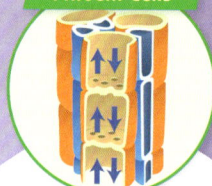

Cell Differentiation

When new cells are formed in organisms, they are simple in form. However, over time, they differentiate (become specialised) to form different types of cells.

Most types of animal cell differentiate early in life – many in the embryo – whereas many types of plant cell retain the ability to differentiate throughout their life.

In mature animals, new cells are still formed by cell division to replace old cells and to repair tissues. As the cell differentiates into a specialised cell, it adopts different subcellular structures. For example, cells in the bone marrow differentiate into new red blood cells. The cells lose their nucleus, change shape and become filled with the red, oxygen-carrying pigment, haemoglobin.

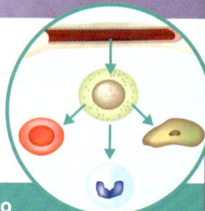

daydream EDUCATION

Binary Fission

Prokaryotes, such as bacteria, multiply by simple cell division, known as binary fission. Under ideal conditions (at a suitable temperature and with sufficient nutrients), a bacterium can divide once every 20 minutes.

The **mean division time** is the average amount of time it takes for one bacterium to divide.

Step 1

DNA Replication
The one circular chromosome replicates.

Step 2

Growth
The cell gets bigger and becomes elongated as the two chromosomes move to opposite ends of the cell.

Step 3

Cell Separation
A septum forms down the middle of the cell, and a cell wall begins to develop.

Step 4

Daughter Cells Form
The cell divides into two daughter cells that are genetically identical.

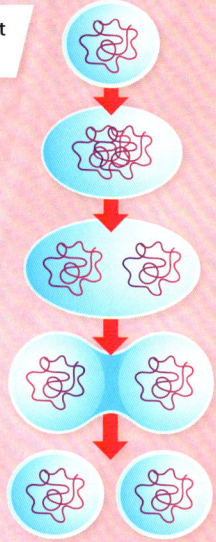

Bacteria and other prokaryotic cells are less complex than eukaryotic cells. Therefore, binary fission is a faster means of cellular division than **mitosis**.

Estimating Bacterial Populations

If a bacterium divides once every 20 minutes (its mean division time), the population of the bacteria will double every 20 minutes. If there are 100 bacteria to begin, how large would the bacterial population be 4 hours later?

1	Calculate how many times each bacterium will divide in 4 hours.	4 hours = 240 minutes $240 \div 20 = 12$ Each bacterium will divide 12 times.
2	Find the population size by using the following equation:	Population size = starting amount $\times 2^{\text{number of divisions}}$ $= 100 \times 2^{12}$ $= 409{,}600$

The answer expressed in **standard form** is 4.096×10^5.

daydream EDUCATION

Culturing Microorganisms

Aseptic Technique

Many bacteria have similar requirements. Therefore, when growing bacteria, it is essential that the cultures are not contaminated by other unwanted bacteria.

Aseptic technique involves practices and procedures to prevent microorganisms from contaminating cultures or escaping into the environment. Although most microorganisms are harmless, some can be dangerous to health.

Culture Media

The culture medium is the material in which microorganisms are grown. There are two main types of culture medium.

Nutrient Broth

The microorganisms live in this liquid, which contains essential nutrients.

Agar

The microorganisms grow and form visible colonies on the surface of this jelly, to which essential nutrients have been added.

The culture medium and any container it is put into, such as a petri dish or test tube, must be sterilised before use, to prevent unknown bacteria being transferred into the culture.

Similarly, care must be taken when transferring bacteria from a broth culture to an agar 'plate' with an inoculating loop. Follow the steps outlined below to prevent contamination.

1 Pass the loop through a flame.

2 Remove the bung, and flame the mouth of the tube.

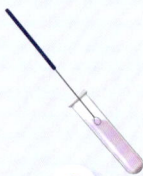

3 Dip the loop into the broth to pick up the bacteria.

4 Flame the mouth of the tube, and replace the bung.

5 Streak the loop across the agar surface to inoculate the agar plate with the bacteria.

Flaming kills bacteria so no live bacteria enter or leave the tube. Carrying out the technique near a lit Bunsen burner also creates a convection current that carries any bacteria in the air upward, away from the agar plate.

Uncontaminated cultures of microorganisms are vital for investigating the action of disinfectants and antibiotics.

daydream
EDUCATION

Individual microorganisms are invisible to the naked eye. To work with them, scientists must grow them into populations that are large enough to see.

Incubation

Once the bacteria have been transferred to an agar plate, they are then incubated so that the microorganisms can grow.

The incubation temperature should not be near 37°C (human body temperature) as this will encourage the growth of dangerous bacteria. In school labs, 25°C is recommended.

- During incubation, the lid of the Petri dish containing the agar plate should be lightly fastened with sticky tape.

- When lifting the Petri dish lid, open it very slightly. Do not remove it completely. This will prevent bacteria in the air dropping onto the plate.

Colony

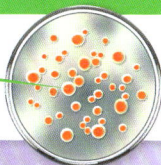

After incubation, each bacterium will have grown into a circular colony. By counting the colonies, we know how many bacteria were initially placed on the plate.

Calculating Colony Areas

Bacterial colonies usually grow in a circular form so their areas can be calculated using the formula:

$$Area = \pi r^2$$

$\pi = 3.142$ r = radius of circle

Investigating the Effects of Antiseptics or Antibiotics on Bacterial Growth

The area of the inhibition zone indicates the effectiveness of the antiseptic or antibiotic on the bacteria. The larger the area, the more effective the antiseptic or antibiotic.

When a sterile antiseptic or antibiotic disc is placed on a bacterial culture, it diffuses out, destroying or inhibiting the growth of bacteria over a certain area, the inhibition zone. The size of the inhibition zone can be calculated by using the area of a circle formula above.

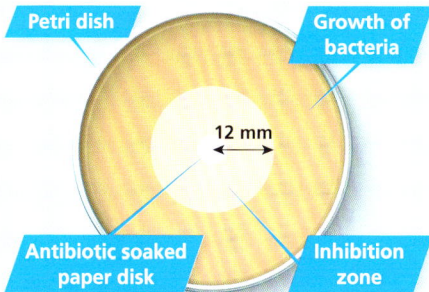

Petri dish

Growth of bacteria

12 mm

Antibiotic soaked paper disk

Inhibition zone

The diagram opposite shows the inhibition zone produced by a new antibiotic. Calculate the area of the inhibition zone:

Calculate the area of the inhibition zone:

$$Area = \pi r^2$$
$$= 3.142 \times 12^2$$
$$= 452.4 \text{ mm}^2$$

Cell Division & the Cell Cycle

Cells divide in a series of stages called the cell cycle. In multicellular organisms, cell division is used for growth and repairing damaged tissues. It is also used by some organisms for asexual reproduction.

Chromosomes

The nucleus of a cell contains structures called chromosomes, which are made of DNA molecules. Along each chromosome are sections called genes.

Each gene controls the manufacture of a particular protein, and these proteins determine the characteristics of the organism. In body cells, the chromosomes exist in pairs. For instance, in humans, there are 23 pairs.

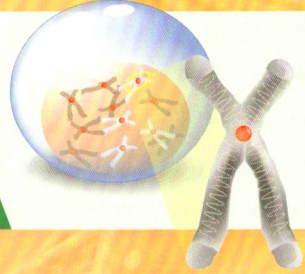

Mitosis and the Cell Cycle

During the cell cycle, a cell's DNA and subcellular structures are replicated before the cell divides by a process called mitosis to produce two identical daughter cells.

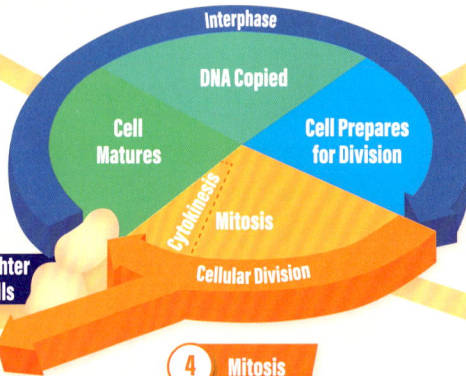

2 DNA Copied

The DNA replicates to form two copies of each chromosome, and the copies form an X shape.

Interphase

DNA Copied

Cell Matures

Cell Prepares for Division

Cytokinesis

Mitosis

Cellular Division

Daughter Cells

1 Cell Matures

Before dividing, a cell needs to grow and increase the number of subcellular structures such as ribosomes and mitochondria.

3 Cell Prepares for Division

The cell grows quickly and continues with protein synthesis in preparation for mitosis. Any damaged DNA is also repaired.

4 Mitosis

During mitosis, cells divide into identical cells. Each set of chromosomes is pulled to either end of the cell, and the nucleus divides.

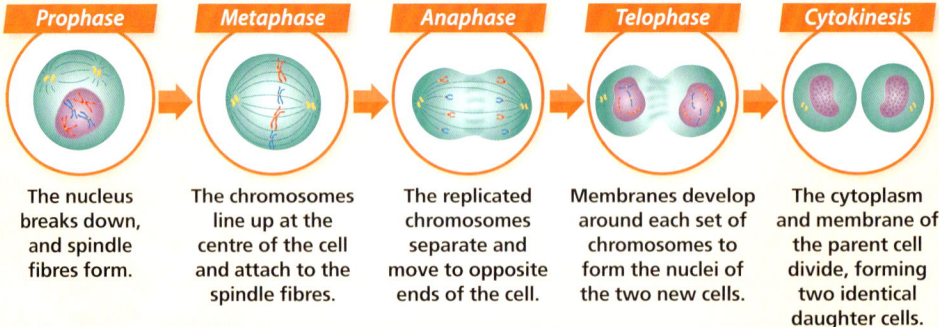

Prophase	Metaphase	Anaphase	Telophase	Cytokinesis
The nucleus breaks down, and spindle fibres form.	The chromosomes line up at the centre of the cell and attach to the spindle fibres.	The replicated chromosomes separate and move to opposite ends of the cell.	Membranes develop around each set of chromosomes to form the nuclei of the two new cells.	The cytoplasm and membrane of the parent cell divide, forming two identical daughter cells.

In plant cells, a new cell wall will form to divide the cells.

daydream EDUCATION

Stem Cells

A stem cell is an undifferentiated cell (i.e. one that has not yet specialised) that can give rise to more cells of the same type or can develop into certain other cells by differentiation.

Stem Cells in Embryos

At an early stage of development, an embryo is a ball of cells. Each cell will divide and later give rise to all the different types of cells in the body.

These cells can be cloned and made to develop into most cell types in a laboratory.

Stem Cells in Adult Animals

Stem cells are present in adult animals. For example, bone marrow inside the cavities of bones can naturally form blood cells.

These cells can also be manipulated in a laboratory to differentiate into some other cell types.

Stem Cells in Plants

Plants have stem cells that can develop into all types of plant cell throughout the life of the plant.

They are mainly found in specific growing points, called meristems, at the tips of roots and shoots.

Medical Uses of Stem Cells

Stem cells can potentially be used to replace damaged cells and repair tissues. Therefore, they can be used to help with conditions such as type 1 diabetes and paralysis. However, if a patient is treated with stem cells from another individual, the immune system may attack the new cells and reject them.

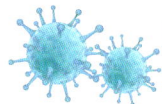

The use of stem cells has some potential risks. For example, viruses live inside cells, and it is possible that a viral infection could be transferred in the stem cells.

Some people also have ethical or religious objections because embryos are destroyed when obtaining stem cells. Although adult stem cells can be used for some treatments, they cannot develop into as many types of cell as embryonic stem cells can.

In therapeutic cloning, a nucleus is taken from a cell of the patient and transplanted into an unfertilised egg cell. The egg cell can then produce stem cells that are genetically identical to those of the patient and will not be rejected.

Uses of Plant Stem Cells

Meristem cells in plants are mainly used to produce clones – and specifically, large numbers of genetically identical plants.

Rare species can be cloned to protect from extinction, and when new varieties of crop plants are produced with beneficial features (e.g. disease resistance), they can be cloned to produce large numbers of plants quickly.

daydream EDUCATION

Diffusion

Diffusion is the spreading out of gas or solute particles from an area of higher concentration to an area of lower concentration.

Diffusion takes place across cell membranes to enable the movement of substances into and out of cells.

Particles move both ways across a membrane. However, if there are more particles on one side, the net (overall) movement will be from an area of higher concentration to an area of lower concentration until the concentrations on both sides are equal.

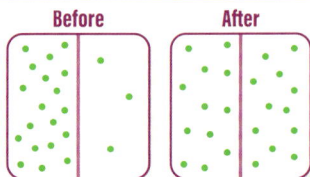

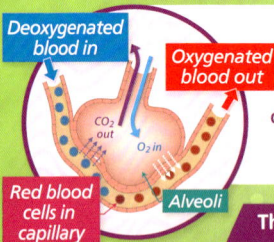

Before   After

In the lungs, oxygen from the air diffuses into the blood in the capillaries. Carbon dioxide from the blood diffuses into the air in the alveoli.

Deoxygenated blood in
Oxygenated blood out
CO_2 out
O_2 in
Red blood cells in capillary
Alveoli

Urea is a waste product produced in liver cells. It diffuses from cells into the blood, and then travels to the kidneys where it is excreted.

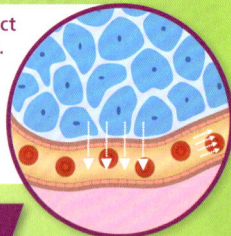

The following factors affect the rate of diffusion:

Concentration Gradient

The bigger the difference between the concentrations, the faster the rate of diffusion.

Membrane Surface Area

The larger the surface area of the membrane, the faster the rate of diffusion, because more particles can pass through at the same time.

Temperature

At a higher temperature, particles have more energy and therefore move quicker.

Surface Area to Volume Ratio

As a cell gets larger, its **surface area** to **volume ratio** gets smaller. You can calculate and compare **surface area** to **volume ratio** as follows.

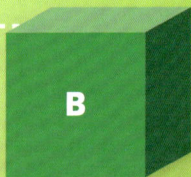

A

B

Shape	Side Length	Area of Each Face	Total Surface Area	Volume	Surface Area to Volume Ratio
A	2 cm	$2 \times 2 = 4$ cm^2	$4 \times 6 = 24$ cm^2	$2 \times 2 \times 2 = 8$ cm^3	24:8 = 3:1
B	4 cm	$4 \times 4 = 16$ cm^2	$16 \times 6 = 96$ cm^2	$4 \times 4 \times 4 = 64$ cm^3	96:64 = 3:2

The table above shows that shape A has a surface area to volume ratio of 3:1, and that shape B has a surface area to volume ratio of 3:2. Therefore, the surface area to volume ratio of shape A (the smaller shape) is larger than surface area to volume ratio of shape B.

daydream EDUCATION

Single-Celled Organisms and Multicellular Organisms

A single-celled organism has a large surface area to volume ratio. As a result, its surface area is large enough to allow sufficient diffusion of substances through its membranes to meet its needs.

However, larger multicellular organisms have smaller surface area to volume ratios and therefore need specialised gas exchange surfaces and transport systems to assist with the exchange of substances.

Capillary
Alveoli
Bronchus
Ciliated cell
Goblet cell

Look at how the lungs are adapted to increase gas exchange.

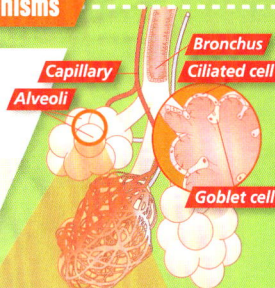

1 The lungs contain millions of tiny air sacs called alveoli, which provide a **large surface area** for gas exchange.

2 The walls of the alveoli are only one cell thick, creating a **short diffusion path**. They are also moist, so oxygen and carbon dioxide can be dissolved and diffused more quickly.

3 The alveoli are covered in a mesh of capillaries, which provide a **constant supply of blood** so that large volumes of gases can be exchanged.

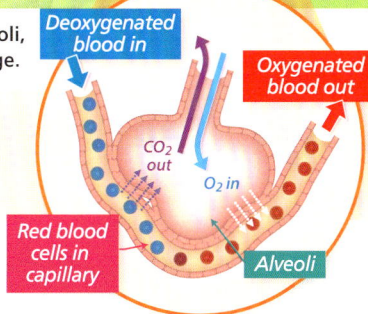

Deoxygenated blood in
Oxygenated blood out
CO_2 out
O_2 in
Red blood cells in capillary
Alveoli

Oxygen diffuses from the air into the blood, and carbon dioxide diffuses from the blood into the air. Both do so along **steep concentration gradients**, which are maintained by **ventilation** and the flow of blood through capillaries in the lungs.

Other Examples

Mammals

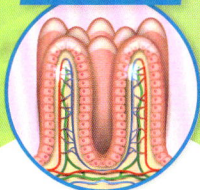

The small intestines are lined with tiny projections called villi, which aid the absorption of nutrients. They have a large surface area, thin walls (one cell thick) and a good blood supply.

Plants

Plant leaves have a large surface area to maximise the absorption of carbon dioxide. They are also thin so that carbon dioxide does not have far to diffuse into the leaf.

Fish

Fish have specially adapted gills that are highly folded to provide a large surface area. The flow of water and blood through the gills also ensures steep concentration gradients.

Active Transport & Osmosis

Active Transport

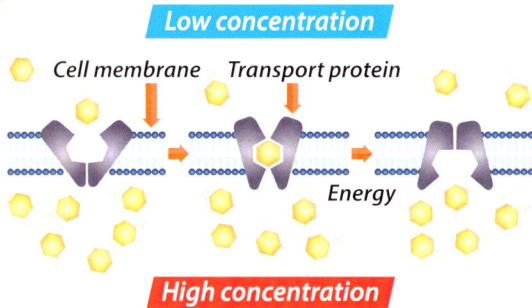

Low concentration

Cell membrane   Transport protein

Energy

High concentration

Active transport occurs when molecules need to be moved against a concentration gradient or they are too big to diffuse through the membrane. This process requires energy from respiration.

Transport proteins capture the molecules and transfer them across the cell membrane.

Active transport is used by plants to take up mineral ions from the soil because the concentration of mineral ions is much lower in the soil than in the root cells.

Active transport is also used to absorb sugar molecules from the gut into the blood. This allows absorption to continue even if the concentration of sugar in the gut is lower than in the blood.

Osmosis

Osmosis is the diffusion of water across a partially permeable membrane from a dilute solution to a concentrated solution.

A partially permeable membrane allows molecules to pass through it in both directions. However, large molecules, such as salt, are too big to fit through.

If the concentration of water is higher on one side of the membrane, it will diffuse through the membrane to the side where the concentration is lower. The net movement will stop when the concentration of water is the same on both sides.

Osmosis is used by plants to absorb water from the soil through their root hair cells.

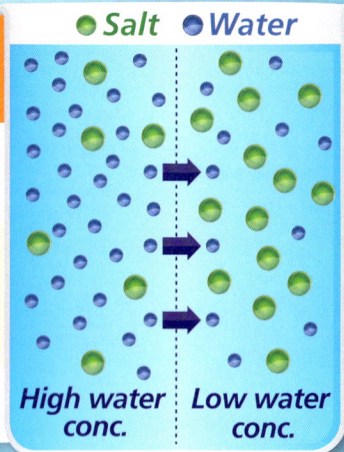

● **Salt**   ● **Water**

High water conc.   **Low water conc.**

Osmosis can cause tissue to gain or lose mass. To calculate the change in mass, the following formula can be used:

$$\text{Percentage change in mass} = \frac{\text{Change in mass}}{\text{Initial mass}} \times 100$$

daydream EDUCATION

Osmosis can be investigated by placing cylinders of potato into different concentrations of salt or sugar solution. In this activity, we will use sugar.

1 Cut the potatoes into evenly sized cylinders so that they have the same surface area.

2 Pour different concentrations of sugar solution (0.2 molL^{-1}, 0.4 molL^{-1}, 0.6 molL^{-1}, 0.8 molL^{-1}) into beakers.

3 Measure the mass of each cylinder.
Then place one in each beaker and leave them for 24 hours.

4 Take the cylinders out of the solution, dry them and then measure their masses again.

5 Calculate the percentage change in mass of each potato using the formula:

$$\% \text{ Change in mass} = \frac{\text{Change in mass}}{\text{Original mass}} \times 100$$

6 Plot a graph to show the results, with sugar concentration on the x-axis and percentage change in mass on the y-axis.

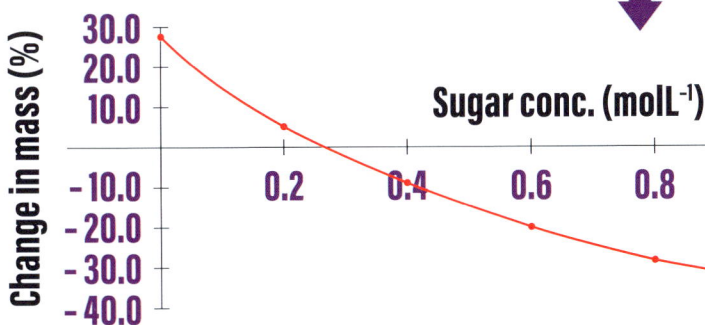

If the cylinder has decreased in mass, it has lost water. If the cylinder has increased in mass, it has gained water. If there is no change in mass, the concentrations of the solution and the potato sap are the same, and water moves in and out at equal rates.

Cell Organisation & Organ Systems

Cells	Tissue	Organs	Organ Systems
Cells are the basic building blocks of all living organisms.	A tissue is a group of cells with a similar structure and function.	Organs are collections of different tissues that perform specific functions.	Organs work together in systems to form organisms.

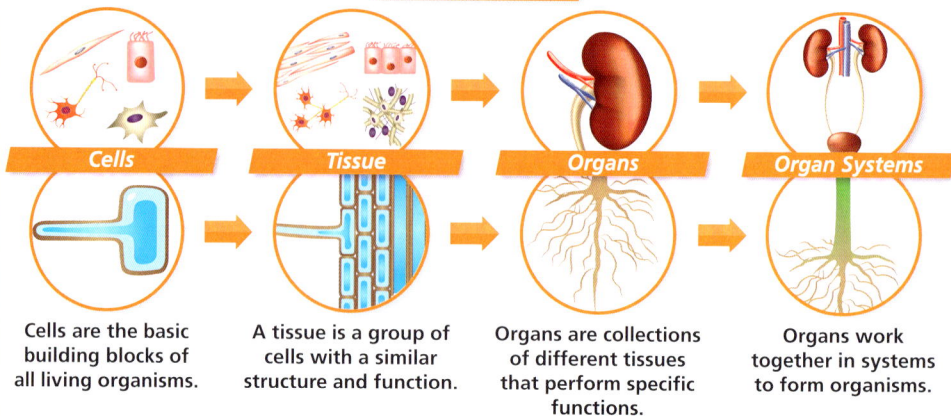

Some Human Organs

Lungs
The lungs help us breathe. They take in oxygen from the air and expel carbon dioxide into the air.

Heart
The heart is a pump. It pumps blood around the body.

Stomach
The stomach helps to digest food before it passes into the intestines.

Pancreas
The pancreas helps with the digestion of food by secreting digestive enzymes. It also secretes the hormones insulin and glucagon to help control blood sugar levels.

Kidneys
The kidneys filter waste from the blood and expel excess water and salts from the body in the form of urine.

Brain
The brain is the control centre for movement, sleep, hunger, thirst and virtually every other vital activity necessary for survival.

Liver
The liver is like a chemical factory that adjusts food levels in the blood. It removes toxins from the blood and generates body heat.

Small Intestine
The small intestine is the longest section of the digestive system and is where most digestion occurs.

Large Intestine
Indigestible food goes to the large intestine. Water is absorbed, and the remaining food becomes faeces.

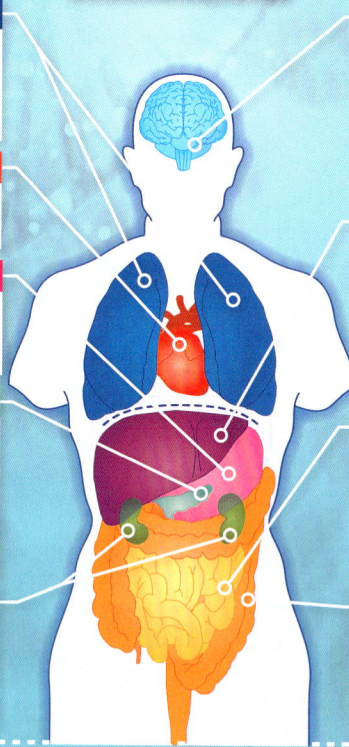

daydream
EDUCATION

The 11 Human Organ Systems

The human body is made up of 11 major organ systems.

Digestive System

Digests (breaks down) and absorbs food so that it can be used by the body

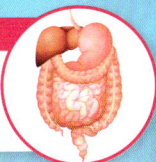

Muscular System

Controls movement and helps to maintain posture

Circulatory System

Circulates blood and transports oxygen, carbon dioxide and nutrients around the body

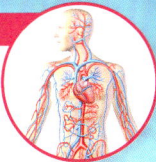

Respiratory System

Facilitates gaseous exchange by moving air into the lungs and removing carbon dioxide

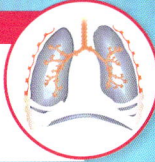

Skeletal System

Performs vital functions, including support, movement, protection, blood cell production, calcium storage and endocrine regulation

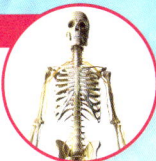

Integumentary System

Protects the body from damage and helps with the retention of body fluids, removal of waste and regulation of body temperature

Lymphatic & Immune System

Protects against infection, returns excess interstitial fluid to the circulatory system and transports dietary fats

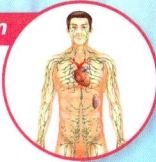

Endocrine System

Secretes hormones into the bloodstream to regulate bodily functions such as metabolism, growth and tissue function

Urinary System

Removes waste from the body as urine; regulates water and salt levels in the blood

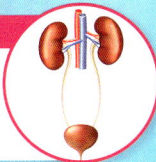

Nervous System

Coordinates actions and transmits signals to and from different parts of the body

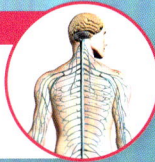

Reproductive System

Female
Produces egg cells and supports the development of offspring

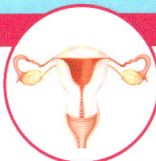

Male
Produces and transports sperm for reproduction

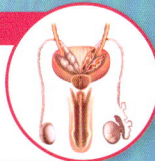

daydream
EDUCATION

The Human Digestive System

In the human digestive system, several organs work together to digest and absorb food.

Food is mostly made up of complex organic compounds (e.g. carbohydrates, proteins, fats) that must be broken down into simple inorganic compounds so that they can be absorbed into the blood system. This breakdown is catalysed by enzymes.

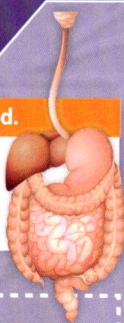

Structure and Function in the Human Digestive System

Mouth
Saliva in the mouth lubricates food and contains the enzyme, amylase, which breaks down starch (a carbohydrate) into maltose sugar.

Liver
The liver makes bile, which is stored in the gall bladder and helps break down fats.

Gall Bladder
The gall bladder stores bile.

Pancreas
The pancreas secretes enzymes that break down various food chemicals in the small intestine.

Rectum
The rectum stores solid waste and then passes it out via the anus.

Oesophagus
The oesophagus moves food to the stomach using peristalsis (wave-like muscle contractions).

Stomach
The stomach releases the enzyme protease, which breaks down proteins into amino acids. Hydrochloric acid in the stomach also kills harmful pathogens.

Small Intestine
Enzymes complete digestion, and nutrients are then absorbed into the blood, so they can be transported around the body.

Large Intestine
The large intestine reabsorbs water.

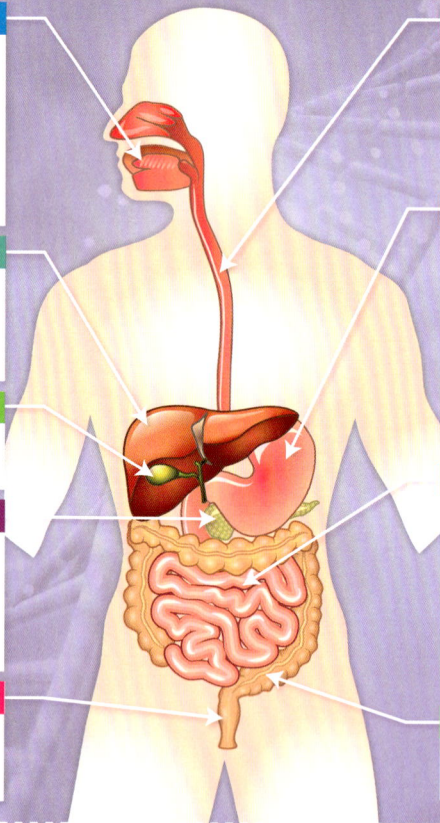

Food Type	Enzymes Used	End Product
Complex carbohydrates	Carbohydrases	Simple sugars
Proteins	Proteases	Amino acids
Lipids (fats)	Lipases	Glycerol and fatty acids

daydream EDUCATION

Bile

Bile is an alkaline digestive fluid produced in the liver and stored in the gall bladder. It is released into the small intestine via the bile duct. It contains no enzymes but serves two vital functions:

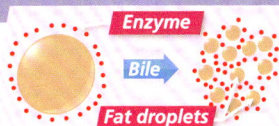

Enzyme
Bile
Fat droplets

1 It neutralises the acid that is added to food in the stomach. If the pH level in the small intestine is too low, the enzymes won't work properly.

2 It emulsifies fats. Large fat droplets are broken up into many smaller ones, so that there is a greater surface area over which enzymes can act.

The products of digestion are used in the body to build new carbohydrates, proteins and fats. Some glucose is used directly to provide energy by respiration.

Practical Activity

There are a wide variety of tests that are used to identify carbohydrates, lipids and proteins.

Testing for Starch

Add iodine solution to the sample. If starch is present, the mixture of the sample and iodine solution will change colour from orange-brown to blue-black.

Iodine solution

Test sample   Positive result

Testing for Simple Sugars

Add Benedict's solution to the sample, and place it in a hot water bath (75–80°C). If sugar is present, a colour change occurs from blue to green, yellow, orange and then red. A precipitate will form, making the sample cloudy.

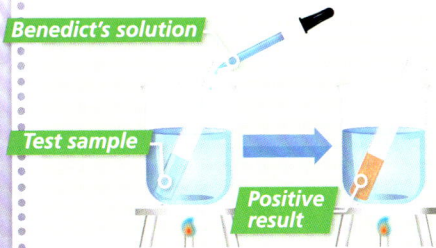

Benedict's solution

Test sample

Positive result

Testing for Protein

Biuret solution is added to the sample, sometimes in two parts: biuret A (sodium hydroxide) and biuret B (copper sulfate). If protein is present, the solution will change colour from blue to purple.

Biuret solution

Test sample   Positive result

Testing for Lipids

Lipids are detected using the emulsion test. Mix the test sample with 2 cm³ of ethanol and add an equal volume of distilled water. If lipids are present a milky-white emulsion will form.

Test sample + ethanol

Distilled water

Positive result

Enzymes

Enzymes are proteins that act as biological catalysts. They are produced by living organisms to speed up chemical reactions in the body.

Key Terminology

Catalyst: Catalysts increase the rate of chemical reactions but are not used up during the reaction. Different reactions need different catalysts.

Enzyme Action

Enzymes are formed from chains of amino acids that are folded in a particular way to create a small pocket called the active site.

The molecule upon which an enzyme acts, or the substrate, also has a specific shape, which fits together with the shape of the active site. This is known as the lock-and-key mechanism. Enzymes can both split apart and join substrates to form products.

The Lock-and-Key Mechanism

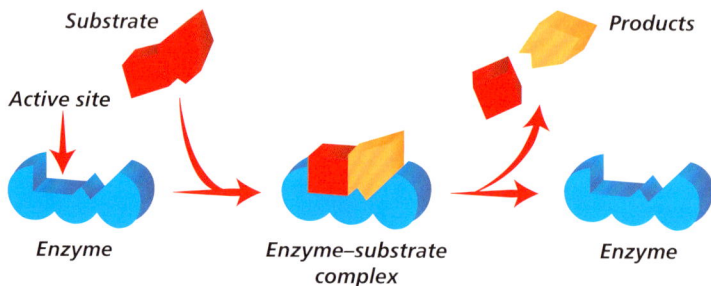

Substrate

Active site

Enzyme

Enzyme–substrate complex

Products

Enzyme

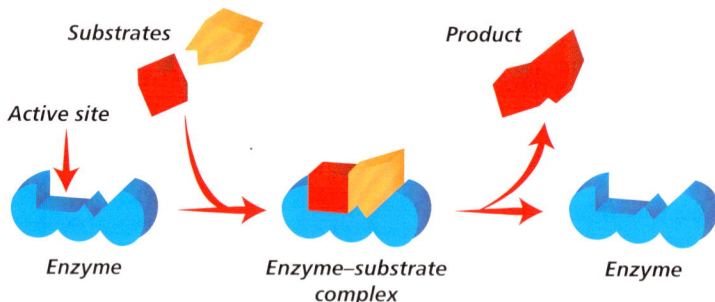

Substrates

Active site

Enzyme

Enzyme–substrate complex

Product

Enzyme

If the shapes of the enzyme and substrate do not match, then the reaction will not be catalysed. Therefore, enzymes can only work with specific substrates. It is now known that the enzyme needs to change its shape slightly to perfectly match the shape of the substrate. This is called the induced-fit model.

daydream EDUCATION

Enzyme Activity

Enzymes are affected by their surrounding conditions. Temperature, pH, and substrate and enzyme concentration are all factors that can affect the rate of enzyme-controlled reactions.

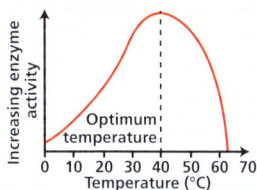

As temperature increases, so does the rate of reaction. However, at high temperatures, some of the bonds that hold the enzyme together break, changing the shape of the active site so the enzyme becomes denatured.

Different enzymes work best at different pHs. If the pH changes too far from the optimum, the bonds holding the enzyme together weaken, changing the shape of the active site so the enzyme becomes denatured.

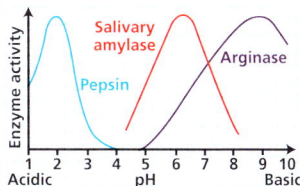

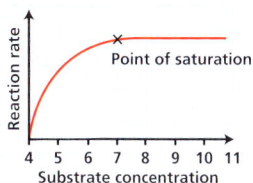

As substrate concentration increases, so does the rate of reaction as there are more substrate molecules to collide with enzyme molecules. However, after a certain concentration, any increase has no effect on the rate of reaction because the enzymes are working at their maximum rate.

Uses of Enzymes

1 Digestion

Enzymes break down large molecules into smaller molecules so they can be used for growth, respiration and other life processes.

Part of a starch molecule → Separate glucose molecules

Complex carbohydrates (starches) are broken down into glucose by carbohydrases such as amylase.

Protein → Amino acids

Proteins are broken down into amino acids by proteases.

Lipid molecule → Fatty acids   Glycerol

Lipids are converted into glycerol and fatty acids by lipases.

2 Metabolism

Metabolism refers to all the chemical reactions in an organism. These reactions use energy and are catalysed by enzymes. Examples include:

| Conversion of glucose to starch, glycogen and cellulose | Formation of lipids from a molecule of glycerol and three molecules of fatty acids | Using glucose and nitrate ions to form amino acids, which form proteins | Breakdown of excess proteins to form the waste product urea | Respiration |

daydream EDUCATION

The Heart & Blood Vessels

The Heart

Superior vena cava

Pulmonary artery

Aortic semilunar valve

Right atrium

Tricuspid valve

Right ventricle

Inferior vena cava

● Veins ● Chambers ● Valves ● Arteries

Aorta

Pulmonary semilunar valve

Pulmonary veins

Left atrium

Bicuspid (mitral) valve

Left ventricle

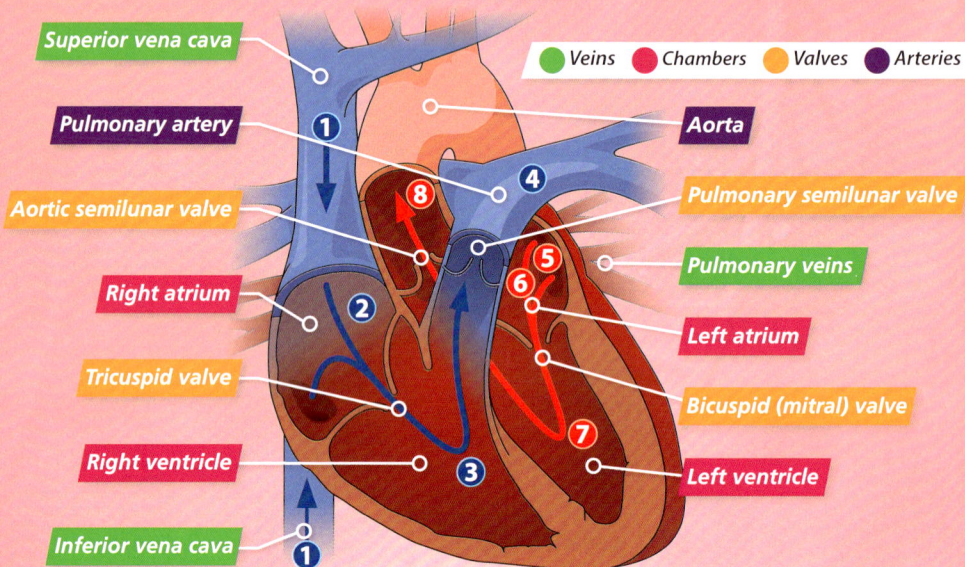

1 Deoxygenated blood from the body is carried by the venae cavae into the right atrium.

2 The right atrium contracts, pushing blood through the tricuspid valve into the right ventricle.

3 The right ventricle contracts, pushing blood through the pulmonary semilunar valve into the pulmonary artery.

4 The blood travels to the lungs, where carbon dioxide is exchanged for oxygen from the air.

5 Oxygenated blood from the lungs is carried by the pulmonary veins into the left atrium.

6 The left atrium contracts, pushing blood through the bicuspid valve into the left ventricle.

7 The left ventricle contracts, pushing blood through the aortic semilunar valve into the aorta.

8 The aorta delivers oxygenated blood to the body, where it is used for energy production.

The heart pumps blood around the body in a double circulatory system.

- The **pulmonary circuit** carries deoxygenated blood away from the heart to the lungs and returns oxygenated (oxygen-rich) blood to the heart.
- The **systemic circuit** carries oxygenated blood away from the heart to the body and returns deoxygenated blood to the heart.

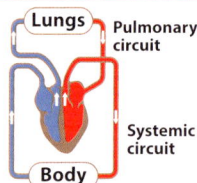

Lungs
Pulmonary circuit
Systemic circuit
Body

daydream
EDUCATION

The circulatory system consists of the heart, blood vessels and blood. It is responsible for circulating blood and transporting oxygen, carbon dioxide and nutrients around the body.

Controlling Heart Rate

The rate at which the heart beats is controlled by a group of cells in the wall of the right atrium. This is referred to as the heart's pacemaker. Whenever extra oxygen is needed by the tissues (e.g. during exercise), the pacemaker cells will increase the heart rate so that oxygen can be pumped around the body faster.

Sometimes the pacemaker can develop a fault or be damaged. In such cases, it is possible to have surgery to fit an artificial pacemaker – an electrical device, which corrects any irregularities in the heart rate.

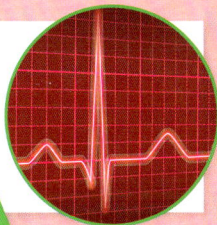

Blood Vessels

Arteries

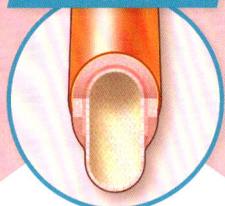

- Carry oxygenated blood (except pulmonary artery) at high pressure, from the heart to the body

- Have thick walls made of elastic fibres
- Have narrow channels (lumen) to maintain high pressure

Veins

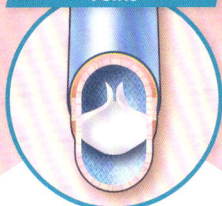

- Carry deoxygenated blood (except pulmonary veins) at low pressure, from the body to the heart

- Have thin walls and contain valves that prevent the backflow of blood
- Have wide channels (lumen) to ease the flow of blood

Capillaries

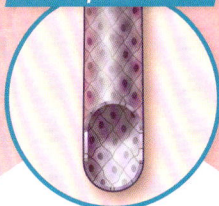

- Allow the exchange of materials between tissues and blood

- Have walls that are only one cell thick
- Have channels (lumen) the width of one blood cell, which distort the cells and aid gaseous exchange

Blood

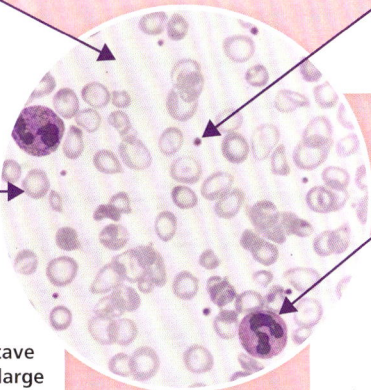

Plasma

Plasma is the fluid part of blood that carries the other components (platelets, red blood cells and white blood cells) throughout the body. It also carries dissolved nutrients and carbon dioxide.

Platelets

Platelets are tiny cell fragments that clump together to help blood clot and to stop bleeding.

Red Blood Cells

Red blood cells transport oxygen from the lungs to the body's cells. They have no nucleus so that there is more space for haemoglobin, which carries oxygen. Also, the biconcave shape of these cells provides a large surface area to volume ratio for gaseous exchange.

White Blood Cells

There are different types of white blood cells, all of which contain a nucleus. One type, lymphocytes, produce antibodies that destroy pathogens. Another type, phagocytes, ingest pathogens and release enzymes to destroy them.

daydream
EDUCATION

The Lungs and Gas Exchange

The respiratory system delivers oxygen to the circulatory system and removes carbon dioxide from the body. The circulatory system delivers carbon dioxide to the lungs and carries oxygen away to the body.

The Gaseous Exchange System in Humans

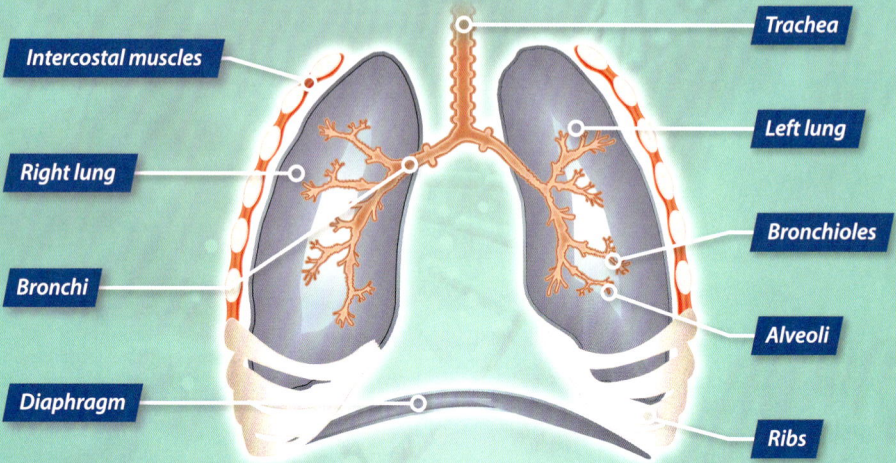

- Trachea
- Intercostal muscles
- Left lung
- Right lung
- Bronchioles
- Bronchi
- Alveoli
- Diaphragm
- Ribs

The Alveoli

The lungs contain millions of alveoli that, combined, provide a large surface area.

Their walls are one single epithelial cell thick and provide a thin, permeable surface for gas exchange.

Alveoli are moist to ease gaseous diffusion.

Oxygen diffuses from the air to the blood, and carbon dioxide diffuses from the blood to the air. Diffusion occurs along steep concentration gradients.

The alveoli are rich in blood supply.

Alveoli contain phagocyte cells that destroy any bacteria not trapped by mucus in the bronchi and trachea.

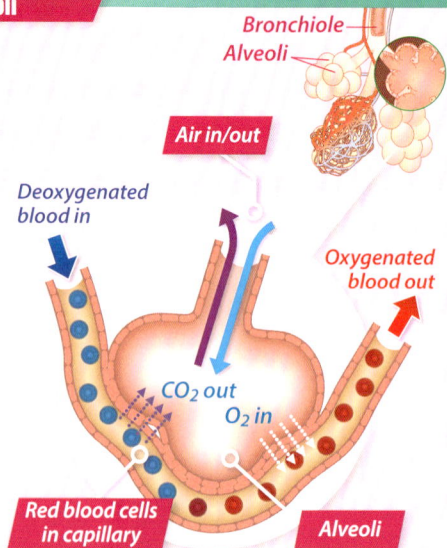

Bronchiole
Alveoli
Air in/out
Deoxygenated blood in
Oxygenated blood out
CO_2 out
O_2 in
Red blood cells in capillary
Alveoli

daydream
EDUCATION

Cardiovascular Disease

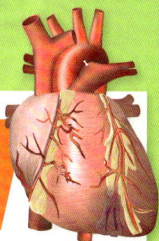

Cardiovascular diseases are diseases of the heart and blood vessels.

Coronary Heart Disease

Coronary arteries supply the heart muscle with blood. In coronary heart disease, layers of fatty material build up in the walls of the coronary arteries, causing their channels to narrow and reducing blood supply to the heart. The reduced flow of oxygen-rich blood through the arteries can damage cells and eventually lead to a heart attack.

Healthy Artery

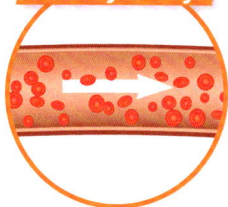

Plaque Build-up

Blocked Artery

The fatty material is made of fat, cholesterol and calcium. It is more likely to build up in people who are overweight or obese and/or who have a diet high in cholesterol.

Treatments for Coronary Heart Disease

There are a number of different treatments for coronary heart disease, depending on the stage and severity of the disease.

Stent

- Sections of blocked arteries can be replaced through surgery.
- A plastic or metal mesh tube called a stent can be inserted into a blocked artery to keep it open.
- Patients can be placed on drugs called statins, which reduce blood cholesterol and therefore slow the build-up of fatty materials.
- In severe cases, a heart transplant can be performed.

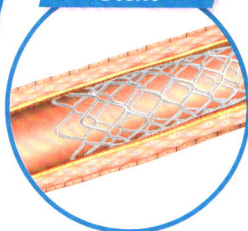

A healthy diet and active lifestyle can reduce the risk of coronary heart disease.

Faulty Heart Valves

In some people, heart valves may become damaged, reducing the efficiency of blood flow in the heart. This can cause tiredness, breathlessness and chest pains.

Faulty valves can be replaced with transplanted (biological) or artificial (mechanical) valves.

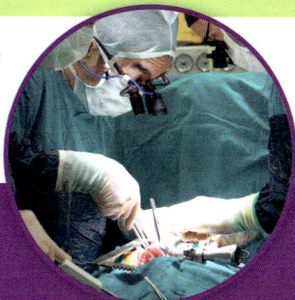

Heart Failure

When a person's heart stops beating, a heart, or heart and lung, transplant is required. This is where a heart from a matching donor is transplanted into the patient.

A donor is not always easy to find so as a temporary measure, patients can be attached to an artificial heart while they await a transplant.

Coronary heart disease is a non-communicable disease – a medical condition or disease that is not caused by infectious agents and can therefore not be passed from person to person.

daydream EDUCATION

Health

Health is defined as the state of physical and mental well-being. Both communicable and non-communicable diseases are major causes of ill health. Other important factors include diet, stress and life situations.

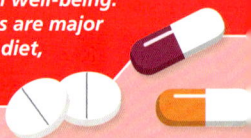

Health and Disease

Communicable Diseases

Communicable diseases are infectious; they can be spread from person to person through pathogens, such as viruses and bacteria.

Examples: influenza (flu), chicken pox and measles

Non-Communicable Diseases

Non-communicable diseases are caused by non-infectious agents and therefore cannot be passed from person to person.

Examples: cancer, dementia and diabetes

Different types of disease may interact to cause health problems.

- Immune system defects can increase the risk of catching infectious diseases.
- Viral infections can trigger some types of cancers.
- Immune reactions to a pathogen can set off allergies such as asthma.
- Severe physical illnesses can lead to mental health issues such as depression.

Lifestyle and Non-Communicable Diseases

There are various risk factors that are linked to an increased rate of a disease. People's lifestyles and their surrounding environment can have a significant impact on their health.

In some but not all cases, there is a direct link between the risk factor and the disease. However, many diseases are caused by interactions of several factors, so it is difficult to identify direct causation.

Smoking causes an increased risk of lung disease, lung cancer, mouth cancer, cardiovascular disease and damage to unborn babies.

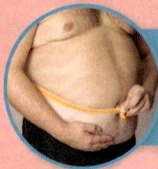

Poor diet and obesity can cause various health problems including, cardiovascular disease, type 2 diabetes and various cancers.

daydream
EDUCATION

Lifestyle and Non-Communicable Diseases Continued

Lack of exercise can lead to various health problems, which are linked to an increased risk of cardiovascular disease.

Drinking excess alcohol can directly cause an increased risk of liver disease, reduced brain function and damage to unborn babies.

Radiation and exposure to certain chemicals can directly cause certain cancers. Cancer-causing substances are called carcinogens.

A balanced diet and exercising regularly will help reduce the risk of ill health. If you are experiencing any physical or mental difficulties always seek medical help.

Cost of Non-Communicable Diseases

Non-communicable diseases have significant human and financial costs. Individuals with non-communicable diseases may have a low quality of life and a lower than average life expectancy. They may also require support from family and friends.

On a national and global scale, the cost of non-communicable diseases is huge, with billions of pounds being spent annually on researching and treating the diseases.

daydream
EDUCATION

Cancer

Cancer is caused by changes in cells that lead to the uncontrolled growth and division of cells. The resulting mass of cells is known as a tumour. However, not all tumours are cancerous.

Benign Tumours

Benign tumours are growths of abnormal cells that are contained in one area, usually surrounded by a membrane.

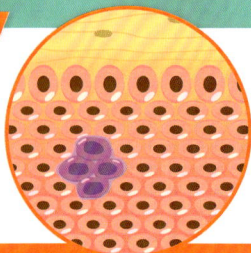

These tumours are not cancerous and do not invade other parts of the body. However, they can be very large and unsightly, so they are often surgically removed.

Malignant Tumours

Malignant tumours spread and invade neighbouring tissues. If the cells get into the blood, they can be carried around the body, leading to secondary tumours in other organs.

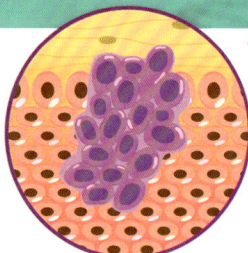

These tumours are cancerous and very dangerous, so they require prompt medical treatment to prevent the cancer spreading.

Symptoms of Cancer

There are over 200 types of cancer, each of which has its own specific symptoms. However, there are several common symptoms to look out for.

If you have any of these symptoms or are worried that you may have cancer, visit your doctor immediately.

Symptoms

- ✓ Lumps on or below the surface of the skin
- ✓ Unexplainable weight loss
- ✓ Bleeding
- ✓ Coughing and breathlessness
- ✓ Changes in bowel habits

Cancer and Lifestyle

Anyone can develop cancer. However, scientists have identified several lifestyle factors that can increase the risk of developing different cancers.

Smoking	This is linked to over 1 in 5 cancer deaths in the UK.
UV Exposure	UV radiation is a major risk factor for most skin cancers.
Alcohol	This is linked to several cancers, including bowel and mouth.
Obesity	Obesity is the second largest preventable cause of cancer in the UK.
Infections	Infections such as hepatitis C can cause changes in cells and eventually lead to cancer. They can also damage the immune system.

Additionally, there are genetic risk factors for some cancers. For example, mutations in inherited *BRCA* genes are linked to an increased likelihood of developing breast cancer.

daydream
EDUCATION

Plant Tissues, Organs & Systems

Just like animal cells, plant cells are organised into tissues, organs and organ systems.

Plant Tissues

Plant tissues are made up of plant cells with a similar structure and function.

Epidermal Tissue	A single layer of cells that covers the whole plant (epidermis)
Xylem	Found in roots, stems and leaves; gives support and transports water and minerals
Phloem	Found in roots, stems and leaves; transports sugars
Spongy Mesophyll	Found in leaves; helps facilitate gas exchange
Palisade Mesophyll	Found in leaves; the main site of photosynthesis
Meristem Tissue	Found at the tips of roots and shoots; enables the plant to grow

Plant Organs

Plant organs are collections of plant tissues that perform specific functions. The three main plant organs are the root, stem and leaf.

The function of the leaf is to convert carbon dioxide and water into sugar by using light energy.

Epidermis

The lower epidermis contains pores called stomata that can open to allow carbon dioxide into the leaf. The upper epidermis is transparent to allow sunlight to pass through to the palisade layer. It also helps protect against water loss.

Palisade Mesophyll

The elongated cells in the palisade mesophyll are closely packed with many chloroplasts to absorb light energy and perform photosynthesis.

Spongy Mesophyll

Spongy mesophyll cells contain chloroplasts, but they are loosely arranged with many air spaces to allow carbon dioxide to travel up to the palisade layer.

Veins

The veins contain two tissues; xylem, which transports water to the leaf, and phloem, which transports the sugar made by photosynthesis around the plant.

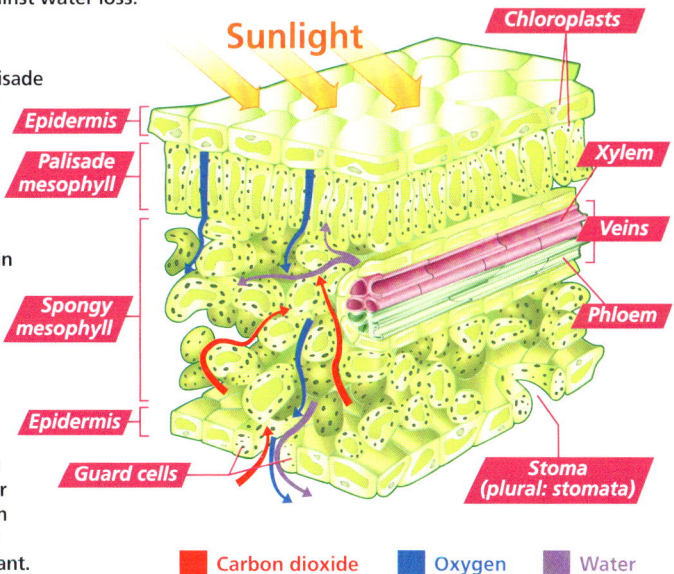

Sunlight

Chloroplasts

Epidermis

Palisade mesophyll

Xylem

Veins

Spongy mesophyll

Phloem

Epidermis

Guard cells

Stoma (plural: stomata)

■ Carbon dioxide   ■ Oxygen   ■ Water

daydream EDUCATION

Plant Transport

Stomata

Stomata are tiny pores that control gas exchange and water loss. They allow carbon dioxide to diffuse into the leaves and oxygen to diffuse out, along with water vapour. The stomata are surrounded by guard cells. The stomata open when the cells fill with water and become turgid; they close when the cells lose water and become flaccid.

During transpiration, water vapour diffuses out of a plant through its leaves because there is more water inside the plant than outside it. This water then needs to be replaced so more water is drawn up through the xylem vessels.

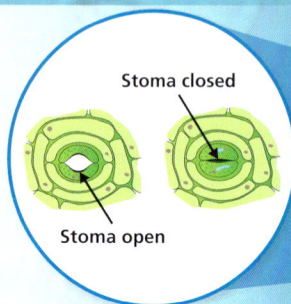

Stoma closed

Stoma open

Xylem Tissue

During their development, xylem cells die, and their top and bottom walls disintegrate to form long vessels, which are supported by a material called lignin. The vessels transport water and dissolved mineral ions from a plant's roots to its stems and leaves.

Inside xylem vessels, there is an unbroken chain of water. As the water evaporates out of the leaves through the stomata, more water is pulled up the xylem vessels to replace the water lost through evaporation.

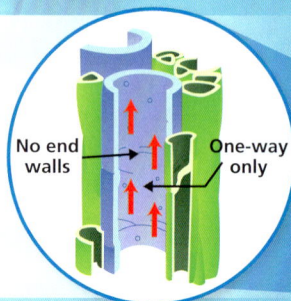

No end walls

One-way only

Phloem Tissue

Phloem is made of columns of elongated cells. These cells transport sugars made in the leaves to other parts of the plant for immediate use or storage. Phloem vessels have pores in the ends of their walls that allow food to move between them.

Phloem is not part of the transpiration process. It is used for translocation.

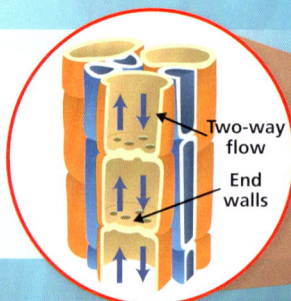

Two-way flow

End walls

Root Hair Cells

Millions of specialised root hair cells are located on the surface of plant roots. These cells stick out into the soil to provide the plant with a large surface area to absorb more water and mineral ions.

Because the concentration of minerals is greater in the root hair cells than in the surrounding soil, the plant uses active transport to absorb minerals from an area of lower concentration to an area of higher concentration.

To ensure there is a constant stream of water through the plant, any water flowing out of the xylem must be replaced by water from the roots.

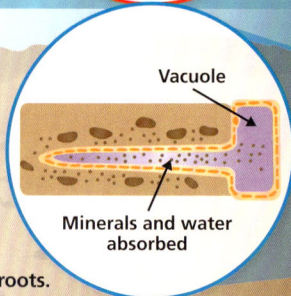

Vacuole

Minerals and water absorbed

daydream
EDUCATIO

Plants are made of specialised cells, tissues and organs that work together to allow substances to move around the plant.

Transpiration

Transpiration is the process by which moisture is transported through a plant, from its roots to the small pores on the underside of its leaves. From the leaves, it is released into the atmosphere through evaporation and diffusion.

Translocation

Translocation is the process by which food substances, such as sucrose and amino acids, are transported through a plant.

Factors Affecting the Rate of Transpiration

Light Intensity

The greater the light intensity, the greater the rate of transpiration. When it is dark, photosynthesis cannot take place, and the stomata close. This means that little water can diffuse out of the leaves.

Temperature

The greater the temperature, the greater the rate of transpiration. Water particles have more energy when it is warm, and they evaporate and diffuse out of the stomata at a faster rate.

Air Flow

The greater the air flow, the greater the rate of transpiration. When air flow is fast, water vapour is moved away quickly to create a high concentration gradient for diffusion.

Humidity

The lower the humidity, the faster the rate of transpiration. When the air is dry, there is a high concentration gradient for diffusion.

daydream EDUCATION

Communicable Diseases

Bacteria

Bacteria are microscopic living cells. Some bacteria are helpful and protect against disease, whereas others, such as pathogenic bacteria, are harmful and cause disease. Pathogenic bacteria can release poisonous toxins that damage cells and make people feel ill.

The Growth of Bacteria

Bacterial cells reproduce asexually through a process called binary fission. In binary fission, a cell splits into two genetically identical daughter cells. Bacteria can reproduce rapidly in the right conditions. Most bacteria thrive in warm, moist environments that have a good source of nutrients.

Bacterial Diseases

Salmonella

Salmonella is spread by bacteria ingested in food or on food prepared in unhygienic conditions.

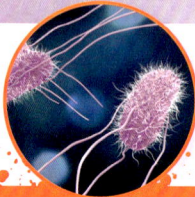

Symptoms include vomiting, fever, abdominal cramps and diarrhoea and are caused by the toxins the bacteria produce. In the UK, poultry is vaccinated against salmonella to control the spread.

Gonorrhoea

Gonorrhoea is a sexually transmitted disease (STD) that causes pain when urinating and a thick yellow or green discharge from the penis or vagina.

It used to be easily treated with the antibiotic penicillin, but new drug-resistant strains of the bacteria have made treatment harder. Infection can be prevented by using barrier contraception such as condoms.

Protist Diseases

Malaria

Protists are single-celled organisms, some of which are pathogens. Malaria is a serious disease that causes episodes of fever, and it can be fatal. The pathogen that causes malaria is transmitted by mosquitos. Mosquitos pick up the pathogen when they feed on infected organisms and then transmit the disease to other organisms through their saliva when they bite.

The spread of malaria is controlled by preventing mosquitos from breeding and by using mosquito nets to avoid being bitten.

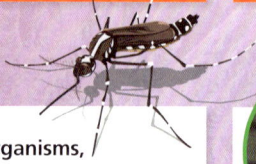

Fungal Diseases

Rose Black Spot

Rose black spot is a fungus that causes purple or black spots to develop on leaves, which often turn yellow and fall off. This reduces photosynthesis and growth.

The fungal spores are spread by water and wind. Rose black spot is treated using fungicides, and the spread can be avoided by removing and destroying affected leaves.

Fungi can also cause disease in animals, such as athlete's foot and ringworm in humans.

daydream
EDUCATION

Pathogens are microorganisms (viruses, bacteria, fungi or protists) that cause communicable (infectious and contagious) disease. They infect plants or animals and can be spread through air, water, food and direct contact.

Viruses

Viruses are smaller than bacteria and harder to detect by the body's defences because they are hidden inside cells. Viruses inject their genes into a host cell and use the cell to produce thousands of copies of themselves. These copies fill the cell until it bursts, releasing the virus into the body.

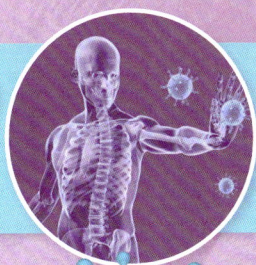

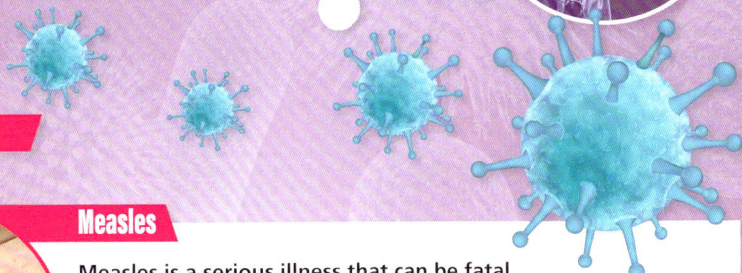

Viral Diseases

Measles

Measles is a serious illness that can be fatal if complications arise. As a result, most young children are vaccinated against it.

The measles virus is spread through the inhalation of droplets from sneezes and coughs of infected people. Symptoms include fever and a red skin rash.

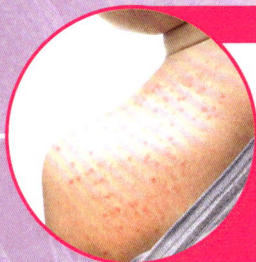

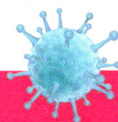

HIV

HIV is a virus that causes the disease AIDS. It can initially cause flu-like symptoms, but after this, there are usually no other symptoms for several years. The virus attacks the immune system, but this can be controlled by using antiretroviral drugs.

Late-stage HIV, or AIDS, develops once the immune system is so badly damaged that it cannot cope with other infections or cancers. HIV is spread through the exchange of bodily fluids, often during sex or through the sharing of needles by drug users.

TMV

Tobacco mosaic virus (TMV) is a widespread plant pathogen. It affects many different plants including tomato plants.

Its symptoms include a distinctive 'mosaic' pattern of discoloration on the leaves, which limits photosynthesis and therefore affects the growth of the plant.

daydream
EDUCATION

Fighting Disease

The body has several ways of defending itself against pathogens.

Eyes – Tears remove unwanted particles and contain an enzyme that can kill bacteria.

Skin – Skin is difficult to penetrate, and skin cells produce oils that can kill microbes.

Nose – Mucus in the nose traps microbes, which are removed by sneezing or blowing the nose. Hairs also stop large particles containing pathogens from entering the lungs.

White Blood Cells – White blood cells protect the body from infections.

Trachea and Bronchi – The trachea and bronchi produce mucus to trap microbes, which are then carried out of the body by tiny hairs known as cilia.

Stomach – The stomach contains hydrochloric acid and enzymes that can kill microbes that enter the body through food and drink.

Blood Clotting – Microbes can enter the body through open wounds. Blood cells, known as platelets, help blood clot quickly and seal wounds to reduce the risk of infection.

White Blood Cells

1 **Ingestion** – White blood cells (phagocytes) engulf pathogens and then digest them. This process is called phagocytosis.

2 **Producing Antibodies** – Antibodies are produced by specialised white blood cells (**lymphocytes**) when they detect **antigens**, a protein found on the surface of pathogens. The antibodies, which are specific to the **antigen** detected, then find and destroy the pathogen. Some white blood cells (**memory cells**) remain in the blood. Therefore, if the same pathogen enters the body again, the antibodies to kill it can be produced quickly.

3 **Producing Antitoxins** – Some white blood cells produce proteins called antitoxins that neutralise the toxins released by pathogens.

daydream EDUCATION

Vaccinations

Vaccinations are used to protect against infections. They involve injecting a small amount of dead or inactive pathogens into the body. These harmless pathogens contain antigens that provoke white blood cells to produce antibodies to destroy them, while producing memory cells which remain in the blood.

If the same pathogen infects the body again, the memory cells recognise it and produce the appropriate antibodies to help to destroy it. As the pathogens in a vaccine are inactive and do not reproduce, they often do not produce enough memory cells to provide full immunity.

As a result, booster injections are often required to increase the number of memory cells.

Advantages

- Vaccinations prevent lots of people from contracting infectious diseases such as polio and measles.
- Epidemics can be prevented by vaccinating a large percentage of the population.

Disadvantages

- Vaccinations do not guarantee immunity to the illness in the future.
- People can experience side effects from vaccinations such as swelling, high temperatures and rashes. More serious reactions such as seizures are very rare.

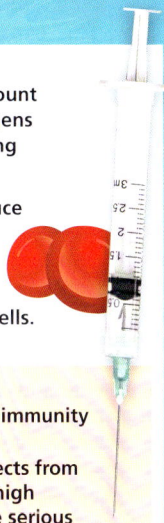

Antibiotics

Antibiotics reduce the growth of bacteria without killing the body's cells. Each type of bacteria requires a different antibiotic. Therefore, if you are prescribed the wrong antibiotic, it will not work.

Antibiotics cannot destroy viruses because they reproduce inside the body's own cells. This makes it difficult to develop drugs that can kill viruses without destroying the body's cells.

Resistance

Mutation can cause bacteria to become resistant to antibiotics, resulting in more serious infections. Doctors try to avoid overprescribing antibiotics to reduce the risk of resistance. Failure to complete a full course of antibiotics can also increase the risk of resistance.

Painkillers

Many different drugs, such as aspirin and paracetamol, act as painkillers. These have no affect on pathogens but can be used to treat the symptoms of a disease. Painkillers, like all drugs, usually have some side effects.

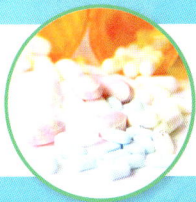

daydream EDUCATION

Developing New Drugs

Traditionally, drugs have been extracted from plants and microorganisms.

The heart drug digitalis originates from foxgloves.

The painkiller aspirin originates from willow.

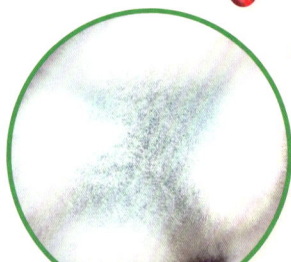

Penicillin originates from the *penicillium* mould.

Most new drugs are synthesised by chemists. However, the starting point may still be a chemical extracted from a plant. New medical drugs have to be tested and trialled before being used.

Preclinical Testing

Preclinical testing is performed in a laboratory using human cells and tissues. However, testing on cells and tissues is ineffective for a drug that affects whole or multiple organ systems. Because of this, the drug then needs to be tested on animals to identify how it works, its toxicity and the best dosage. If animal tests are successful, the drug is then tested on human volunteers in clinical trials.

- At the start of a clinical trial, a very low dose of the drug is given to healthy volunteers to identify if it has any harmful side effects. The dose is gradually increased.

- If the test results are good, the drug is tested on people who have the illness to find the optimum dose.

- Patients are split into two groups: the test group, which is given the new drug, and the control group, which is given a placebo (a substance that does not have any physical effect). Any changes to the patients' condition are monitored. If changes are only seen in the test group, the scientists know that the drug works.

- Clinical trials are performed either blind, meaning patients do not know which group they are in, or double-blind, meaning neither the doctors nor patients know. This is to remove any bias that may affect the results of the trial.

daydream
EDUCATION

Monoclonal Antibodies

Monoclonal antibodies are made by identical immune cells that are clones of a unique parent cell. They are identical copies of one type of antibody, so they can only target one protein antigen.

Making Monoclonal Antibodies

Monoclonal antibodies are generally produced by injecting mammals (usually mice) with an antigen to prompt their B-lymphocyte (a type of white blood cell) to produce a particular antibody.

The lymphocytes can be collected directly from the mice. However, they divide slowly and cannot produce a large amount of antibody quickly.

To increase production, lymphocytes are fused with cancer cells, which divide very rapidly, to create new cells known as a hybridoma cells.

Hybridoma cells can divide quickly. Therefore, they are cloned to produce large quantities of a single, monoclonal antibody.

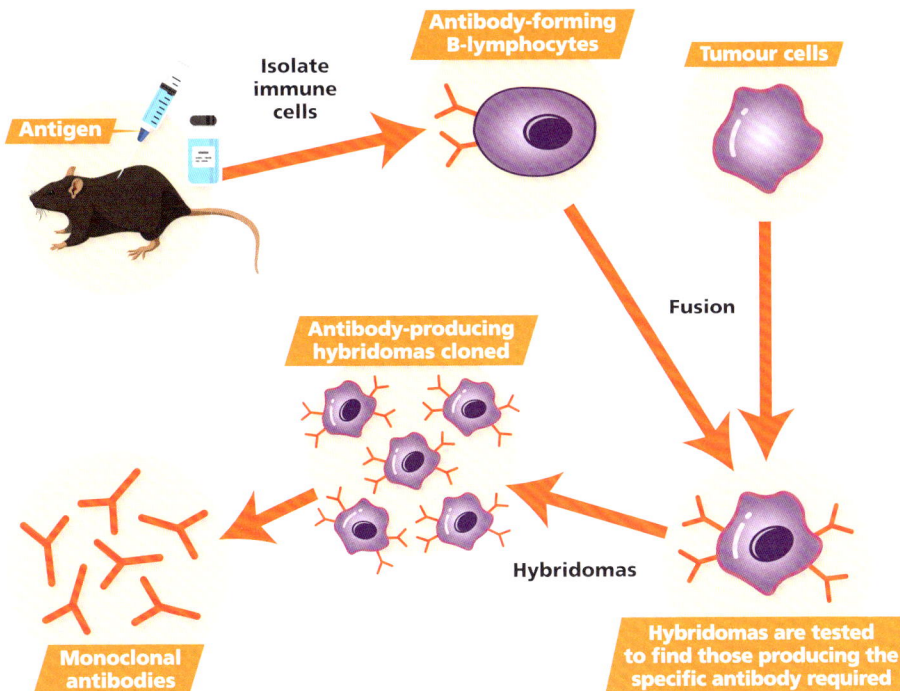

Antigen

Isolate immune cells

Antibody-forming B-lymphocytes

Tumour cells

Fusion

Antibody-producing hybridomas cloned

Hybridomas

Hybridomas are tested to find those producing the specific antibody required

Monoclonal antibodies

daydream
EDUCATION

Uses of Monoclonal Antibodies

Scientists design and produce monoclonal antibodies for several reasons. As well as being used to fight disease directly, they are made to target a specific antigen or type of cell. Substances that interact with the target cell or chemical can then be attached to the antibody.

Pregnancy Testing

During pregnancy, the placenta produces a hormone called human chorionic gonadotropin (hCG) which is then present in the pregnant woman's urine.

Pregnancy tests contain monoclonal antibodies that attach to hCG. These antibodies have dye molecules attached to them that change colour if hCG is present, indicating the woman is pregnant.

The ELISA Test

Similar to a pregnancy test, the ELISA test uses monoclonal antibodies to detect a specific antigen in the blood or urine.

It is used to test for drug use (e.g. in athletes) and for HIV antigens, which indicate if a person is HIV-positive.

Cancer Treatment

Monoclonal antibodies with drugs attached can be designed to attach to cancer cells and kill them.

Unlike chemotherapy and radiotherapy, which can also kill other body cells, only the cancer cells are targeted.

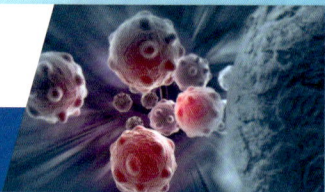

Detecting Pathogens

In addition to detecting HIV, specific monoclonal antibodies can be used to detect other pathogens, such as the bacteria which cause gonorrhoea, a sexually transmitted infection.

Problems with Monoclonal Antibodies

Although monoclonal antibodies are designed to target a single antigen, side-effects, such as vomiting and low blood pressure, have occured in humans. As a result, their use in treating diseases has been limited.

Scientists did not expect these side effects, and research is ongoing to try to understand and address this problem.

daydream
EDUCATION

Plant Diseases

Symptoms of Plant Diseases

Plants that have a disease are likely to show one symptom or more, including:

- Stunted or distorted growth
- Discolouration, often of the leaves
- Spots on the leaves
- Patches of rot
- Lumps or unusual growths
- The presence of pests

Plant diseases can be identified by:

- **Reference to gardening manual**
- **Identifying the pathogen**
- **Using testing kits that contain monoclonal antibodies**

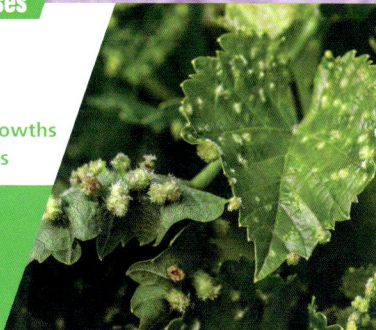

Deficiency Diseases

Plants need a variety of minerals from the soil. Most minerals are required in tiny amounts, but some, such as nitrogen, magnesium and potassium, are needed in larger quantities.

Nitrates are required to make proteins for growth. A lack of **nitrates** will cause weak, spindly growth, and older leaves may turn yellow as a result of chlorosis.

Magnesium ions are needed to manufacture chlorophyll. When chlorophyll is in short supply the leaves turn yellow, primarily between the veins.

Diseases Caused by Pathogens

Viruses, bacteria and fungi can cause disease in plants, like they do in animals.

The **tobacco mosaic virus** infects tobacco and related plants. It causes a mosaic pattern of discolouration on the leaves.

Crown gall is a bacterial disease that causes abnormal growths.

Black spot disease is a fungal disease that causes roses to develop black spots on their leaves.

Pests can also infest plants. Common pests include blackflies and greenflies, which are types of insects known as **aphids**.

Plant Defences

Chemical defences: Some plants produce chemicals that kill bacteria, and others produce poisons that deter herbivores from feeding on them.

Physical defences: An outer covering like bark can help prevent bacterial entry. The waxy cuticle of leaves and the cellulose cell walls also form a barrier to entry.

Mechanical defences: Some plants, such as mimosas, have leaves that droop suddenly when touched; any insect landing on them to feed may fall off.

Photosynthesis

Photosynthesis is the process by which plants, algae and other organisms produce their own food (glucose). It is an endothermic reaction that uses light energy, carbon dioxide and water to produce glucose and oxygen.

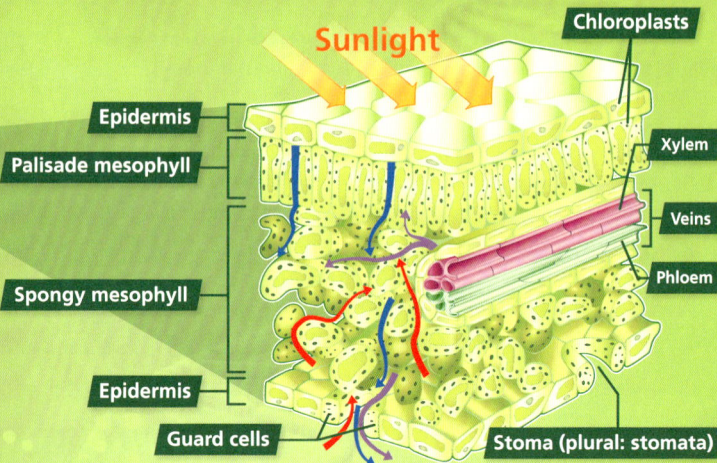

Sunlight

Chloroplasts

Epidermis

Palisade mesophyll

Xylem

Veins

Phloem

Spongy mesophyll

Epidermis

Key
- Oxygen
- Water
- Carbon dioxide

Guard cells

Stoma (plural: stomata)

1 Sunlight is absorbed by chlorophyll, a green pigment within the chloroplasts.

2 Water enters a plant through its roots by osmosis and then travels to the leaves through tubes called xylem vessels.

3 Carbon dioxide from the air diffuses into leaves through the stomata. Guard cells surrounding the stomata control their size depending on the amount of light being received.

4 Photosynthesis takes place in the chloroplasts. Light energy is used to convert water and carbon dioxide into glucose and oxygen.

5 Oxygen, a by-product of photosynthesis, leaves the plant through the stomata.

Leaves are broad and flat to provide a large surface area for the absorption of light. They are also thin, which means that carbon dioxide does not have far to diffuse into the leaf.

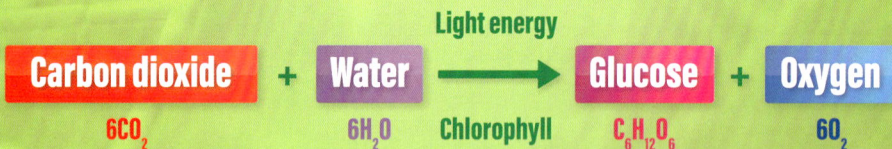

Light energy

Carbon dioxide	+	Water	→	Glucose	+	Oxygen
$6CO_2$		$6H_2O$	Chlorophyll	$C_6H_{12}O_6$		$6O_2$

How the glucose produced in photosynthesis is used:

For respiration	To produce cellulose, which strengthens cell walls	To produce fat or oil for storage	To produce amino acids for protein synthesis	Converted to insoluble starch and stored for later use

daydream EDUCATION

Limiting Factors

In this part of the graph, light intensity and rate of photosynthesis are directly proportional as they increase at the same rate.

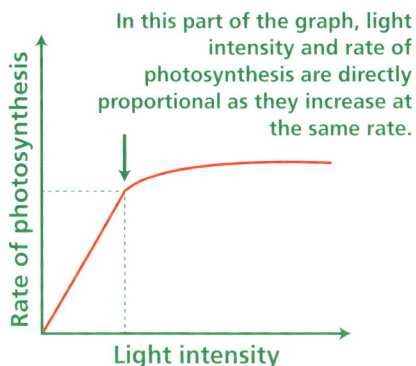

Rate of photosynthesis / Light intensity

Light Intensity

Increasing light intensity boosts the rate of photosynthesis to a certain level. Beyond this, other factors, such as temperature and carbon dioxide, limit the rate.

Temperature

Photosynthesis will not take place if the temperature is below approximately 0°C or above 45°C. This is because the reactions involved are catalysed by enzymes.

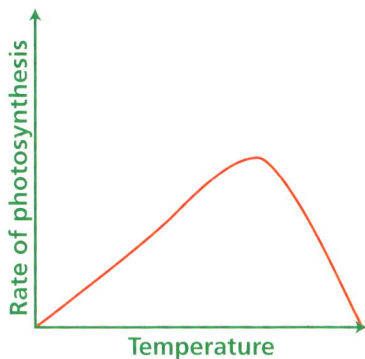

Rate of photosynthesis / Temperature

Carbon Dioxide Concentration

Increasing carbon dioxide concentration boosts the rate of photosynthesis to a certain level. Beyond this, other factors such as light intensity and temperature, limit the rate.

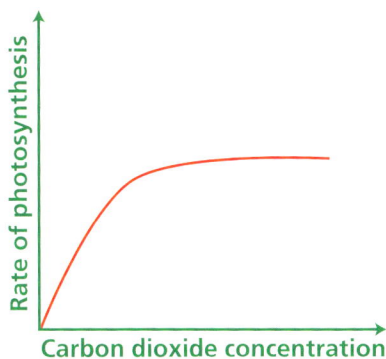

Rate of photosynthesis / Carbon dioxide concentration

Chlorophyll can also limit photosynthesis. If chloroplasts become damaged through disease or lack of nutrients, they cannot absorb as much light, reducing photosynthesis. All of the above factors interact so any one factor, or multiple factors, may be responsible for limiting photosynthesis.

Light Distance and Light Intensity

The light intensity in photosynthesis experiments is often measured as the light's distance from the plant. In such cases, the light intensity is inversely proportional to the square of the distance, according to the inverse square law:

$$\text{Intensity} \propto \frac{1}{\text{Distance}^2}$$

The Economics of Limiting Factors

To maximise photosynthesis in plants for food production, plants are often grown in a greenhouse, so the limiting factors can be manipulated and kept to an optimum level.

However, creating optimum levels is difficult and costs money, so it is important that each factor is adjusted only when it is limiting.

Practical Activity

The effect of light intensity on the rate of photosynthesis can be investigated using an aquatic organism, such as pondweed.

1 Cut a piece of elodea pondweed and place it upside down (cut tip facing up) into a boiling tube filled with water so it is completely submerged. Place the tube into a beaker of water which will absorb any heat from the lamp and keep the temperature around the pondweed constant.

2 Set up a lamp at a fixed distance from the pondweed.

3 Count how many bubbles the pondweed produces over a set period of time, e.g. 1 minute.

4 Repeat this two more times and calculate the mean across the three results.

5 Now repeat the experiment with the lamp at different distances from the pondweed.

If the number of bubbles increases, the pondweed is producing more oxygen, which means it is photosynthesising faster. Conversely, fewer bubbles means less oxygen and a slower rate of photosynthesis.

During an experiment, it is important to keep all control variables the same. In this experiment, carbon dioxide concentration and temperature need to remain constant.

daydream
EDUCATION

Respiration

Respiration is an exothermic reaction that occurs in living cells to release energy stored in glucose. The energy released supplies all the energy needed for living processes.

Organisms need energy for:

Movement

Chemical reactions to build larger molecules from smaller ones

Keeping warm

Aerobic Respiration (Respiration With Oxygen)

In aerobic respiration, oxygen and glucose are used to generate energy.

Glucose + **Oxygen** → **Carbon Dioxide** + **Water** + **Energy**

$C_6H_{12}O_6$ $6O_2$ $6CO_2$ $6H_2O$

Glucose is broken down to produce carbon dioxide and water, and to release energy.

Anaerobic Respiration (Respiration Without Oxygen)

In animals, anaerobic respiration takes places when the body is unable to supply muscles with sufficient oxygen for aerobic respiration.

Glucose → **Lactic Acid** + **Energy**

Glucose is broken down to produce lactic acid and to release energy.

In plant cells, anaerobic respiration takes place when there is insufficient oxygen for plants to respire aerobically.

Glucose → **Ethanol** + **Carbon Dioxide** + **Energy**

Glucose is broken down to produce ethanol (an alcohol) and carbon dioxide, and to release energy.

Anaerobic respiration does not release as much energy as aerobic respiration because the oxidation of glucose is not completed – that is, the glucose is not fully broken down.

Anaerobic Respiration in Yeast

Anaerobic respiration in yeast is called fermentation. Yeast is a fungus, but it respires in the same way as plants do. It is used commercially in the manufacture of bread and alcoholic drinks.

Exercise and Metabolism

Exercise

During exercise, the body reacts to the increased demand for energy.

Breathing rate and breath volume increase to get more oxygen into the blood and to remove carbon dioxide.

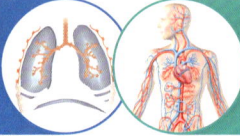

Heart rate also increases to get oxygenated blood to the muscles more rapidly and to remove more carbon dioxide.

During vigorous exercise, the body may be unable to supply the muscles with sufficient oxygen for aerobic respiration. As a result, the muscles also respire anaerobically, and the incomplete oxidation of glucose causes a build up of lactic acid (causing muscle fatigue) and creates an oxygen debt.

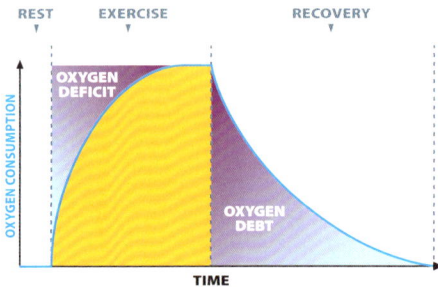

REST   EXERCISE   RECOVERY

OXYGEN CONSUMPTION

OXYGEN DEFICIT

OXYGEN DEBT

TIME

To repay oxygen debt, extra oxygen must be taken on after anaerobic exercise to convert lactic acid into waste products (carbon dioxide and water) that can be removed from the body.

Lactic acid is also transported in the blood to the liver, where it is converted back into glucose.

After exercise, we take deeper or quicker breaths to take in more oxygen and remove more carbon dioxide. Long periods of vigorous activity result in muscles becoming fatigued and then contracting less efficiently.

Metabolism

Metabolism is the sum of all the reactions taking place in a living organism. These reactions are controlled by enzymes and use energy from respiration either to break down large molecules into smaller molecules or to synthesise (make) large molecules from smaller ones.

Carbohydrates

- Broken down into simple sugars, including glucose

- Built up into starch and cellulose (in plants) or glycogen (in animals)

Proteins

- Broken down into amino acids*

- Glucose and nitrate ions form amino acids, which are built up into proteins.

Lipids (fats)

- Broken down into glycerol and fatty acids

- Built up into lipids. It takes a molecule of glycerol and three fatty acid molecules to form a lipid molecule.

Animals cannot store protein, so excess protein is broken down into urea and excreted from the body in urine.

Respiration is a series of reactions. Although respiration releases energy overall, some of the reactions also require energy.

daydream EDUCATION

Homeostasis

Cells can survive only within narrow physical and chemical limits. Homeostasis is the regulation of the conditions within the body to maintain optimal conditions for enzyme action and other cell functions. In the body, homeostasis controls:

Body temperature   **Blood glucose concentration**   **Water levels**

Control Systems

There are various control systems in the body, all of which include:

Receptors

Groups of specialist cells that detect stimuli (changes in the environment).

Light receptor cells in the eye

Coordination Centres

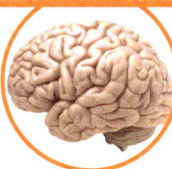

Receive information and coordinate any possible response.

Brain, spinal cord, pancreas

Effectors

Bring about responses to restore optimum conditions.

Muscles or glands

Negative Feedback

Negative feedback is a control mechanism used in homeostasis that maintains optimum conditions within a system. It occurs when a change from normal conditions in the body leads to a series of events that reverse the change.

Example: Body Temperature Control

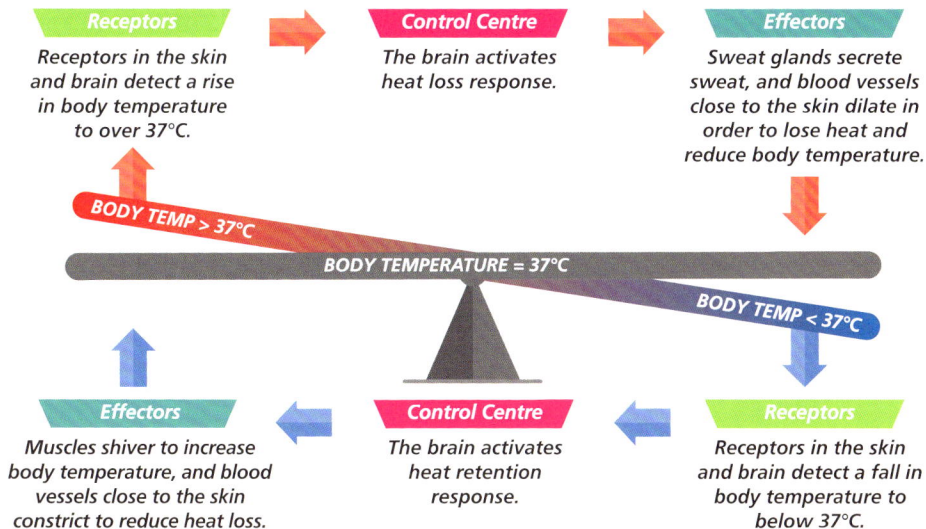

Receptors
Receptors in the skin and brain detect a rise in body temperature to over 37°C.

Control Centre
The brain activates heat loss response.

Effectors
Sweat glands secrete sweat, and blood vessels close to the skin dilate in order to lose heat and reduce body temperature.

BODY TEMP > 37°C

BODY TEMPERATURE = 37°C

BODY TEMP < 37°C

Effectors
Muscles shiver to increase body temperature, and blood vessels close to the skin constrict to reduce heat loss.

Control Centre
The brain activates heat retention response.

Receptors
Receptors in the skin and brain detect a fall in body temperature to below 37°C.

The Human Nervous System

The Human Nervous System

The nervous system enables humans to react to their environment and to coordinate their behaviour. It consists of two parts:

Key
- CNS
- PNS

1 Central Nervous System (CNS), which includes the brain and spinal cord

2 Peripheral Nervous System (PNS), the network of nerves that lead out from the CNS to the rest of the body

Nerves are made of nerve cells called neurones, which carry messages in the form of electrical impulses.

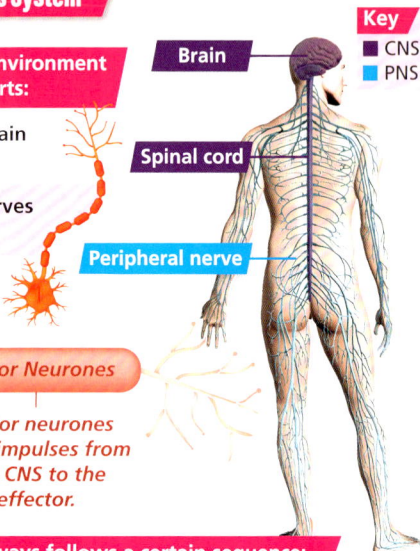

Brain

Spinal cord

Peripheral nerve

Sensory Neurones
Sensory neurones carry impulses from the receptor to the CNS.

Relay Neurones
Relay neurones carry impulses within the CNS.

Motor Neurones
Motor neurones carry impulses from the CNS to the effector.

The coordination of actions in the body always follows a certain sequence:

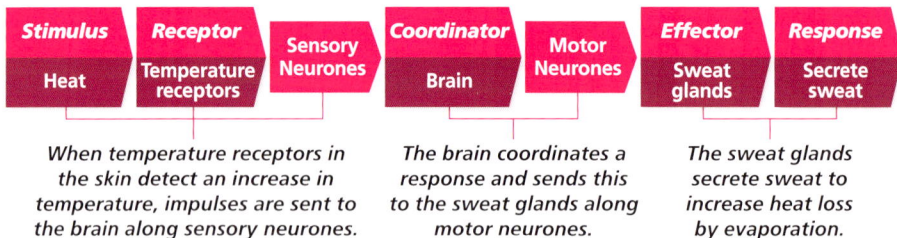

Stimulus	Receptor	Sensory Neurones	Coordinator	Motor Neurones	Effector	Response
Heat	Temperature receptors		Brain		Sweat glands	Secrete sweat

When temperature receptors in the skin detect an increase in temperature, impulses are sent to the brain along sensory neurones.

The brain coordinates a response and sends this to the sweat glands along motor neurones.

The sweat glands secrete sweat to increase heat loss by evaporation.

Other control systems and responses also regulate body temperature.

Reflex Actions

Reflex actions have two important features: they are automatic/involuntary and very rapid. They often have some sort of protective function to prevent injury. Examples include:

- Swallowing
- Blinking
- Pupil reflex
- Breathing
- Coughing
- Sneezing
- Withdrawal reflex (pulling away from a painful stimulus)

daydream EDUCATION

The Reflex Arc

In reflex actions, the nerve impulses always follow a certain pathway.

When a stimulus is detected by the receptor, impulses travel along the sensory neurones to relay neurones in the spinal cord and then out to the effector via the motor neurones.

The impulses do not go through the brain as the response needs to be automatic. However, the brain will still receive the sensory input while the reflex is being carried out.

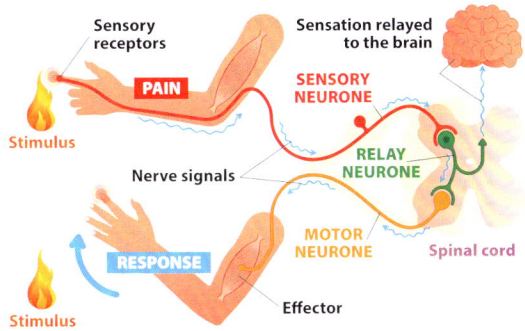

Sensory receptors

Sensation relayed to the brain

PAIN

SENSORY NEURONE

Stimulus

Nerve signals

RELAY NEURONE

MOTOR NEURONE

Spinal cord

RESPONSE

Stimulus

Effector

Synapses

Vesicles

Synapse

Neurotransmitters

Receptors

Synapses, the junctions between neurones, slightly delay impulses: when impulses transfer from one neurone to another across a synapse, they must be converted into chemical signals and back again.

In a reflex arc, the impulses go through only two synapses, so the delay is minimal. In the brain, the impulses would travel through millions of synapses.

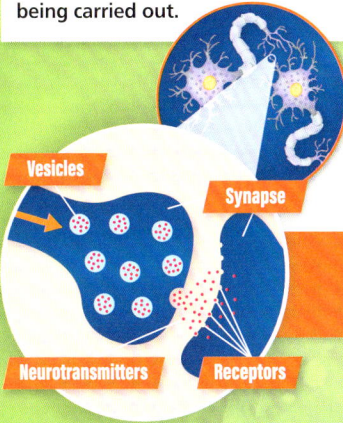

Practical Activity

Reaction time is the time taken to react to a stimulus. The effects of a factor on human reaction time can be investigated using the ruler drop test.

The ruler drop test can be used to measure reaction time in response to external factors such as a visual or audio cue. The test is performed with a partner who holds the ruler.

As your partner holds the ruler, stand with your hand in front of you and position the ruler in between your index finger and thumb. The top of your index finger should be level with 0 cm on the ruler.

Your partner then drops the ruler, and you must catch the ruler as quickly as possible. Measure the point at which you caught the ruler from the top of your thumb. For improved reliability, repeat two more times, and then calculate the mean of your three scores.

The Brain

The brain controls all complex behaviour in mammals. Together with the spinal cord, the brain makes up the **central nervous system.**

The Structure of the Brain

The brain contains billions of interconnected nerve cells (neurones). There are about 10^{11} neurons in a fully grown human brain. The brain is split into two halves: the left and right hemispheres. Different areas of the brain perform specific functions.

The **cerebral cortex** is the outer layer of the cerebrum, the largest area in the brain. It is responsible for intelligence, personality, language and memory.

The **medulla** is at the base of the brain, where it connects to the spinal cord. It controls involuntary processes, e.g. breathing and heart rate.

The **cerebellum** is at the rear of the brain. It mainly controls muscle coordination and balance.

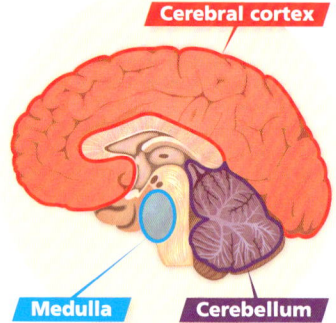

Cerebral cortex

Medulla

Cerebellum

Discovery of Brain Functions

Scientists have used different approaches to identify the functions of various areas of the brain.

Studying the Effects of Brain Damage

When an area of the brain is damaged, the functions it controls may be lost or damaged. For example, a person can become blind when the area of the brain that controls sight is damaged, even if no damage occurs to the eyes.

MRI Scans

An MRI scanner can detect activity in the brain. By giving a subject a particular stimulus, scientists can see which areas of the brain respond. For example, if a subject sees a picture of someone they know, scientists can detect activity in the areas responsible for facial recognition and memory.

Electrical Stimulation

Neurones are activated by electricity. If a small area of the brain is stimulated with an electrode, the effect can be monitored. For example, when stimulating a certain area causes a subject to blink, this identifies that the brain area controls that function.

Investigating and Treating Brain Disorders

A better understanding of the brain has enabled the treatment of some brain disorders. Scientists are constantly increasing their knowledge of brain function and developing new technologies to analyse it.

However, because of the brain's complexity and our limited understanding of its functions, treatments do not always work as intended and may cause physical problems and side-effects.

daydream
EDUCATION

The Eye

The eye is a sense organ. It detects colours, patterns and intensities of light and sends this information to the brain, which builds a picture from it.

Iris

The coloured part of the eye that expands and contracts to **control** the diameter and size of the **pupil** and thus the amount of light reaching the retina

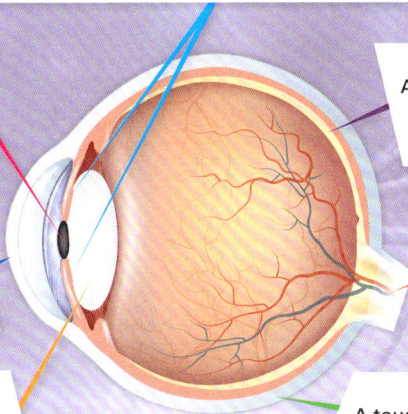

Pupil

A circular gap in the iris that lets light into the eye

Cornea

A transparent protective covering that refracts light into the eye

Lens

Focuses light onto the retina

Retina

A thin layer of tissue containing light receptors that convert light into electrical impulses

Optic nerve

Carries impulses from receptors in the retina to the brain

Sclera

A tough white protective outer layer

The receptors in the retina detect light, but they have limits. They require a minimum level of light to work. Likewise, if there is too much light, too many cells become stimulated, preventing the brain from making out patterns.

The iris contains two sets of muscles that can widen or narrow the pupil to let in more or less light. These changes in pupil diameter ensure that the retinal receptors receive an appropriate amount of light. The muscles act together antagonistically – as one muscle contracts, the other relaxes.

Normal Light

Pupil

Circular muscle

Radial muscle

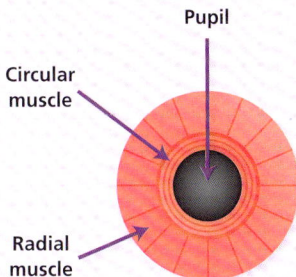

Bright Light

Circular muscles contract to constrict (narrow) the pupil

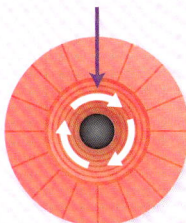

Dim Light

Radial muscles contract to dilate (widen) the pupil

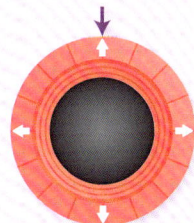

Accommodation

The way the shape of the lens adjusts to focus on objects at varying distances is called accommodation. To obtain a clear image, light hitting the retina must be appropriately focused.

The light rays from close objects need to be **refracted** more than the rays from distant objects. The **ciliary muscles** attached to the lens (via **suspensory ligaments**) alter its shape to increase refraction.

Focusing on a Near Object

Light rays from close objects diverge and need more refraction to bring the objects into focus.

To increase refraction:

- The ciliary muscles contract.

- The suspensory ligaments loosen.

- The lens thickens, strongly refracting the light rays.

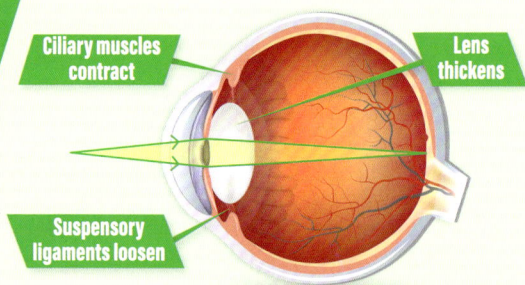

Ciliary muscles contract

Lens thickens

Suspensory ligaments loosen

Focusing on a Distant Object

Light rays from distant objects are parallel and need only a small amount of refraction to focus.

To reduce refraction:

- The ciliary muscles relax.

- The suspensory ligaments are pulled tight.

- The lens thins, lessening the angle at which it refracts light.

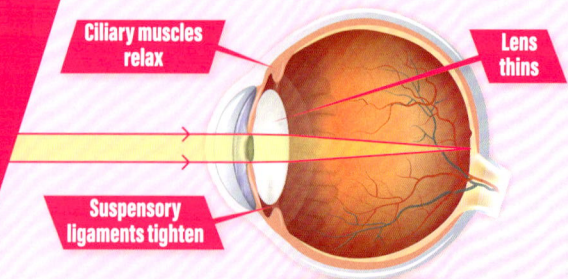

Ciliary muscles relax

Lens thins

Suspensory ligaments tighten

daydream EDUCATION

Eye Defects

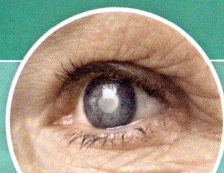

Short-Sightedness (Myopia)

Short-sighted people cannot focus on distant objects but can see close objects clearly.

Myopia commonly occurs when an eyeball's shape is more oval than spherical. This means that light doesn't focus on the retina at the back of the eye. Instead, the light focuses in front of the retina, making **distant** objects appear blurred.

Light is focused in front of the retina — Retina

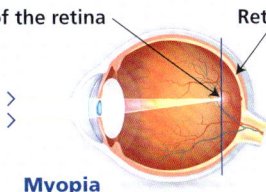

Concave lens — Retina

Wearing glasses with concave lenses, which curve inward, can correct short-sightedness.

Myopia

Myopia corrected

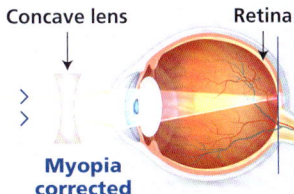

Long-Sightedness (Hyperopia)

Long-sighted people cannot focus on close objects but can see distant objects clearly.

Hyperopia commonly occurs in middle-aged people because the lens in the eye becomes stiffer and less able to focus. The lens does not refract the light sufficiently, so the light focuses behind the retina, making close objects appear blurred.

Light is focused behind the retina — Retina

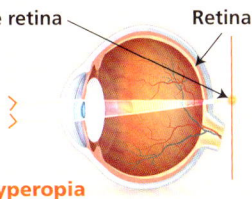

Convex lens — Retina

Wearing glasses with convex lenses, which curve outward, can correct long-sightedness.

Hyperopia

Hyperopia corrected

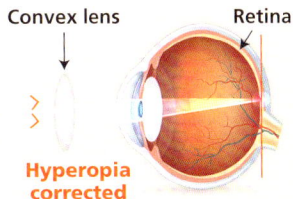

Alternative Treatments

Contact Lenses

Contact lenses are shaped to correct vision defects. Placed directly on the surface of the eye, they are discrete and useful when playing sports. There are two types: hard and soft. Soft lenses are more comfortable but carry a higher risk of infection.

Laser Eye Surgery

In laser eye surgery, a laser is used to burn away some of the cornea to change its shape so it changes the refraction of the light and adjusts the focusing of the eye. The surgery involves a low risk of infection or complication, but eliminates the need for glasses or contact lenses.

Replacement Lens Surgery

Replacement lens surgery involves replacing the lens with an artificial clear plastic one. It is often performed on people with cataracts (cloudy lenses), and can also be used to correct short- and long-sightedness. However, it does pose a higher risk than other treatments.

Controlling Body Temperature

All living processes are controlled by enzymes, which have an optimum temperature. Mammals and birds have internal mechanisms that maintain a constant body temperature, enabling their enzymes to work efficiently.

Detecting Body Temperature

Humans typically have a body temperature of around 37°C. To control internal temperature, the body must be able to detect it. This is done in the brain.

Internal body temperature is detected by receptors in the brain's **thermoregulatory centre** that monitor blood temperature.

Found in the **hypothalamus** region, the thermoregulatory centre also coordinates the responses that raise or lower body temperature.

The thermoregulatory centre also receives information about the external temperature from the skin's thermoreceptors.

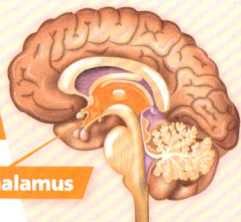

Hypothalamus

Responding to Temperature Changes

The body controls its temperature through a negative feedback mechanism. If the temperature rises or falls, a series of events are initiated to restore it to normal. This negative feedback mechanism can be seen on the *Homeostasis* page.

Body Temperature Too Low

Hair erector muscles contract to raise hairs and provide a thicker insulating layer of air.

No sweat is secreted by the sweat glands.

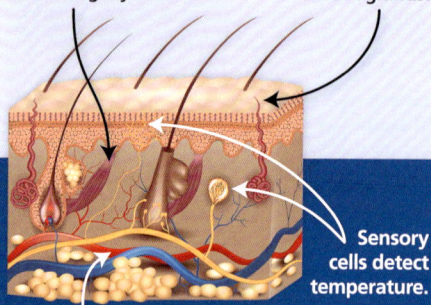

Sensory cells detect temperature.

Blood vessels near the surface of the skin constrict to reduce blood flow to surface capillaries in order to reduce heat loss.

The muscles shiver (contract and relax quickly) to generate heat through respiration.

Body Temperature Too High

Hair erector muscles relax to lower hairs and reduce the insulating layer of air.

Sweat glands secrete sweat, which evaporates on the surface of the skin.

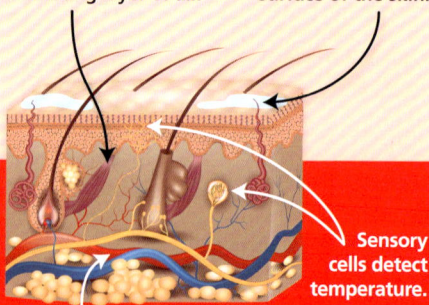

Sensory cells detect temperature.

Blood vessels near the surface of the skin dilate to allow more blood to flow to the surface capillaries in order to lose heat.

Energy is transferred from the skin to the environment.

daydream EDUCATION

The Endocrine System

The endocrine system is made up of glands that secrete hormones into the bloodstream.

Hormones are chemical 'messengers' that travel in the bloodstream from their source to target organs, where they produce an effect. Their effect is slower than that of the nervous system. However, they can target several different locations, and their effects act for longer.

Main Endocrine Glands in the Human Body

Pituitary Gland
The pituitary gland is attached to the underside of the brain. It acts like a 'master gland' because the hormones it secretes act on other glands to stimulate them to produce their own hormones. It secretes its hormones in response to changes in body conditions.

Thyroid Gland
The thyroid gland produces hormones that regulate the rate of metabolism in cells.

Adrenal Glands
The adrenal glands produce hormones that help to regulate metabolism and blood pressure. Also, in response to a perceived threat or danger, they produce adrenaline to prepare the body to either fight or flee.

Pancreas
The pancreas produces the hormones insulin and glucagon, which regulate blood sugar levels.

Ovaries
Ovaries produce the hormone oestrogen, which regulates the monthly menstrual cycle.

Testes
Testes produce the hormone testosterone, which stimulates sperm production.

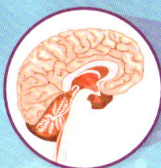

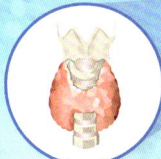

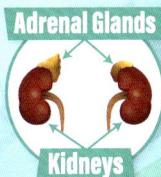

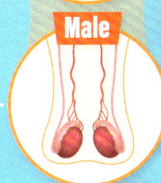

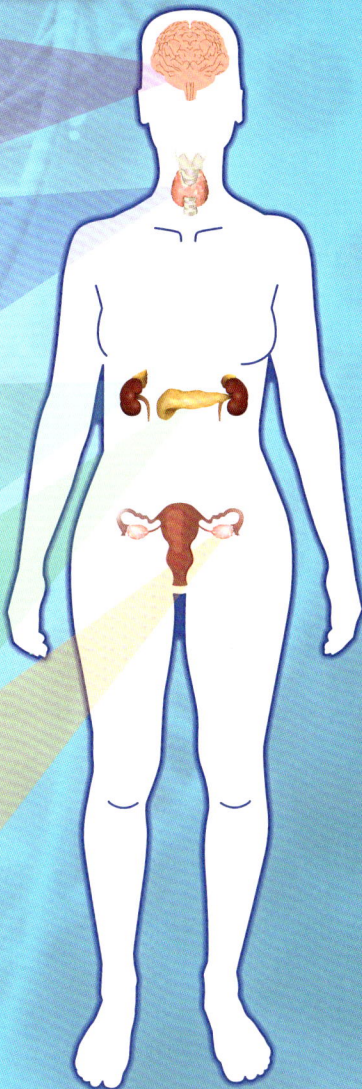

Adrenal Glands

Kidneys

Female

Male

Control of Blood Glucose Concentration

Glucose is needed for energy, but high levels of glucose in the blood can be harmful. Hormones from the pancreas control blood glucose concentration.

Pancreatic Hormones

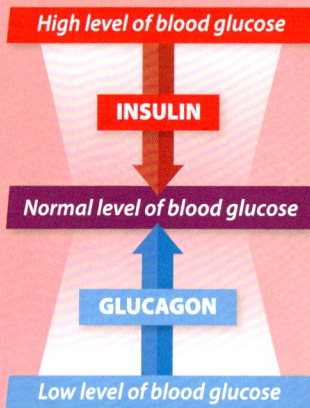

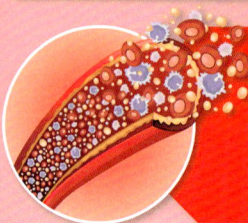

High level of blood glucose

INSULIN

Normal level of blood glucose

GLUCAGON

Low level of blood glucose

If the concentration of blood glucose gets too high, the pancreas secretes **insulin**. This triggers cells to take in glucose from the blood. The glucose is then converted into glycogen in the liver and muscles to **reduce blood glucose concentration**.

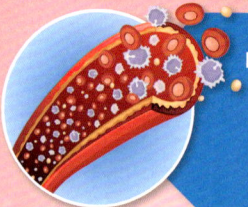

If the level of blood glucose falls too low, the pancreas produces **glucagon**. This triggers the muscles and liver to convert glycogen back into glucose. This glucose is then released into the bloodstream to **increase blood glucose concentration**.

This type of control is an example of negative feedback (see Homeostasis page for more information).

Diabetes

Diabetes is a disorder in which the body is unable to control the blood glucose level effectively. If unmanaged, diabetes can be very dangerous, leading to serious health problems.

Type 1 Diabetes

- The pancreas fails to produce sufficient insulin.
- It is characterised by uncontrolled high blood glucose and by glucose in the urine.
- It is treated with insulin injections.
- Monitoring carbohydrate intake and exercising regularly can help manage blood glucose level.
- It usually develops in children or young people.
- The cause is unknown.

Type 2 Diabetes

- The body cells no longer respond to insulin.
- It is characterised by uncontrolled high blood glucose (often not as high as in type 1) and glucose in the urine.
- Obesity is a big risk factor in the development of type 2 diabetes. As a result, it is usually treated with a carbohydrate-controlled diet and an exercise regime, along with tablets.

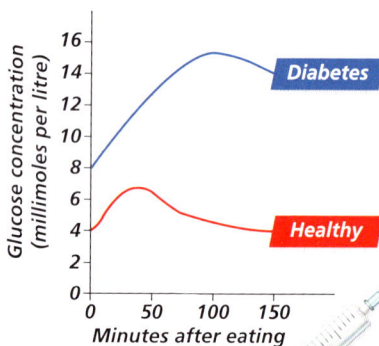

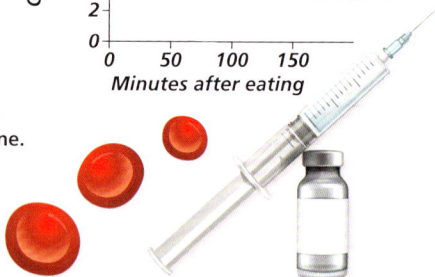

Glucose concentration (millimoles per litre) vs *Minutes after eating*

Diabetes

Healthy

daydream
EDUCATION

The Kidneys

The kidneys do two important jobs: they excrete poisonous nitrogenous waste (urea) and maintain blood and body fluid concentrations within a safe range. This action enables the efficient performance of body functions.

The Kidneys

In the kidneys, blood undergoes **filtration** to remove waste products and small soluble molecules from the blood.

Some of the molecules in the blood (e.g. glucose, amino acids) are useful and are reabsorbed into the blood in a process called **selective absorption**. Water and ions are also reabsorbed as necessary to maintain the blood concentration.

The remaining water, ions and dissolved urea form **urine**, which is stored in the bladder and then excreted from the body.

The Excretory System

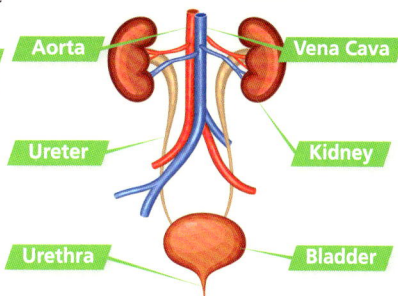

- Aorta
- Vena Cava
- Ureter
- Kidney
- Urethra
- Bladder

Urea

The body has no way to store amino acids, so excess amino acids are converted into carbohydrates or fats in the liver by a process called **deamination**.

During deamination, ammonia forms. Because ammonia is highly toxic, the liver immediately converts it into urea. The urea is then transported in the blood to the kidneys where it is filtered out with ions and water to form urine.

Some urea also leaves the body in sweat, but the amount secreted cannot be controlled.

Maintaining Water Balance

Maintaining a constant level of water in the body is important. Cells are mostly water, and all reactions in the body take place in solution. Gaining or losing too much water through osmosis can damage or kill cells and affect living processes.

The body gains water from:

- Food, which almost always contains water
- Drinks

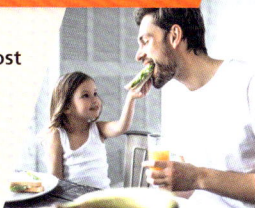

The body loses water through:

- Urination
- Sweat secretion
- Exhalation

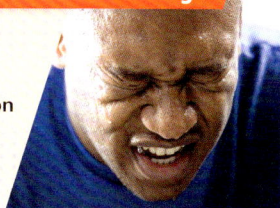

Water lost through sweat secretion and exhalation cannot be controlled. However, the body can adjust the water concentration of urine to control water loss.

If the body's water level gets so low that the kidneys cannot reabsorb enough water, the sensation of thirst kicks in, prompting us to take in fluids.

daydream EDUCATION

Balancing Ions

Ions enter the body in food and drink. The kidneys then re-absorb enough of them to maintain a healthy ion concentration.

If the body's balance of ions and water is not right, cells can become damaged or die. The kidneys regulate ion levels in the blood by filtering out surplus ions in urine.

Ions are also secreted from the body in sweat, but the amount cannot be controlled.

Anti-Diuretic Hormone

Anti-diuretic hormone (ADH) controls the mechanism that allows the kidney to re-absorb the right amount of water from urine.

ADH is released into the bloodstream from the pituitary gland in the brain. The amount of ADH released depends on the blood's water concentration.

If the water concentration in the blood is too high, the pituitary gland releases more ADH. The blood carries the ADH to the kidneys, where the ADH causes renal tubules to re-absorb more water. As a result, water concentration decreases in the urine.

When the water concentration in the blood returns to normal, less ADH is released. If the blood becomes too dilute, ADH production is reduced further, and less water is re-absorbed in the kidneys.

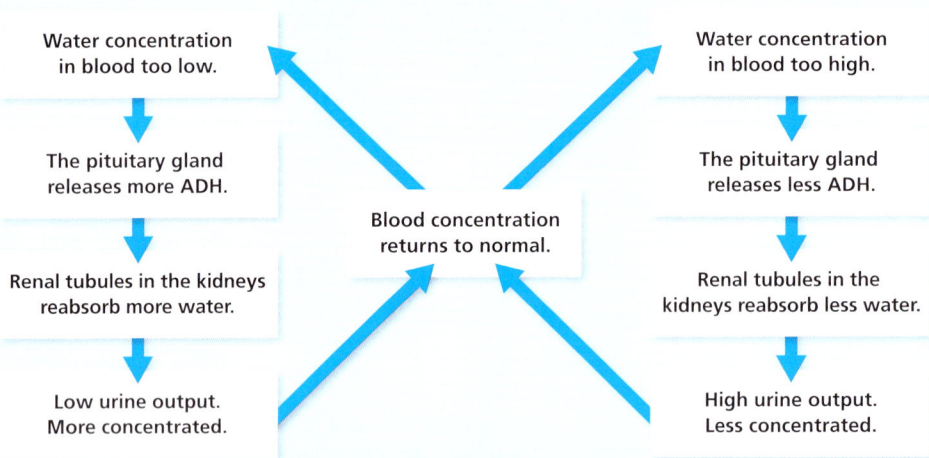

Water concentration in blood too low.
↓
The pituitary gland releases more ADH.
↓
Renal tubules in the kidneys reabsorb more water.
↓
Low urine output. More concentrated.

Blood concentration returns to normal.

Water concentration in blood too high.
↓
The pituitary gland releases less ADH.
↓
Renal tubules in the kidneys reabsorb less water.
↓
High urine output. Less concentrated.

This control mechanism is an example of negative feedback.

daydream EDUCATION

Kidney Failure

The kidneys control the body's water content and remove toxins and waste. Therefore, kidney failure is a serious condition. A person can survive with one working kidney, but if both fail, urgent treatment is required. Death can occur without treatment.

Dialysis

When kidneys stop working, a dialysis machine is used to remove wastes from the body and control water content.

Blood from the patient flows into the dialysis machine, which contains a series of partially permeable membranes surrounded by a fluid called dialysate.

Dialysate contains the same concentrations of glucose and ions as healthy blood, which enables excess glucose and ions to diffuse through the membrane into the dialysate from high concentration to low concentration.

Dialysate does not contain urea, so urea in the blood diffuses into the dialysate.

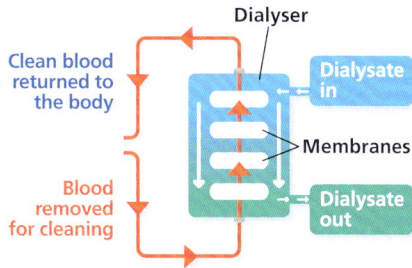

Clean blood returned to the body

Blood removed for cleaning

Dialyser

Dialysate in

Membranes

Dialysate out

During dialysis, the dialysate is constantly replaced to prevent the build-up of concentrations of wastes. The filtered blood is then passed back into the body

Disadvantages of Dialysis

- Dialysis sessions take 3–4 hours and are usually required three times a week.

- Patients must follow a strict diet to avoid waste build-up.

- Patients must be careful about how much fluid they consume between sessions because the body cannot self-regulate its water content.

- Because blood is removed from patients during dialysis, there is a risk of infection.

Kidney Transplants

Kidney disease can be cured by having a kidney transplant. If successful, this is much more convenient than regular dialysis sessions, but transplants also have disadvantages:

- A kidney transplant is a major operation that carries risks.

- Donors and patients must be a tissue match. Moreover, there is a shortage of donors so patients may have to wait years for a transplant.

- Even when there is a tissue match, the patient's immune system can reject the kidney. To prevent rejection, patients must take drugs that suppress their immune system. This can weaken their defences against everyday infections.

- The (transplanted) kidney has a limited lifespan of about 12 years on average.

Hormones in Human Reproduction

The functioning of the human reproductive system is regulated by hormones in both males and females. In females, hormones control the menstrual cycle and pregnancy.

Hormones in Males and Females

♀ Females

In females, the main reproductive hormone, oestrogen, is produced by the ovaries. It helps facilitate the menstrual cycle and the development of female secondary sex characteristics.

At puberty, eggs already formed in the ovaries begin to mature, and one is released approximately every 28 days (ovulation).

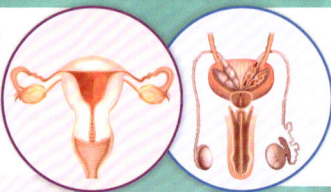

Males ♂

In males, the main reproductive hormone, testosterone, is produced by the testes. Testosterone stimulates sperm development at a constant rate from puberty.

In both sexes, reproductive hormones control the development of secondary sex characteristics, such as breast development, voice breaking and body hair growth.

The Menstrual Cycle

During the menstrual cycle, an egg is released from one ovary, and the female's uterus is prepared for a possible pregnancy. If the egg is not fertilised, the uterus reverts to its original state by shedding its lining in the process of menstruation (a period, when blood is lost).

The process is controlled by several different hormones.

MENSTRUAL CALENDAR

5	6	7	8	9	10	11
12	13	14	15	16	17	18
19	20	21	22	23	24	25
26	27	28	29	30	31	

Follicle-stimulating hormone (FSH) is released by the pituitary gland. It causes the maturation of the egg cell in the ovary and stimulates the production of oestrogen by the ovaries.

Luteinising hormone (LH) is produced by the pituitary gland and stimulates ovulation, the release of eggs from the ovaries, at 14 days.

Oestrogen and progesterone are produced in the ovaries. Both control the development and maintenance of the uterus lining in preparation for pregnancy.

FSH causes the maturation of an egg.

Oestrogen causes growth and repair of uterus lining.

Ovulation is caused by a peak in LH. During this time, there is also a fall in oestrogen.

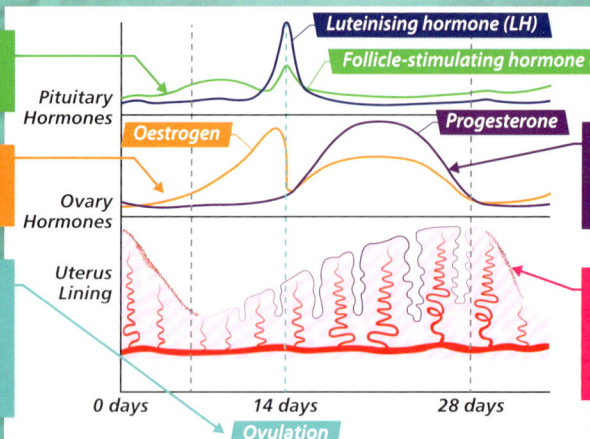

Progesterone continues the development of the uterus lining.

Menstruation is brought about by a fall in progesterone and oestrogen.

Luteinising hormone (LH)

Follicle-stimulating hormone (FSH)

Pituitary Hormones

Oestrogen

Progesterone

Ovary Hormones

Uterus Lining

0 days   14 days   28 days

Ovulation

daydream EDUCATION

Contraction

Hormonal Methods of Contraception

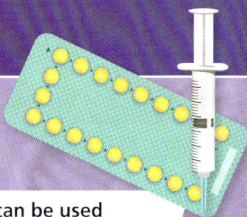

Hormones are used in the natural control of fertility. Hormones can be used artificially to prevent the fertilisation of an egg by a sperm, which results in pregnancy.

Hormonal methods of contraception include:

Oral Contraceptive Pill

The oral contraceptive pill contains oestrogen and progesterone, which inhibit follicle stimulating hormone (FSH) production. In turn, this prevents the maturation of eggs and implantation if fertilisation does occur.

Progesterone

Progesterone can be injected, implanted or delivered via a skin patch to inhibit the maturation and release of eggs naturally and therefore prevents pregnancy.

Non-Hormonal Methods of Contraception

Barrier Contraception

Barrier contraception prevents sperm from reaching the egg.

Condoms are worn over the penis to stop sperm entering the vagina. They also prevent the exchange of bodily fluids so protect against most STDs.

Diaphragms are shallow plastic domes that are placed over a woman's cervix to prevent sperm from entering the uterus. They are often covered in spermicidal agents that kill or damage sperm.

Intrauterine Device

Intrauterine devices (IUDs) are T-shaped 'coils' that are inserted into the uterus to prevent the implanting of an embryo in the uterus.

Some IUDs damage sperm so they cannot reach the egg. There are also hormonal IUDs. These release hormones that can prevent the release of an egg or thicken cervical mucus so the sperm cannot reach the egg.

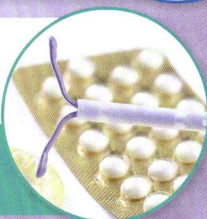

Sterilisation

Sterilisation is a permanent form of contraception.

Male sterilisation (vasectomy) is a surgical procedure that involves the tying or cutting of the sperm ducts between the testes and the penis.

Female sterilisation is a surgical procedure that involves the tying or cutting of the fallopian tubes between the ovaries and the uterus.

People who do not wish to use artificial contraception can prevent pregnancy by abstaining from intercourse during the times when an egg may be in the fallopian tube (oviduct). However, this is not always 100% effective.

Treating Infertility

Some women produce only a small amount of follicle-stimulating hormone (FSH) and luteinising hormone (LH), which leads to reduced ovarian function. This means that ovarian follicles do not grow properly, and an egg may not be released during ovulation.

Developments in modern reproductive technology have enabled hormones to be used to treat infertility. Fertility drugs (clomiphene, taken as a pill, and FSH and LH injections) are the initial main treatment for women with ovulation disorders.

In Vitro Fertilisation (IVF)

In IVF, fertilisation occurs outside the body.

Step 1

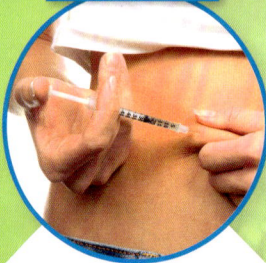

The mother is given FSH and LH to stimulate the production of multiple eggs.

Step 2

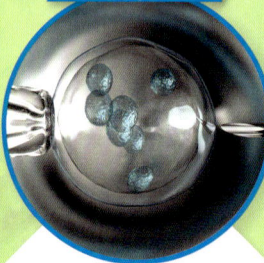

Eggs are collected from the mother and fertilised by sperm from the father in a laboratory.

Step 3

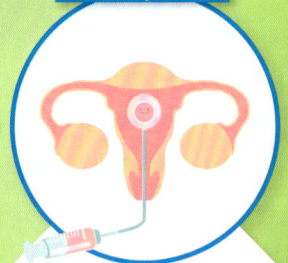

The eggs develop into early-stage embryos, and one or two are inserted into the mother's uterus.

Issues Around Fertility Treatment

Although fertility treatments enable infertile women and couples to have children, success rates are still relatively low (although improving); this can cause a lot of physical and emotional pain. There is also a greater risk of complications due to the increased chance of having multiple children.

During IVF, embryos are often destroyed. As a result, some people argue that IVF treatment is unethical and immoral because it destroys potential lives.

daydream EDUCATION

Adrenaline & Thyroxine

Adrenaline

Adrenaline is a hormone produced by the adrenal glands, which are found on the top of the kidneys. This hormone is produced at times of fear or stress, and prepares the body for 'fight or flight'.

- Adrenaline increases breathing rate to get more oxygen into the body.
- It also increases heart rate to pump oxygen and glucose to muscles more quickly.
- Adrenaline causes the liver to convert glycogen to glucose for increased energy.

The increased oxygen supply allows the body to respond more quickly in an emergency.

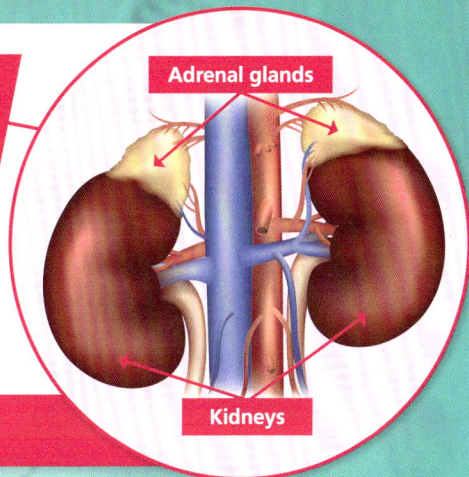

Adrenal glands

Kidneys

Thyroxine

Larynx

Thyroid   Trachea

Thyroxine is a hormone produced by the thyroid gland, which is found at the front of the trachea.

This hormone stimulates metabolism and plays an important role in growth and development. It also helps to maintain body temperature in cold conditions.

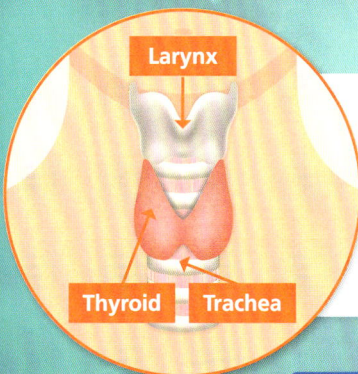

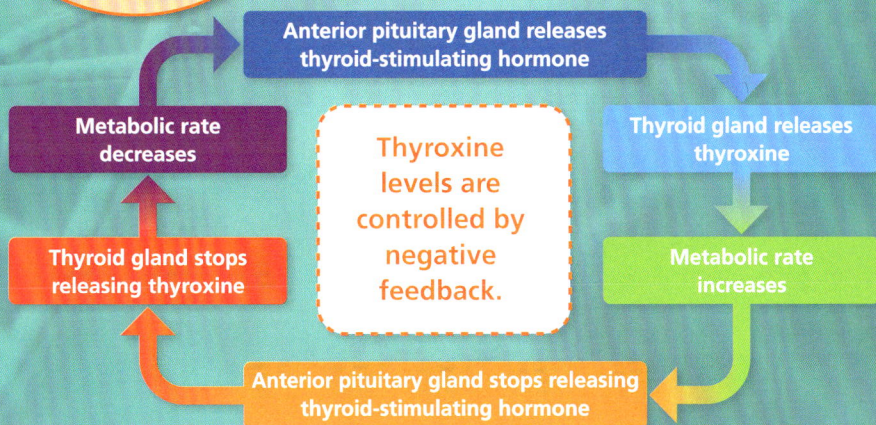

Anterior pituitary gland releases thyroid-stimulating hormone

Metabolic rate decreases

Thyroxine levels are controlled by negative feedback.

Thyroid gland releases thyroxine

Thyroid gland stops releasing thyroxine

Metabolic rate increases

Anterior pituitary gland stops releasing thyroid-stimulating hormone

daydream EDUCATION

Plant Hormones

Like animals, plants respond to stimuli. However, unlike animals, where coordination involves both nerves and hormones, all plant responses are controlled solely by hormones.

Auxin

Auxin, one of the most important plant hormones, affects the growth of plants.

Plants have specific areas where growth occurs, including sections just behind the tips of the roots and the shoots.

Auxin can have different effects on growth depending on its concentration.

Auxin is produced at the tip of a root or shoot.

It diffuses down to the zone of elongation, where it causes growth.

Zone of elongation

Tropisms

A **tropism** is a growth movement in response to a stimulus. Examples are **phototropism**, a response to light, and **gravitropism** (or geotropism), a response to gravity. Tropisms can be **positive** (growth towards the stimulus) or **negative** (growth away from the stimulus).

In stems, **positive phototropism** occurs due to the auxin moving away from the light.

The side where the auxin accumulates grows the most, causing the stem to bend towards the light.

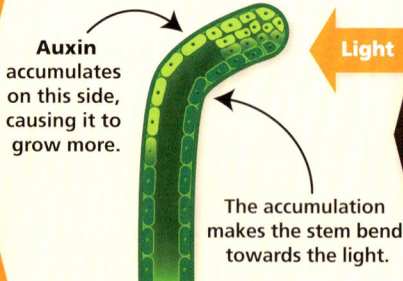

Auxin accumulates on this side, causing it to grow more.

Light

The accumulation makes the stem bend towards the light.

In stems, **negative gravitropism** occurs due to the auxin 'sinking' to the bottom of the stem.

The bottom of the stem grows more than the top, causing the stem to bend upward, away from gravity.

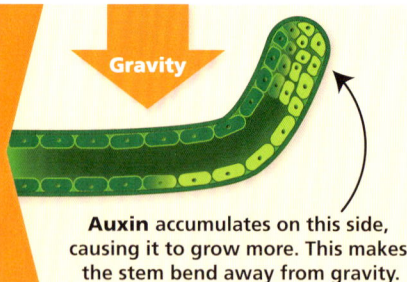

Gravity

Auxin accumulates on this side, causing it to grow more. This makes the stem bend away from gravity.

daydream EDUCATION

In roots, **positive gravitropism** is caused by the same mechanism as negative gravitropism in stems. However, the high concentration of auxin in roots inhibits growth rather than stimulates it.

The bottom of the horizontal root grows less than the top, causing the root to bend towards gravity.

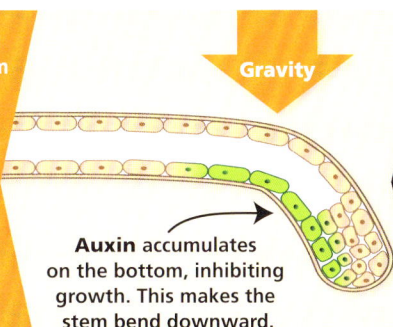

Gravity

Auxin accumulates on the bottom, inhibiting growth. This makes the stem bend downward.

Practical Activity 1

Phototropism can be investigated by analysing how light affects the growth of newly germinated seedlings.

1. Place a petri dish containing recently germinated seedlings (grown on a bed of cotton wool soaked in water) in a darkened room with a light source on just one side.

2. After several days, check on the seedlings. They should be bending towards the light. To obtain quantitative results, measure the angle of the bend.

Practical Activity 2

Gravitropism can be investigated by analysing the effect of gravity on the growth of newly germinated seedlings.

1. Place three seedlings in a Petri dish that contains cotton wool soaked in water. The orientations of the seeds should all be different.

2. Use a clamp stand to hold the Petri dish in a vertical position and place it in a dark room.

3. After a few days, check on the seedlings. All the young roots should be pointing downward in the direction of gravity.

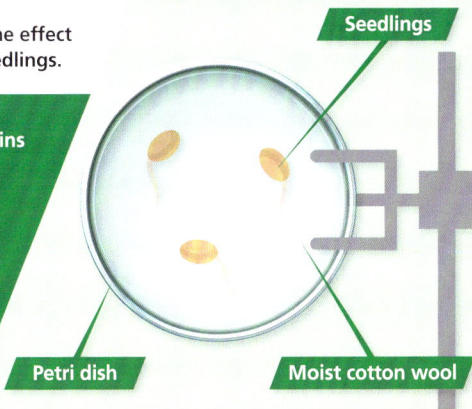

Seedlings

Petri dish

Moist cotton wool

daydream EDUCATION

Uses of Plant Hormones

Ethene

Ethene is a plant hormone that controls cell division and the ripening of fruit. The use of ethene enables growers to harvest and ship unripe fruit, which is hard and less liable to damage in transit. After the fruit arrives at its destination, it is exposed to ethene gas, which causes it to ripen.

Conversely, chemicals are often used to limit ethene production in fruit to prevent ripening. In particular, this is done on fruits that ripen quickly or that are stored for a long time.

Auxins

Auxins are a group of hormones that stimulate growth in plants. They are used in a wide variety of agricultural and horticultural products.

Rooting Powder

Rooting powder containing auxin can be applied to plant cuttings (parts of plants that have been removed from the main plant) to promote new root growth.

Auxin increases the cuttings' chances of survival and enables growers to grow lots of plant clones quickly.

Tissue Culture

Tissue culture is a process that makes it possible to grow whole plants from just a few cells.

The cells are treated with auxin, which stimulates cell division and the growth of roots and shoots.

Weed Killers

Most weeds that affect lawns and fields are broad-leaved plants, whereas grasses and cereals have narrow leaves. Broad-leaved plants are far more sensitive to certain auxins than narrow-leaved plants.

For this reason, auxins are used in weed killers. Auxins cause weeds to grow so rapidly that they essentially pull themselves apart without affecting the grass or cereal crop.

daydrean
EDUCATIE

Gibberellins

Gibberellins stimulate stem growth and promote seed germination and flowering. Because of this, they have a wide range of uses.

Inducing Flowering

Some plants only flower during a short period in the year (connected to day-length and temperature).

Treating plants with gibberellins can make them flower at any time of year, enabling flowers to be harvested and sold year-round.

Breaking Seed Dormancy

Seeds cannot germinate immediately after formation. A period of time must pass or certain conditions, which vary between plants, must be met before they can germinate.

Treating seeds with gibberellins breaks their dormancy, enabling germination at any time of year.

Growing Larger Fruit

Some plants produce fruits that contain no seeds. This occurs either naturally or through the use of plant hormones.

Consumers often prefer seedless varieties of fruit (e.g. grapes, watermelon), but they tend to be smaller than seeded varieties. However, treating fruit with gibberellins makes them grow larger.

daydream
EDUCATION

Reproduction

Reproduction is the process of generating offspring. There are two forms of reproduction: sexual and asexual.

Sexual Reproduction

Sexual reproduction takes place in animals and plants. It involves the joining (fusion) of male and female gametes (sex cells), which are formed through meiosis (see meiosis section for more information).

In both plants and animals, the female gamete is an egg cell. In animals, the male gamete is sperm, and in flowering plants, it is pollen.

Egg (Ovum)	Sperm	Zygote (Fertilised egg)
23 chromosomes	23 chromosomes	46 chromosomes in 23 pairs

 **+** 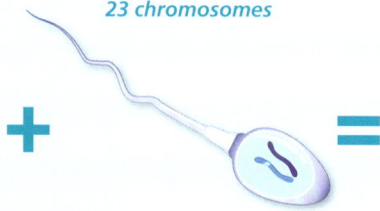 **=**

Human cells contain 46 chromosomes (23 pairs), but gametes (egg and sperm cells) contain only half this amount (one of each pair). When the two gametes fuse together during fertilisation, a cell containing the full set of 46 chromosomes is formed. The resulting cell contains a mixture of genetic material from the mother and the father.

Which of the pair of chromosomes ends up in each gamete is random. Therefore, all of the gametes are genetically different from each other. This also creates genetic variety in the offspring.

Asexual Reproduction

Asexual reproduction occurs in plants, bacteria and other simple organisms.

New cells are formed through mitosis only.

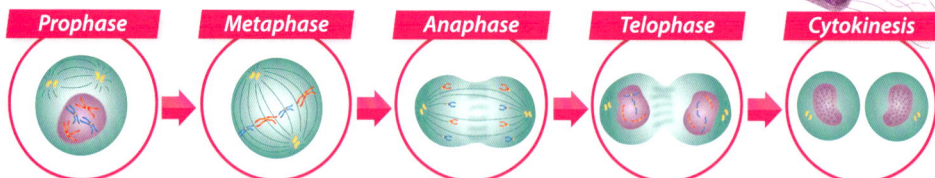

Prophase	Metaphase	Anaphase	Telophase	Cytokinesis

The cell divides to create two daughter cells, each of which has the same number of chromosomes as the parent nucleus.

Asexual reproduction involves one parent and no fusing of gametes, so there is no mixing of genetic material. Therefore, the offspring are genetically identical (clones).

daydream EDUCATIO

Meiosis

Cells in reproductive organs divide by meiosis to form gametes.

Body cells normally divide by the process of mitosis. However, the formation of gametes requires a different form of cell division called **meiosis**. In humans, this process ensures that each gamete contains 23 chromosomes, half the amount of a normal body cell, which contains 46 chromosomes.

In meiosis, there are two divisions so four cells (two daughter cells) are created from one.

The diagram below shows the stages in meiosis in a simplified format.

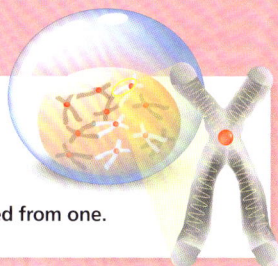

1 Before a cell divides, its genetic information is duplicated, creating a chromosome that consists of two identical chromatids. This process is known as DNA replication.

Duplication

2 The chromosomes line up in pairs at the centre of the cell (equator). The pairs are then pulled apart with half of the pair moving to one side of the cell and the other moving to the opposite side.

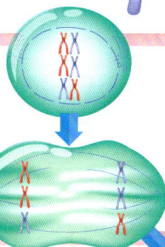

3 The cell divides, and the pairs of chromosomes are split between the two cells.

4 The chromosomes line up at the centre of the cell, and the chromatids separate to create four gametes that have a single set (half the normal number) of chromosomes.

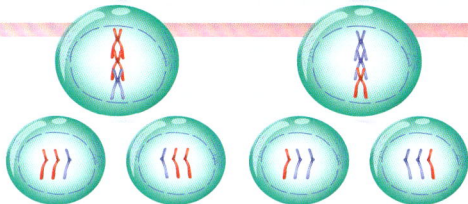

Which half of a pair of chromosomes ends up in each gamete is random. This means that all the gametes genetically differ from each other.

Embryonic Development

When the male and female gametes fuse through fertilisation, the normal number of chromosomes is restored.

The new cell then divides by mitosis during growth into an embryo. As the embryo develops, the cells differentiate into specialised cells that make up the whole organism.

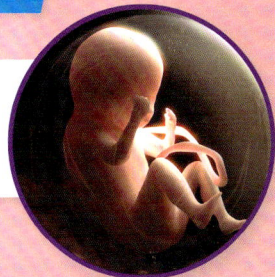

daydream EDUCATION

Sexual & Asexual Reproduction

Advantages of Sexual Reproduction

Sexual reproduction has one big advantage: variation.

Although sexual reproduction involves two parents, lots of flowers can reproduce sexually because they have male and female sex organs. Because this involves two gametes, it is still considered as two parents.

Variation in a population means that if a crisis occurs, such as a deadly epidemic, there is a chance that some individuals will be genetically resistant to it, saving the population from extinction.

Evolution relies on variation. If all the individuals are identical, it is impossible for new and better varieties to evolve. If organisms reproduce asexually, there is no mixing of parental genes and variation can only arise via mutation.

Selective breeding can be used to increase food production. For example, crops can be bred for improved disease resistance, and cows can be bred for greater milk production or improved meat quality.

Advantages of Asexual Reproduction

Widespread in living organisms, particularly in plants, asexual reproduction requires only one parent. Therefore, it is simpler and quicker than sexual reproduction and can produce large numbers of offspring in a short time.

Individuals do not have to find a mate to reproduce. Reproduction can occur even if a population is small and spread out, which is especially important for immobile organisms such as plants.

Using Both Sexual and Asexual Reproduction

Many organisms can reproduce both sexually and asexually.

Malarial Parasite

The malarial parasite is a single-celled organism that lives in humans. It is transferred from one person to another by mosquitoes when they feed on human blood.

The parasite reproduces sexually in mosquitoes but asexually in humans.

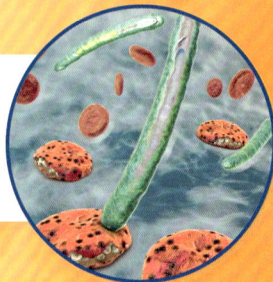

daydream
EDUCATION

Living organisms have two basic methods of reproduction: sexual and asexual.
Many organisms use both sexual and asexual reproduction.

Using Both Sexual and Asexual Reproduction (continued)

Fungi

Fungi reproduce by releasing spores, which can be produced both sexually and asexually, into the environment. Asexually produced spores are identical.

Sexual reproduction tends to occur when there is some sort of environmental stress – that is, when variation has an increased survival value.

Plants

Many plants reproduce asexually to supplement sexual reproduction by pollination. Examples include:

Daffodil Bulbs

Daffodil bulbs produce lateral bulbs that form new plants in the next growing season. The lateral bulbs easily separate from the main plant and grow into an identical plant.

Strawberry Plant Runners

Strawberry plants have runners, stems that grow horizontally across the soil surface. New plants form along the runner, and if the delicate runner breaks, the plants become separated.

Different Scenarios, Different Methods

In your exam, you could be asked to determine which method of reproduction is best in a given scenario. Consider:

- Is there a new environmental factor that could kill the organism? If so, sexual reproduction is best because it may give rise to individuals that can survive the change.

- Are the organisms plentiful enough that finding a mate is easy? If so, sexual reproduction is best. If not, asexual reproduction is best, especially for plants.

- Is a rapid population increase necessary (e.g. when first colonising an area)? If so, asexual reproduction is better because it is quicker.

daydream
EDUCATION

DNA

The genetic material in organisms is composed of a chemical called deoxyribonucleic acid, or DNA. It is found in the nucleus of animal and plant cells in structures called chromosomes.

Cell

Nucleus

The nucleus of a cell contains chromosomes, which are made of DNA molecules.

Chromosomes

Genome

The genome is the entire genetic material of an organism. An understanding of the human genome is vitally important. It enables scientists to:

- Search for genes linked to different types of disease.
- Understand and treat inherited disorders.
- Trace human migration patterns from the past.

The entire human genome has been studied, and the position of every gene is now known.

DNA

Genetic Inheritance

Each human cell with a nucleus (except gametes) contains 23 pairs of chromosomes (46 in total).

In each pair, one chromosome is inherited from the person's mother and one is inherited from the father.

The chromosomes contain the genes inherited from both parents. There may be different forms of the same genes called alleles.

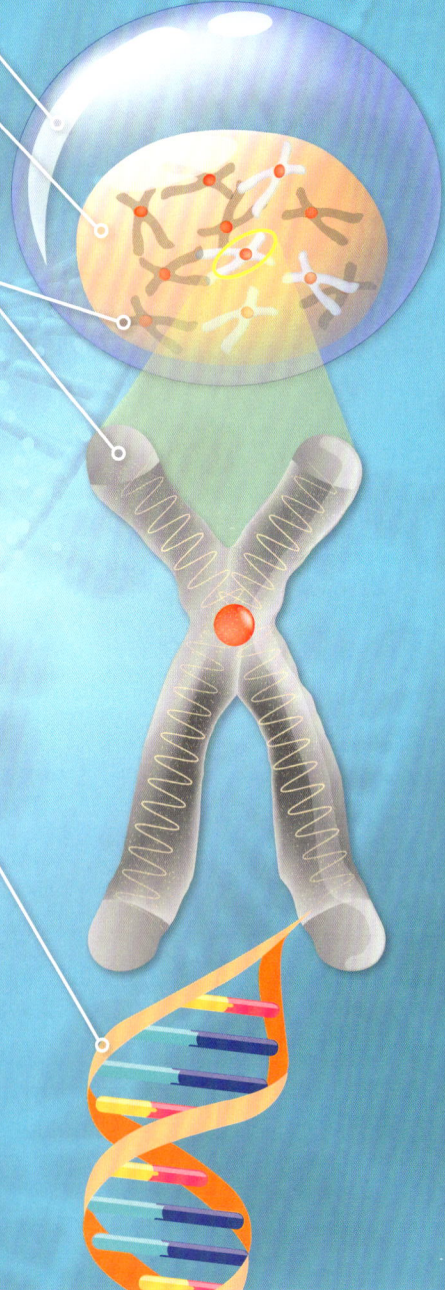

daydream EDUCATION

DNA

DNA contains the genetic instructions for the development and function of organisms. It is a polymer consisting of two strands that are wound into a double helix (twisted ladder shape).

The strands are made of repeating units called **nucleotides**.

Each nucleotide consists of a sugar and phosphate group linked to one of four bases: thymine (T), adenine (A), guanine (G) and cytosine (C).

These bases pair up in a specific way, known as complementary base pairing.

Nucleotide

G always binds to **C**

Guanine   Cytosine

T always binds to **A**

Thymine   Adenine

These base pairs hold the DNA strands together.

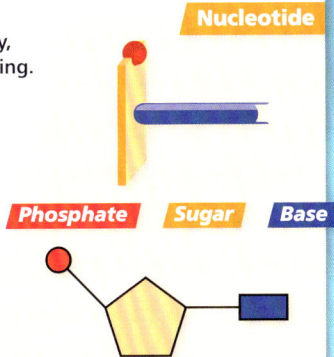

Phosphate   **Sugar**   **Base**

Genes

Genes are sections of DNA in a chromosome that code for proteins.

Proteins are made of long chains of amino acids.

Genes instruct cells how to sequence amino acids to make different proteins.

Each gene codes for a particular sequence of amino acids to make a specific protein.

Each amino acid is coded by a sequence of three bases (triplet). For example, the amino acid glycine is coded by the triplet GGA.

There are 64 different possible triplet codes but only 20 amino acids, so some amino acids have multiple triplets.

Glycine

G

G

A

Not all sections of DNA code for proteins. The functions of these non-coding sections are uncertain. Some genes may switch others on or off, so variations in these DNA sections may affect how genes are expressed.

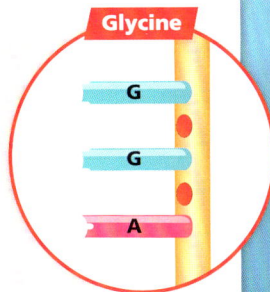

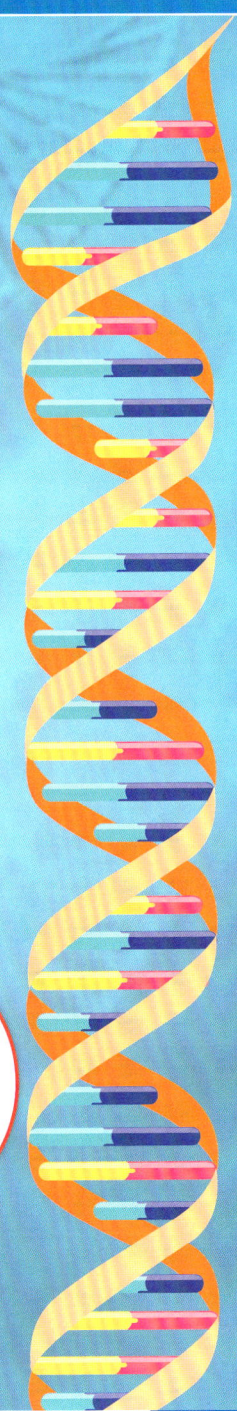

Protein Synthesis

Proteins are assembled in ribosomes, tiny structures in the cell cytoplasm. Because DNA is too big to pass through the nucleus, the DNA code is copied to another molecule, **messenger RNA (mRNA)**, which transports it to the ribosomes.

The following is a simplified description of the process of protein synthesis.

DNA strand **mRNA** 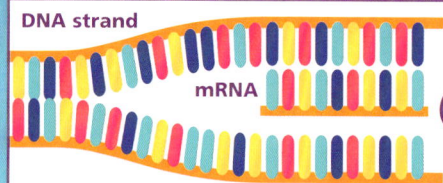	**1** The DNA double helix unwinds and the strands split apart. DNA from one of the strands is then copied to mRNA.
Ribosome **Nucleus** 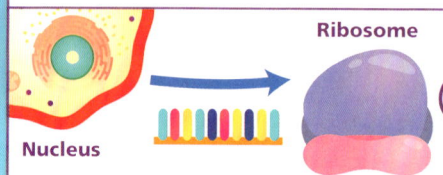	**2** The mRNA travels from the nucleus to the ribosomes in the cytoplasm.
Amino acid **tRNA** **Base** 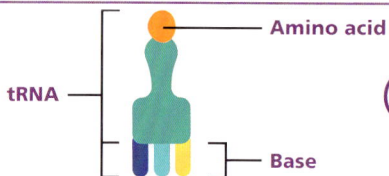	**3** Carrier molecules, called **transfer RNA (tRNA)**, bring amino acids to the ribosomes. tRNA have three specific bases that pair with the complementary triplet code on the mRNA.
	**4** As the tRNA bases attach to the mRNA bases, the amino acids on the tRNA join to form the protein specified by the DNA.

Once the chain of amino acids is complete, it folds to form a protein with a specific shape, which enables it to perform its function correctly.

Proteins play a very important role in the function of living things.

- Enzymes are proteins that catalyse all the chemical reactions in the body.

- Most hormones are proteins. They act as chemical messengers in the body, travelling in the blood and causing events in cells some distance from where the hormones are produced.

- Structural proteins, such as collagen, are important in strengthening tissues like ligaments and cartilage. Proteins also form part of the structure of cell membranes.

daydream EDUCATION

Mutations

DNA is replicated when new cells form. However, mistakes occasionally occur during replication, and the base sequence of the DNA changes, resulting in mutations. Factors such as radiation, and certain chemicals can increase the rate of mutation.

Effects of Mutations

Most mutations have very little or no effect. Proteins are large, complex molecules and many of the amino acids they contain are not vital to their function. Also, mutations may occur in areas of the DNA that do not actually code for proteins.

Mutations can be beneficial. For example, features that have become common in a species because their development aided survival often began as mutations. However, some mutations are harmful:

- If an amino acid in an enzyme's active site is changed, the enzyme may be unable to function because it no longer binds to its specific substrate.
- The function of a hormone may be disrupted by a change in its structure.
- Changes in a structural protein, such as collagen, may weaken its structure.

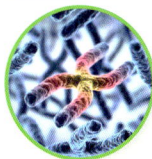

Mutations can occur in genes that control other genes, resulting in changes to the function of the 'controlled' genes.

Insertion

Sometime an extra base is inserted into a DNA sequence, disrupting the sequence of the bases and altering the genetic code.

For example, inserting guanine disrupts and changes the amino acid coding.

Deletion Sometimes a base may be removed from the sequence. This changes the amino acid coding in a similar way to insertion.

Both insertion and deletion completely alter all the amino acids encoded by the gene following the mutation.

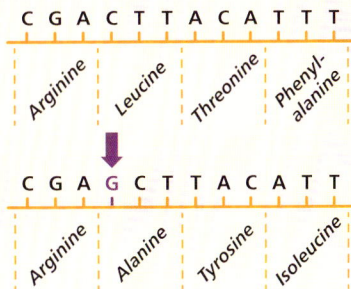

C G A C T T A C A T T T
Arginine | Leucine | Threonine | Phenyl-alanine

C G A G C T T A C A T T
Arginine | Alanine | Tyrosine | Isoleucine

Substitution

Sometimes a base may be changed to another base, altering the code for just one amino acid. However, it may not change the amino acid produced because many amino acids have more than one code.

CCC, CCA, CCT and CCG all code for the amino acid proline. Therefore, if A (in CCA) is changed to G, the amino acid will not change.

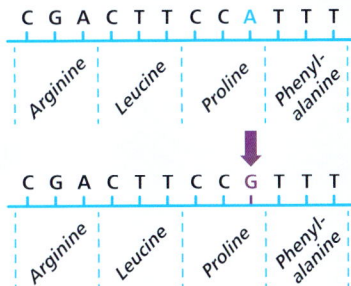

C G A C T T C C A T T T
Arginine | Leucine | Proline | Phenyl-alanine

C G A C T T C C G T T T
Arginine | Leucine | Proline | Phenyl-alanine

daydream
EDUCATION

Genetic Inheritance

Control Systems

Every cell in the human body, except gametes, contains 23 pairs of chromosomes. One chromosome in each pair is inherited from the mother's ovum and one is inherited from the father's sperm.

The **genes that an organism** inherits from its parents determine its characteristics.

Some characteristics are controlled by a single gene (e.g. fur colour in mice, red–green colour blindness in humans), but most are a result of multiple genes interacting (e.g. height in humans).

Variations of a given gene are called **alleles**, and **every gene has more than one allele**. Alleles operate at a molecular level to determine the genetic makeup of an organism (genotype), and therefore, its physical (phenotypic) characteristics.

Alleles are either dominant or recessive.

A **dominant allele** will always be expressed, even if only one copy is present.

For example, the allele for brown eyes is dominant. Therefore, only one copy is needed to have brown eyes. (Two copies will also result in brown eyes.)

A **recessive allele** is not always expressed. For a recessive allele to be expressed, two copies must be present.

For example, the allele for blue eyes is recessive. Therefore, two copies of this allele are needed to have blue eyes.

Two alleles can be equally dominant. In such cases, both alleles are expressed equally. For example, the blood group **AB** is the result of codominance of the **A** and **B** dominant alleles.

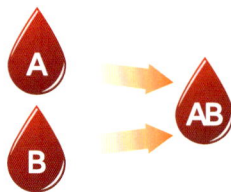

If the two alleles present are the same, the organism is **homozygous** for that trait. However, if the alleles are different, they are **heterozygous**.

Key Terms

Term	Definition
Gene	A small section of DNA
Alleles	Variations of a given gene
Homozygous	Two identical alleles
Heterozygous	Two different alleles
Genotype	The genetic makeup of an individual organism (i.e. the alleles it contains)
Phenotype	The way a gene is expressed; its observable characteristics
Dominant	An allele that is always expressed in the phenotype
Recessive	An allele that shows in the phenotype only when it is homozygous

daydream EDUCATION

Genetic Prediction Using Punnet Squares

It is possible to work out the possible genotypes of offspring using diagrams called punnet squares. In these tables, alleles are given single letter symbols. **Dominant alleles are always capital letters**, and **recessive alleles are always lower-case letters**.

Rr

The example below shows a cross that could result in a plant with red or white flowers.

Red is dominant and white is recessive. Therefore, red is the capitalised letter (R) and white is the lower-case letter (r). The same letter is always used for both alleles.

	Plant 1 🌷	Plant 2 🌷
Phenotypes	Red	Red
Genotypes	Rr	Rr
Gametes	R or r	R or r

These are the possible **gametes** that each plant can produce. A gamete has only one allele.

Although both plants are red, they are heterozygous, with red and white alleles. They have the genotype **Rr**.

The punnet square below shows all the ways in which parents' gametes can combine to produce different genotypes in the offspring.

Plant 1 *Gametes*

	R	r
R	RR 🌷	Rr 🌷
r	Rr 🌷	rr

Plant 2 *Gametes*

The letters on the outside of the grid represent the parents' gametes. The combinations of letters inside the grid show the possible genotypes of the offspring.

Using the punnet square, you can calculate the outcomes of the cross as follows.

Outcome	Genome	Chance	Percentage
Homozygous dominant red flower	RR	1 in 4	25%
Heterozygous red flower	Rr	2 in 4	50%
Homozygous recessive white flower	rr	1 in 4	25%
Red flower	RR or Rr	3 in 4	75%
White flower	rr	1 in 4	25%

We say that the offspring have a 3:1 ratio of red to white.

The ratio indicates the probability of getting each type of plant. It is three times more likely that a red-flowered plant will be produced than a white-flowered one. It does not mean that there will always be **exactly** three times as many red-flowered plants as white-flowered ones.

Genetic inheritance can also be shown using a family tree (see Inherited Disorders section).

Inherited Disorders

Certain alleles can be harmful and cause genetic disorders. Many of these alleles are recessive, but some are dominant.

Genetic Disorders

Polydactyly (having extra fingers and toes) is a rare genetic disorder that is caused by a dominant allele.

Because the allele is dominant, it is inherited when only one parent has a defective allele. It also means that any parent with the defective gene will also have the disorder.

In the examples below, the allele for polydactyly is Y. The recessive, normal allele is y.

If one parent in a couple has polydactyly and a genotype of Yy, the offspring has a 50% chance of having the disorder (Yy).

	y	y
Y	**Yy**	**Yy**
y	yy	yy

Cystic fibrosis (CF) is a disorder of the cell membrane caused by a recessive allele.

The faulty gene causes the production of thick sticky mucus which results in a wide range of health problems, including breathing problems.

Because the allele is recessive, a person with only one defective allele will not have cystic fibrosis, but they will be a carrier. To have cystic fibrosis, a person needs to inherit a defective allele from both parents.

In the examples below, the allele for cystic fibrosis is f. The dominant, normal allele is F.

One Parent Carries

	F	f
F	FF	Ff
F	FF	Ff

If only one parent is a carrier, the offspring has a 50% chance of being a carrier (Ff) but cannot have the disorder.

Both Parents Carry

	F	f
F	FF	Ff
f	Ff	ff

If both parents are carriers, the offspring has a 50% chance of being a carrier (Ff) and a 25% chance of having the disorder (ff).

One Parent with CF

	f	f
F	Ff	Ff
F	Ff	Ff

If one parent has CF and the other is not a carrier, the offspring cannot have the disorder but will definitely be a carrier (Ff).

daydream EDUCATION

Family trees can be used to show how genetic disorders have been inherited in a family over multiple generations. Each generation is connected to the next by a vertical line, with the oldest generation at the top of the tree.

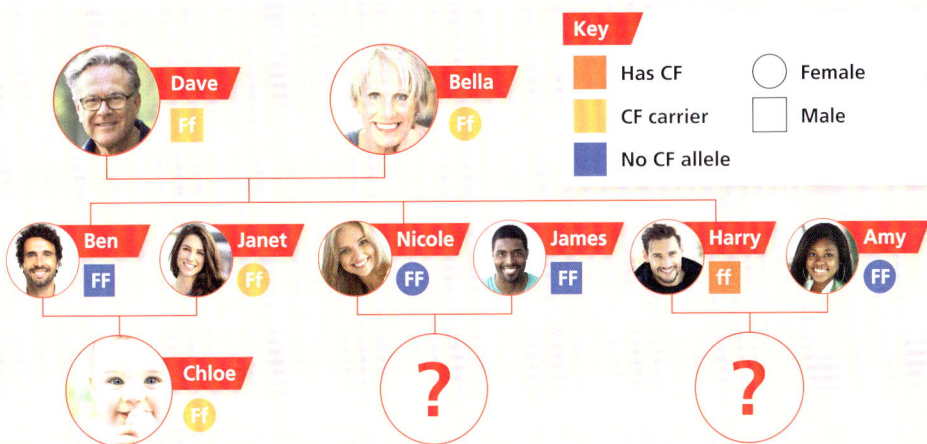

Key

- Has CF
- CF carrier
- No CF allele
- Female
- Male

Dave Ff

Bella Ff

Ben FF | **Janet** Ff | **Nicole** FF | **James** FF | **Harry** ff | **Amy** FF

Chloe Ff | **?** | **?**

Dave and Bella are both carriers of cystic fibrosis, so their chance of having a child with cystic fibrosis is 25%, or 1 in 4. This does not mean that if they have four children, one will definitely have cystic fibrosis; each child's chance of having the disorder is independent.

In reality, the family tree shows that they had three children: one, Harry, with cystic fibrosis and two, Ben and Nicole, who are completely free of the defective allele.

Ben and Janet's child, Chloe, is a carrier.

As neither Nicole nor James are carriers, their children will also be free of cystic fibrosis.

Harry has cystic fibrosis. If he has a child with his non-carrier partner, Amy, their child will not have the disorder. However, it will definitely be a carrier of the defective allele.

	F	F
f	Ff	Ff
f	Ff	Ff

Embryo Screening

Embryo screening involves examining the genetic makeup of embryos to check for disorders such as cystic fibrosis or Down's syndrome.

There are many economic, social and ethical issues concerning embryo screening because it gives parents the opportunity to abort the embryo if a problem is detected. Screening is also expensive and can damage healthy embryos.

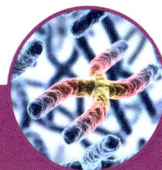

daydream
EDUCATION

Sex Determination

In humans, ordinary body cells contain 23 pairs of chromosomes. Of these 23 pairs, 22 control characteristics only, and one carries the genes that determine sex.

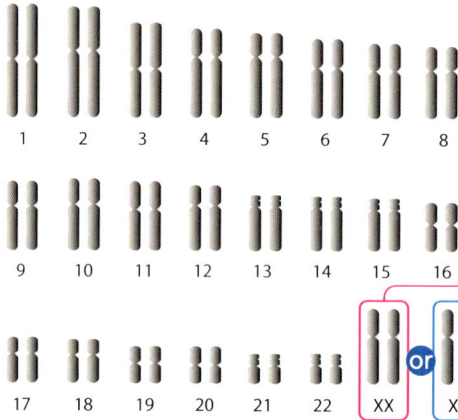

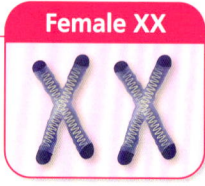

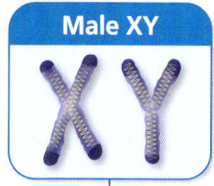

1 2 3 4 5 6 7 8

9 10 11 12 13 14 15 16

17 18 19 20 21 22 XX or XY

Female XX

Male XY

Females have two X chromosomes, so the female genotype is XX.
In males, the paired chromosomes are not identical, and the genotype is described as XY.

Gametes form from cell division during meiosis.

When the female sex chromosome pair divides, each gamete (egg) gets an X chromosome.

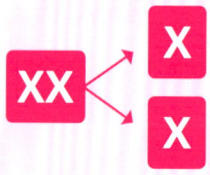

XX → X
X

When the male sex chromosome pair divides, each gamete (sperm) either gets an X chromosome or a Y chromosome.

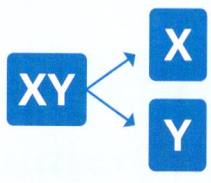

XY → X
Y

Sex Inheritance

A genetic cross can be used to show sex inheritance.

		Mother gametes	
		X	X
Father gametes	X	XX	XX
	Y	XY	XY

The genetic cross shows that there is an equal chance of having a boy or girl.

There is a 50% (2 in 4) chance of having a boy (XY).

There is a 50% (2 in 4) chance of having a girl (XX).

daydream EDUCATION

Variation

Populations of living organisms show extensive variation, with all organisms displaying different characteristics.

What Causes Variation?

The phenotype of an organism is determined by a combination of its genotype (genetic makeup) and how it interacts with the environment.

Even within the same species and breed, there is variation. For example, no two humans are genetically identical.

Genetic Factors

Variation is caused by differences in genes inherited from parents' genotypes.

Examples: blood group, fur colour, leaf shape

Combination of Factors

Some variations are caused by an interaction of genetics and the environment.

Examples: weight, skin colour, plant height

Environmental Factors

Variation is caused by environmental influences or interactions with the environment.

Examples: piercings, scars, leaf discolouration

Mutations and the Origin of Variety

All genetic variations in a population originate from past mutations (changes in DNA).

Mutations occur naturally and continually, and most have little to no effect on the organism's phenotype. However, some mutations do influence the phenotype, either causing harm or improvement, but very rarely does a mutation produce a completely new phenotype.

If a mutation benefits the survival chances of an organism, it can lead to a relatively rapid change in the species. For example, if the new phenotype is suited to a change in the environment, it can lead to rapid change.

Mutations can also be caused by outside factors, such as certain chemicals and radiation.

The Theory of Evolution

Over time, the inherited characteristics of a population change through the process of natural selection. This may eventually lead to the formation of a new species.

According to the theory of evolution by natural selection, all species have evolved from simple life forms that first developed more than three billion years ago. Charles Darwin and Alfred Russell Wallace first published this theory in 1858.

Previous Theories

Before Darwin and Wallace, the most accepted theory of 'evolution' had been proposed by Jean-Baptiste Lamarck (1744-1829).

Lamarck believed that characteristics acquired during an organism's lifetime could be passed on to the next generation.

For example, if a giraffe spent its entire lifetime stretching its neck to reach high leaves, its neck would get longer, and this characteristic could be passed to its offspring.

Except in rare cases in which a lifetime of experience causes a genetic change, we now know this theory is incorrect.

Charles Darwin

Charles Darwin developed his theory of evolution by natural selection based on observations made on a round-the-world voyage, years of experimentation and a growing body of knowledge regarding geology and fossils.

In 1859, the year after his and Wallace's theory was published, Darwin's book, *On the Origin of Species*, which fully described the theory of evolution by natural selection, was released. Darwin's ideas were controversial for the following reasons:

- The theory contradicted the idea held by many religious people that God created all life on Earth.
- Some scientists did not feel there was enough evidence to support the theory.
- Nobody knew about genetics until 50 years later, so Darwin could not explain how characteristics are passed from one generation to the next.

As the study of genetics emerged and developed the theory of natural selection became accepted by virtually all the scientific community.

A common misconception about Darwin's theory is that it suggests humans evolved from monkeys. Instead, the theory suggests that humans and monkeys have a common ancestor.

daydream
EDUCATION

Natural Selection

Natural selection is the theory that individuals best adapted to their environment are likely to outcompete those less adapted to survive. They are also likely to produce more offspring.

- Mutations result in variation in the population.
- Some phenotypes have an increased chance of survival.
- More of the phenotypes best suited to the environment will survive to breed, passing on their advantageous alleles.
- A greater proportion of the next generation will have the advantageous phenotype.
- The process repeats itself each generation, making the advantageous phenotype more and more common.

Example Over time, giraffes evolved to have longer necks and legs to increase their chance of survival.

1 There are giraffes with varying neck and leg lengths in a population.

2 The giraffes with longer necks and legs can reach food that is higher up. Therefore, they have a greater chance of survival.

3 Shorter giraffes have less chance of survival, so fewer remain in the population and reproduce. Conversely, a greater number of taller giraffes remain to produce offspring with the more desirable traits.

4 A greater proportion of the taller giraffes remain in the population generation after generation, making the better phenotype more and more common.

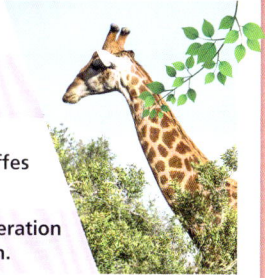

In gathering further evidence on the theory of natural selection, Alfred Russell Wallace also studied warning colouration and speciation.

Warning Colouration

Warning colouration is the opposite of camouflage. Animals use warning colours for protection to make predators think that they are dangerous in some way (e.g. poisonous). Warning colours usually consist of a combination of yellow, red, black and white.

Speciation

A species is a group of organisms that can breed with each other to produce fertile offspring.

Sometimes, evolution causes populations within a species to become so different in phenotype that they can no longer interbreed to produce fertile offspring. Therefore, creating two new species. This process is known as speciation, and it usually occurs as follows:

- The population splits into groups that become isolated from each other, often because of a natural barrier (e.g. a river or mountain range).
- If the conditions on each side of the barrier vary, natural selection and, thus, evolution, will occur differently for the groups.
- Some of these differences may prevent the two populations interbreeding if they ever meet up again (e.g. they may evolve different breeding seasons).

daydream EDUCATION

Selective Breeding

Selective breeding, or artificial selection, is the process by which plants and animals are bred for particular genetic characteristics.

It involves breeding organisms with desirable characteristics to produce offspring that share these characteristics. This is then repeated over multiple generations to continually improve the characteristics and spread them across the whole of the population.

Breeding Sheep for Wool

From an existing flock, males and females with the best quality wool are separated out and bred together.

Their offspring are once again assessed, and those with the best quality wool are used for breeding.

In each generation, the quality of the wool is better than the last because those with poorer quality wool have been removed from the breeding programme.

Other Examples of Selective Breeding

Crops have been bred for improved disease resistance.

Cows have been bred for either greater milk production or improved meat quality.

Plants have been bred to produce large or unusually coloured flowers.

Dogs have been bred for intelligence and a calm temperament.

Disadvantages of Selective Breeding

Animals or plants that are selectively bred are often closely related, which reduces the gene pool (the total set of genes in a population) and increases the chances of inbreeding.

As well as amplifying desirable characteristics, selective breeding can increase the chances of organisms inheriting defective genes that cause diseases and other health problems. The lack of variation in a population can also reduce resistance to new communicable diseases.

The English bulldog, which has been bred for appearance, now suffers from a wide variety of health problems due to inherited defects. Furthermore, the dogs now lack the genetic diversity needed for breeders to selectively breed unhealthy dogs with healthier phenotypes.

daydream
EDUCATION

Genetic Engineering

Genetic engineering involves modifying the genome of an organism by inserting a gene cut out from the DNA of another organism to provide useful characteristics.

Genetically Modified Crops

Plants have been genetically engineered to be resistant to diseases or to produce bigger and better-quality crops. Plants that have been changed in this way are called genetically modified (GM) crops.

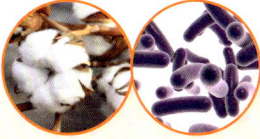

Cotton plants + genes from bacteria for toxin resistance

⬇

Cotton plants that are resistant to insect attack

⬇

Higher yields of cotton

Tomato plants + antifreeze genes from cold-water fish

⬇

Tomato plants that are resistant to frost

⬇

Tomatoes that can be grown outside in cold climates all year round

Corn plants + genes from soil bacteria for herbicide resistance

⬇

Corn plants that are resistant to herbicides

⬇

Fields that can be sprayed with herbicide and only the weeds will die

There are benefits and possible risks of GM crops.

Benefits
- Increased crop yields = more food
- Better quality food
- Reduction in use of chemical insecticides

Possible Risks
- Health risks from eating GM crops
- Reduced biodiversity caused by killing weeds and insects
- Herbicide resistance passing to weeds

Human Proteins

Bacteria can be genetically modified to produce human proteins, such as insulin, which is used to treat people with diabetes.

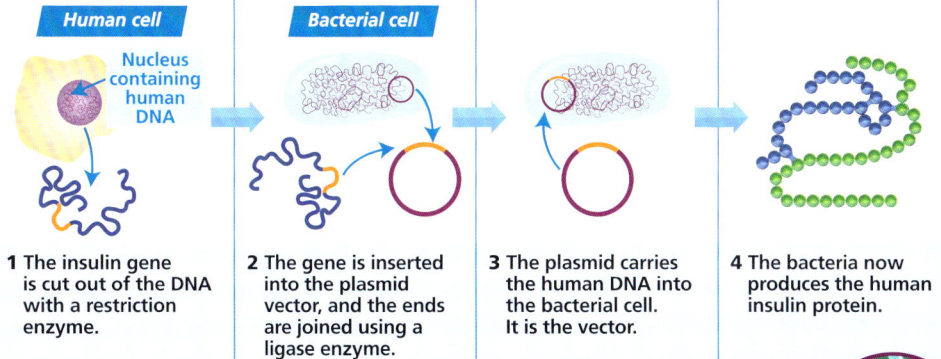

Human cell

Nucleus containing human DNA

Bacterial cell

1 The insulin gene is cut out of the DNA with a restriction enzyme.

2 The gene is inserted into the plasmid vector, and the ends are joined using a ligase enzyme.

3 The plasmid carries the human DNA into the bacterial cell. It is the vector.

4 The bacteria now produces the human insulin protein.

Gene Therapy

Researchers are currently investigating possible ways to cure inherited disorders (e.g. cystic fibrosis) by replacing faulty alleles in the human genome with healthy alleles.

There are ethical concerns that people may use this process to have 'designer' children with particular characteristics, such as sporting talent or high intelligence. Some people are also concerned that genetic engineering could result in unknown problems for future generations.

daydream EDUCATION

Cloning

Clones are living organisms that are genetically identical. Cloning is the process of creating a genetically identical copy of an existing organism. It can happen naturally by asexual reproduction in plants and artificially in both animals and plants.

Cloning Plants

Cuttings

Plants have been cloned for a long time by taking cuttings and growing them.

Because the new plant is a part of the original, it is genetically identical to it. Cuttings are a cheap and quick way of growing new plants.

Tissue Culture

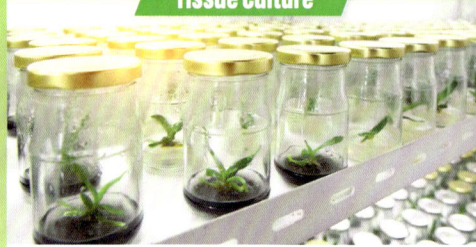

Tissue culture involves growing plant tissue or cells in a growth medium to produce clones of a parent plant. It enables large numbers of plants to be produced in a short time.

This process has been used to build up rare plant populations. Also, nurseries use it to mass-produce plants for sale.

Cloning Animals

Embryo Cloning

Identical twins are natural clones, formed when an early embryo, from a single fertilisation, splits into two parts, each of which develops into a baby.

Scientists can extend this process by fertilising an egg outside the body of an animal.

The early embryo is split into individual cells before they become specialised.

Each cell is then grown into an embryo, and implanted into the uteruses of different mothers.

The resulting offspring are genetically identical.

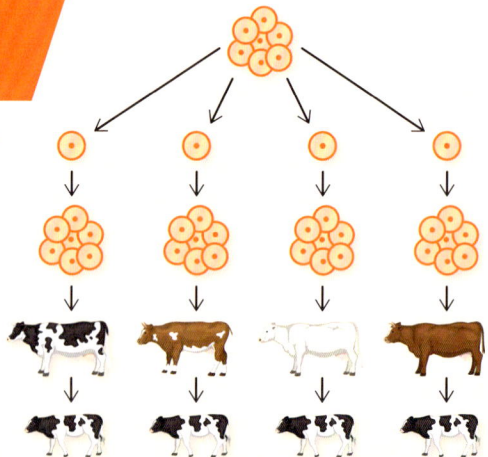

daydream
EDUCATIO

Adult Cloning

An unfertilised egg cell can have its nucleus removed and replaced with one from an adult cell, such as a skin cell. The egg cell is then stimulated by electric shock so that it divides and forms an embryo.

The resulting embryo can be implanted into a surrogate mother to continue its development. The baby will be genetically identical to the animal that provided the adult cell nucleus.

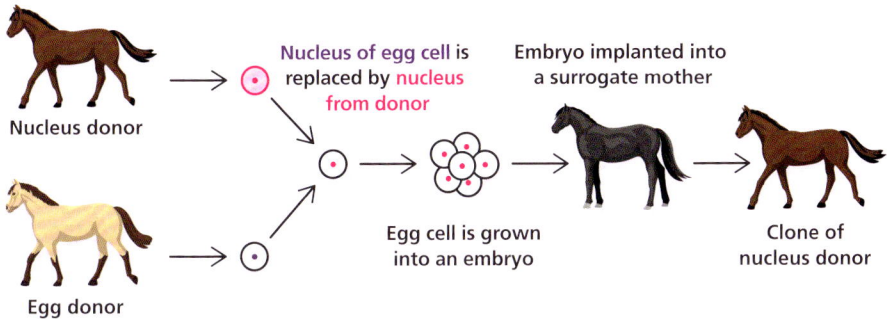

Nucleus donor

Egg donor

Nucleus of egg cell is replaced by **nucleus from donor**

Egg cell is grown into an embryo

Embryo implanted into a surrogate mother

Clone of nucleus donor

Cloning Controversy

Cloning has benefits, but many people are opposed to it, especially in animals.

Benefits

- Breeders can produce animals and plants with known characteristics (e.g. cows with high milk yield, fast racing horses) that will be genetically identical to the original.

- Because genetically identical animals or plants can be created, cloning can be useful for fair testing in science.

- Cloning can conserve endangered plant species. In the future, it may be used similarly for animals.

Concerns

- Some religious groups feel that it is wrong for humans to make life to a 'design'.

- Some evidence suggests that animals produced by adult cloning have a shorter life expectancy or may be less healthy than normal animals.

- There are concerns that humans could have 'designer babies' or clone themselves. Human cloning research is banned in many countries, including the UK.

Understanding Genetics

Gregor Mendel was an Austrian monk who, through his work on pea plants, first discovered the basic theory of inheritance: the idea that information is passed from one generation to the next by hereditary units, or genes.

His work remained largely unknown until after his death, but now he is known as the 'Father of Genetics'.

Mendel's Garden Experiments

Mendel performed various breeding experiments in his monastery garden. One reason for Mendel's success was that he worked with pea plants. Inheritance in peas is much less complex than in humans and other animals, which had been the subject of earlier efforts.

In his experiments, Mendel crossed a tall plant with a dwarf plant. He expected the offspring to be medium-sized, but they were all tall.

He concluded that the tall plant had a hereditary unit that was dominant over the dwarf unit. Therefore, the offspring inherited the dominant unit.

He did not know if the dwarf unit had been destroyed or had simply become hidden.

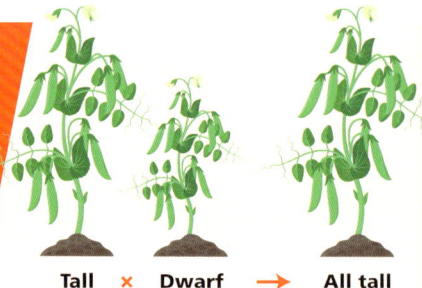

Tall × Dwarf → All tall

Mendel then self-pollinated the tall plants from his first cross. This time, about one-quarter of the plants were dwarf.

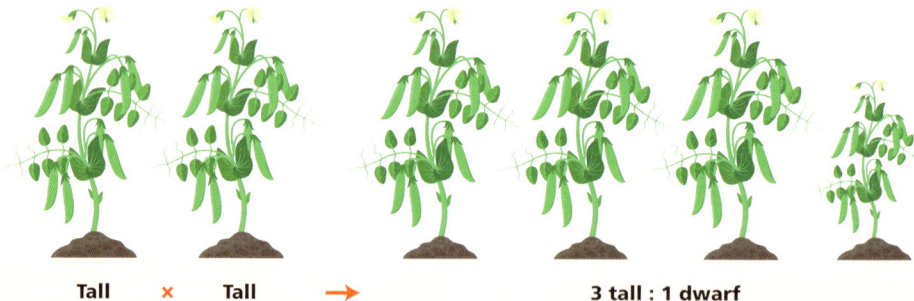

Tall × Tall → 3 tall : 1 dwarf

This indicated that the dwarf unit, which was recessive, had not been destroyed in the first cross but was simply hidden.

It also showed that there were two units, now called alleles, for height in each plant. As a result, Mendel concluded that the offspring inherited one hereditary unit from each parent.

daydream EDUCATIO

Genetic Notation

Mendel's crosses can be explained by using modern genetic notation as shown.

T	=	**Tall allele (dominant)**
t	=	**Dwarf allele (recessive)**
TT	=	**Homozygous tall plant**
Tt	=	**Heterozygous tall plant**
tt	=	**Homozygous dwarf plant**

First cross:

$$TT \times tt \longrightarrow Tt$$

Second cross:

$$Tt \times Tt$$

Gametes	T	t
T	TT	Tt
t	Tt	tt

Later Developments

Mendel published his results in an obscure magazine, which meant his work remained largely unknown until after his death. Regardless, during the 19th century, Mendel would have been unlikely to prove his theory because there was no knowledge of genes or DNA.

Mendel's findings were rediscovered at the beginning of the 20th century, by which time the behaviour of chromosomes during cell division had been observed.

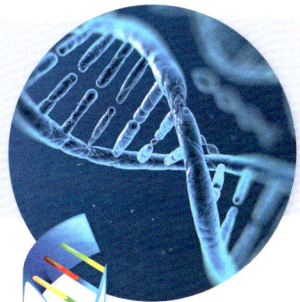

It was discovered that chromosomes and Mendel's units behaved in similar ways. This led to the idea that the units were located on chromosomes, and the units were renamed **genes**.

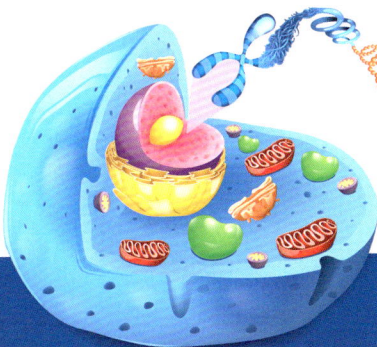

When the structure of DNA was discovered in the mid-20th century, scientists were able to determine how genes functioned.

Although Mendel is credited with first devising the theory of genetics, the development of gene theory involved the scientific work of many scientists.

Evidence for Evolution

Evidence For Evolution by Natural Selection

The theory of evolution by natural selection is now widely accepted because of evidence that it has happened in the past and is still happening today.

The fossil record shows a sequence of progressive changes in body form, leading from ancient ancestors to modern species.

The theory of genetics has shown how characteristics can be inherited from one generation to the next, in the form of genes.

There are examples of natural selection occurring today – for example, the evolution of antibiotic resistance in bacteria.

Fossils

Fossils are the remains of organisms from millions of years ago, found in rocks.

Fossil Formation

- Organisms or parts of them may be preserved when the conditions needed for decay are absent (e.g. insects preserved in amber).
- The hard parts of organisms may be replaced by minerals as they decay, leaving an impression in the rock formed around them.
- Traces of organisms such as footprints, burrows and rootlet traces may be preserved when the mud they were formed in turns to rock.

Fossilisation usually preserves only the hard parts of an organism. Therefore, there are few traces of the earliest forms of life, which were mainly soft-bodied organisms.

Whatever traces may have existed have been destroyed by geological activity. As a result, scientists cannot be certain how and when life first evolved. The whole fossil record is very incomplete because the conditions for fossilisation rarely occur.

daydream
EDUCATION

Extinction

Extinction occurs when there are no remaining individuals of a species left alive.
Extinction can occur for a variety of reasons:

- The climate may change, and the species cannot adapt to the new climate quickly enough.

- The species' habitat may be destroyed, leaving it nowhere to live.

- Another similar species may arrive and out-compete the existing species.

- A predator may wipe out the entire population. Humans are the most common cause of this.

Resistant Bacteria

Evolution is a process that occurs gradually over many generations. As a result, until recently, it has only been possible to find evidence of evolution through fossils.

However, some simple organisms, such as bacteria, reproduce at a rapid rate, so they evolve quickly. This enables scientists to monitor how such organisms evolve through natural selection.

Some bacteria, such as the MRSA bacterium, have evolved a resistance to most antibiotics.

Natural Selection in Antibiotic-Resistant Bacteria

1 Resistant strains of bacteria are not killed when infections are treated with antibiotics.

2 Whilst non-resistant strains die, the resistant strains survive, reproduce and increase in numbers.

3 The resistant strain spreads because people are not immune to it and antibiotics are unable to treat it.

The overuse and misuse of antibiotics has led to an increase in antibiotic-resistant bacteria.

Slowing the Development Rate of Resistant Bacteria

- Overuse of antibiotics causes bacteria to mutate, so doctors are encouraged not to prescribe antibiotics for viral or non-serious infections.

- Failing to complete a full course of antibiotics can result in bacteria surviving and mutating into resistant forms. Therefore, patients must complete their full course of antibiotics.

- Overuse of antibiotics in agriculture (e.g. dosing cattle with antibiotics to prevent infection) should be restricted.

These measures are very important because new forms of antibiotics cannot be developed as quickly as new resistant strains of bacteria emerge. This may mean that some infections can no longer be controlled.

Classification of Living Organisms

Linnaeus's Classification Model

Traditionally, living things have been classified into groups depending on their characteristics. The Linnaeus system divides living organisms into five kingdoms, which are then subdivided into smaller and smaller groups.

Each species is given a scientific name, which consists of two words. The first indicates the genus, the second the species. This is known as the binomial system.

Tiger (*Panthera tigris*)

Increase in numbers / Decrease in similarity

Decrease in numbers / Increase in similarity

Kingdom	Animalia
Phylum	Chordata
Class	Mammalia
Order	Carnivora
Family	Felidae
Genus	Panthera
Species	*Panthera tigris*

French rose (*Rosa gallica*)

Increase in numbers / Decrease in similarity

Decrease in numbers / Increase in similarity

Kingdom	Plantae
Phylum	Angiospermae
Class	Dicotyledoneae
Order	Rosales
Family	Rosaceae
Genus	Rosa
Species	*Rosa gallica*

Members of the same species can appear to be very different from each other. If they are the same species, they can breed together to produce fertile offspring.

daydream
EDUCATION

Three-Domain System

Improvements in microscopes and the understanding of biochemical processes have meant that classification systems have had to be updated. Based on evidence from the chemical analysis of genetic material, a new three-domain system was proposed by Carl Woese in 1977.

In this system, organisms are divided into:

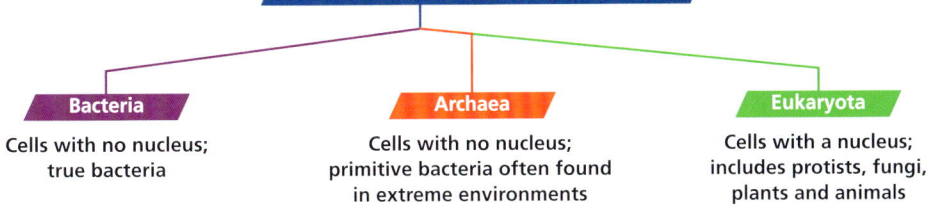

Bacteria

Cells with no nucleus; true bacteria

Archaea

Cells with no nucleus; primitive bacteria often found in extreme environments

Eukaryota

Cells with a nucleus; includes protists, fungi, plants and animals

These are then subdivided into the smaller groups used in the five-kingdom system.

Evolutionary Trees

Evolutionary trees are used by scientists to show how they believe organisms are related.

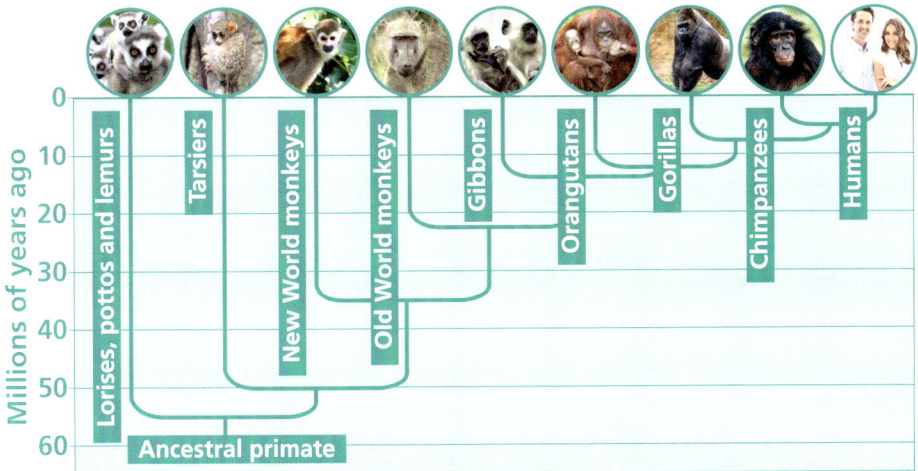

Millions of years ago

Lorises, pottos and lemurs
Tarsiers
New World monkeys
Old World monkeys
Gibbons
Orangutans
Gorillas
Chimpanzees
Humans

Ancestral primate

To show common ancestors and relationships between species, scientists use current classification data for living organisms and fossil data for extinct organisms.

The further up the evolutionary tree an organism is, the more recently it branched from the other species on the tree from a common ancestor. Species that are closer on the tree are more closely related.

Evolutionary trees are also known as phylogenetic trees.

Adaptations, Interdependence & Competition

Communities

An ecosystem is a community of living organisms together with their physical environment. It includes the interactions between the living (**biotic**) and non-living (**abiotic**) components.

Key Terms

Habitat	The place where organisms live
Community	All the living things in an ecosystem
Population	All the organisms of any one species living in a habitat
Organism	An individual living thing

Competition and Interdependence

In ecosystems, living things interact with each other and their habitat in different ways. **Interspecific competition** is competition between organisms of different species, whereas **intraspecific competition** is competition between organisms of the same species.

Organisms compete for resources from their surroundings and from other living organisms, but they also depend on each other to survive and reproduce.

Within a community, plants compete for light, space, water and minerals, whereas animals compete for food, water, territory and mates.

	Tomato Plant 	**Bee** 	**Thrush** 
Organism			
Competes with	Other plants for light, water and minerals.	Other bees and some other insects for food	Other birds for food and nesting sites
Depends on	Insects for pollination; animals to distribute seeds (by eating fruit)	Plants for food (nectar)	Invertebrates for food; plants for nesting sites

Interdependence

All parts of an ecosystem are interdependent. This means that if one factor changes, it will affect the other parts of the ecosystem.

The weather is hot and little rainfall occurs. → Fewer plants grow. → Less food & shelter cause grasshopper and mouse populations to shrink. → Less food causes rat and snake populations to shrink. → Less food causes the owl population to shrink.

The more interactions there are within a community, the greater the level of interdependence. A high level of interdependence often leads to a stable community where all the biotic and abiotic factors are in balance. As a result, the population sizes remain fairly constant. In small communities, the removal of a single species can have major effects.

daydream EDUCATION

There are various factors within an environment that can affect the function of ecosystems. These factors are categorised as abiotic or biotic.

Abiotic Factors

An abiotic factor in an ecosystem is one that is non-living. These include:

light intensity   temperature   moisture levels   oxygen levels

carbon dioxide levels   wind intensity and direction   soil pH and mineral content

The importance of these factors varies in different ecosystems and for different organisms. Light intensity, soil type and carbon dioxide levels are usually only significant for plants, whereas oxygen levels are most important for aquatic animals that need oxygen dissolved in the water for aerobic respiration.

The example in the Interdependence section shows how an abiotic factor (lack of rainfall) can affect the whole community within an ecosystem.

Biotic Factors

A biotic factor in an ecosystem is one that is living. These include:

Introduction of predators

Availability of food

Competing species

Introduction of diseases (pathogens)

These biotic factors can have devastating effects on a community, causing imbalances in organism populations and an unstable community.

Each factor has direct and indirect effects on a community. For example, the introduction of a new predator into a community will not only lead to a decrease in the prey population, but it will also indirectly affect other organisms in the community that are dependent on the prey.

Adaptation

Organisms have features (adaptations) that help them to survive in their natural habitat.

Structural

Physical features that help organisms to survive

Cacti have spines instead of leaves to reduce water loss by evaporation and transpiration, and to protect them from predators.

Behavioural

Learned or inborn behaviours that help organisms to survive

Polar bears dig deep dens in the snow to protect themselves from strong winds.

Functional

Bodily processes that help organisms to survive

Snakes and spiders produce poisonous venom, which helps with protection and immobilising prey.

Some organisms, known as extremophiles, are highly specialised so that they can live in extreme conditions, such as high temperatures (thermophiles) or high salt concentrations (halophiles).

daydream
EDUCATION

Organisation of an Ecosystem

Levels of Organisation

All living organisms need a supply of nutrients to survive and build biomass.

Photosynthetic organisms (mainly green plants and algae) can produce their own food using light energy and inorganic materials through photosynthesis. They are called **producers**. They use this food to provide energy for other life processes.

All other organisms obtain energy from eating other organisms. They are called **consumers**. The original source of all the energy in living organisms is the Sun.

Food Chains

The feeding relationships in a community can be represented in the form of food chains, which show the direct transfer of energy between organisms in an ecosystem.

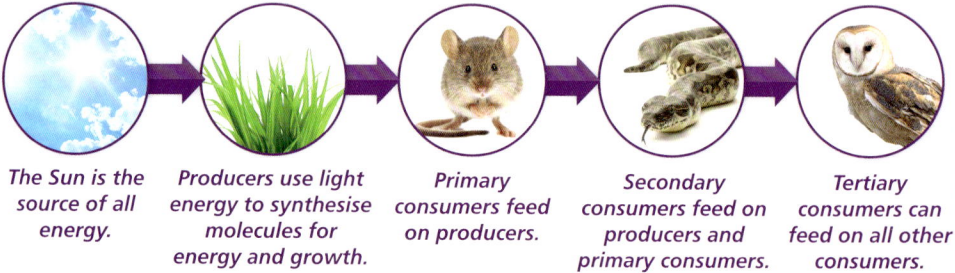

The Sun is the source of all energy.

Producers use light energy to synthesise molecules for energy and growth.

Primary consumers feed on producers.

Secondary consumers feed on producers and primary consumers.

Tertiary consumers can feed on all other consumers.

Predator and Prey Relationships

Consumers that eat other animals are predators, and those that are eaten are prey. In stable communities, the numbers of predators and prey rise and fall in cycles.

An increase in prey will support a larger number of predators. However, when the predators increase, they will eat more prey, reducing their numbers.

When the prey population is reduced, the population will be able to support fewer predators. This occurs in a continuous cycle.

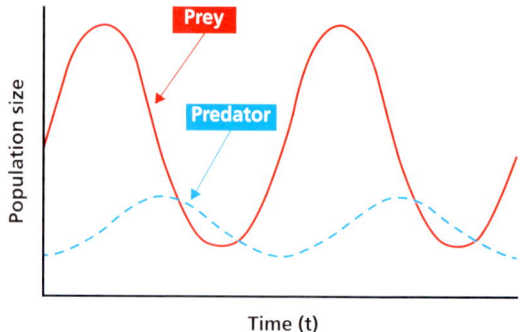

daydream EDUCATION

Measuring the Abundance and Distribution of Organisms

It is not always possible to collect information on a whole population. In such instances, a proportion (sample) of the population is used instead. Ecologists use a wide range of sampling methods to determine the abundance and distribution of species in an ecosystem.

Quadrats

A quadrat is a square frame of a specific size (often 0.5 × 0.5 m). It is used to sample an area that is too big to completely survey.

The number of one or more species in each quadrat is counted and then scaled up to estimate the number in the whole area.

Rules for Using Quadrats

The positioning of the quadrats must be random to avoid bias.	The number of quadrats must be sufficient to give a representative picture of the whole area.	Diverse habitats need a larger number of quadrats than uniform habitats.

Quadrat Example: Estimate the total number of snails in a habitat that is 4,000 m^2.

Total area of habitat = 4,000 m^2

Number of quadrats used = 100

Area of 1 quadrat = 0.25 m^2

Total area sampled = 0.25 × 100 = 25 m^2

Number of snails in sample area (100 quadrats or 25 m^2) = 80

Total number of snails in whole habitat = $\frac{4,000}{25}$ × 80 = 12,800

Transects

A transect is a line, usually marked by a rope or tape measure, that is used to measure the distribution of organisms, not their numbers.

Samples are taken at regular intervals along the line, and the species seen at each point are recorded. The line is usually laid along some sort of gradient to see its effect on distribution (e.g. low tide mark to high tide mark).

Mathematical Terms Used in Ecology

When collecting data on the abundance of organisms in an ecosystem, you will often need to calculate averages, or the middle value of a data set. There are three main types of averages.

Mean	Median	Mode
The sum of all values divided by the number of values	The middle value when data is arranged in order of size (If there is an even number of values, it is the mean of the two middle numbers.)	The value that occurs most often

Cycling Materials

The materials that living things need to survive and reproduce are in limited supply. Therefore, they must be constantly recycled for life to persist.

The Carbon Cycle

All life on earth is carbon based. Therefore, a constant supply of carbon is needed to support life. Carbon is cycled mainly through the processes of respiration and photosynthesis, but also through combustion and decay.

Respiration, combustion and decay release carbon dioxide into the atmosphere, whereas photosynthesis removes it from the atmosphere.

Key Terms

Combustion

Energy and carbon dioxide are released when fossil fuels are burned.

Photosynthesis

Sunlight is used to convert carbon dioxide and water into glucose (which contains carbon) and oxygen.

Respiration

Glucose and oxygen are converted into energy, carbon dioxide and water.

Decay

Organic matter decomposes, releasing carbon dioxide, methane, energy, water and minerals.

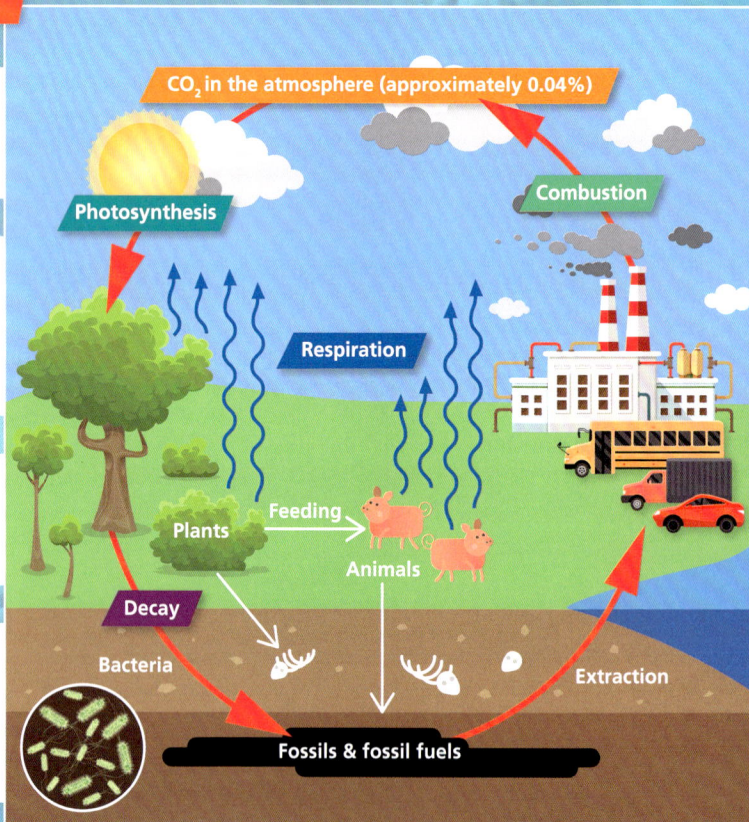

CO$_2$ in the atmosphere (approximately 0.04%)

Photosynthesis

Combustion

Respiration

Feeding

Plants

Animals

Decay

Bacteria

Extraction

Fossils & fossil fuels

Microorganisms in the Carbon Cycle

Microorganisms play a vital role in the carbon cycle (and other cycles). They decay the remains of plants and animals and return the carbon in them to the atmosphere by respiration.

Decay also releases important mineral ions back into the soil.

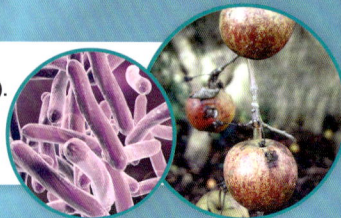

daydream
EDUCATIO

The Water Cycle

All living organisms need water. Therefore, a constant supply of water is needed to support life.

Water is the only chemical compound that occurs naturally on Earth's surface in all three physical states: solid, liquid and gas.

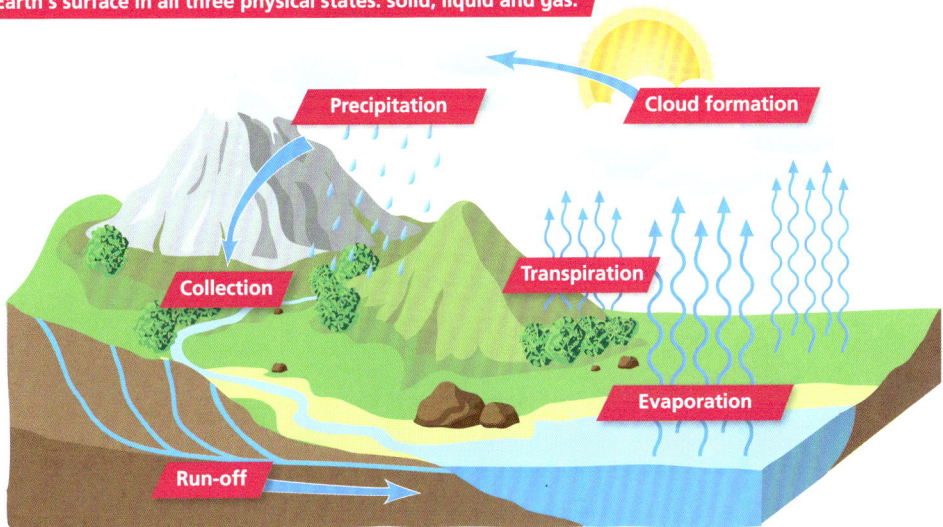

Precipitation

Cloud formation

Transpiration

Collection

Evaporation

Run-off

1 Water in oceans, rivers and lakes evaporates and, as it is heated, turns into water vapour.

2 Water also evaporates from the leaves of green plants by transpiration.

3 As the water vapour rises, it cools and condenses into clouds.

4 The water in clouds eventually falls as precipitation (rain, sleet, snow).

5 The water provides fresh water for plants and animals on land.

6 Water runs back into the sea at different rates through surface flow and groundwater flow.

The Nitrogen Cycle

Nitrogen makes up almost 80% of the atmosphere and is found in all proteins and DNA. Like water and carbon, it is recycled to provide the building blocks for future organisms.

Because nitrogen is so unreactive, it cannot be used directly by plants and animals. Therefore, it must be converted into other chemical forms before it is usable.

Bacteria and other single-celled prokaryotes convert nitrogen into usable forms in a process called nitrogen fixation. This releases nitrates into the soil which are then absorbed by plants. Animals obtain nitrogen by eating plants and other animals.

daydream
EDUCATION

Decomposition

Decomposition involves the breakdown of dead material. Environmental factors, such as temperature, water and the availability of oxygen determine the rate at which it occurs.

Factors Affecting the Rate of Decomposition

Bacteria and fungi are decomposers, which means they break down organic material. The more of them there are, the faster decomposition will occur. Environmental factors affect the survival and population size of decomposers and, therefore, decomposition rates.

Decayed organic material, or compost, is a natural plant fertiliser that contains nutrients. When making compost, gardeners and farmers try to provide optimum conditions for decay.

Conversely, householders and food retailers try to create conditions that will slow or stop decay so that food will last longer.

Temperature

Decomposers use enzymes to decompose matter.

- At cold temperatures, decomposition is slow because the enzymes cannot work efficiently.

- As temperatures rise, the enzymes work more rapidly, and the rate of decomposition rises.

- At high temperatures enzymes become denatured, so decomposition slows and eventually stops when the decomposers die.

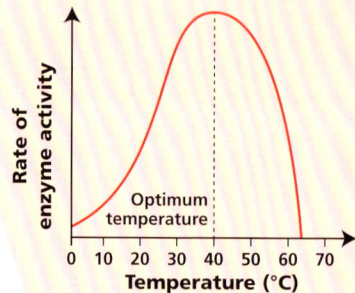

Graph: Rate of enzyme activity (y-axis) against Temperature (°C) (x-axis), marked 0 10 20 30 40 50 60 70, with Optimum temperature indicated.

Water

Like all living things, decomposers require water, which affects the rate of decomposition. Moist conditions increase the rate, whereas extremely dry conditions stop or slow decomposition because decomposers cannot survive in dry conditions.

Decomposition is slow in waterlogged soil because of the lack of oxygen.

Oxygen

Most (but not all) of the bacteria and fungi that act as decomposers are aerobic and require oxygen to survive. Decomposition is slower but does not stop in anaerobic conditions because anaerobic bacteria can survive. Anaerobic decay produces methane.

daydream
EDUCATIO

Biogas

Biogas is a fuel made up mostly of methane gas. It is formed when anaerobic bacteria feed on plant and animal waste (e.g. sewage sludge). This occurs in structures called biogas generators, which may be continuous or batch generators.

Continuous: Sewage is constantly fed into the generator, and biogas is drawn off.

Batch: Sewage is left to decompose, and then the gas is drawn off. Before a further batch is prepared and added, the generator is cleaned.

This diagram shows how a very simple biogas generator works.

Waste is input, and as bacteria anaerobically decompose it, biogas is released. The digested slurry is extracted for use as fertiliser.

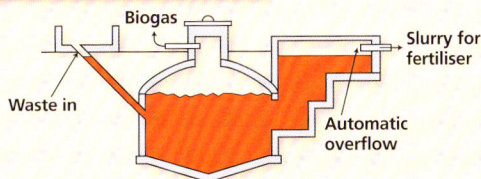

Practical Activity: Investigate the Effect of Temperature on the Rate of Decay

Bacteria in milk produce the lipase enzyme, which breaks down the fat in milk, producing fatty acids and glycerol. The fatty acids cause the pH of the milk to fall.

An indicator, phenolphthalein, can be added to the milk to track the decline in pH. It is pink at high pH values but turns colourless when the pH drops below 8.3.

1 Add 5 cm³ of the lipase solution to a boiling tube and label it 'lipase'.

2 Add 5 cm³ of milk and five drops of phenolphthalein to another tube labelled 'milk'.

3 Add 7 cm³ of sodium carbonate solution to the 'milk' tube. The solution should turn pink.

4 Add both tubes to a water bath that is set to 10°C, and wait until the contents reach the same temperature as the water bath.

5 Transfer 1 cm³ of the lipase to the 'milk' tube and immediately begin timing the reaction.

6 Stir the 'milk' tube contents until the solution turns colourless or yellow.

7 Record how long (in seconds) it takes for the colour to change.

8 Repeat the investigation at different water bath temperatures, and record your results in a table.

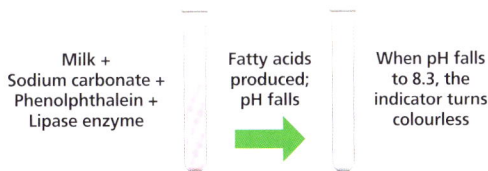

Milk +
Sodium carbonate +
Phenolphthalein +
Lipase enzyme

→

Fatty acids produced; pH falls

When pH falls to 8.3, the indicator turns colourless

Measuring the time taken for the indicator to turn colourless gives an indication of the rate of decomposition. The rate of decomposition can be calculated by using this formula:

$$\text{Rate (s}^{-1}\text{)} = \frac{1000}{\text{Time for colour change (seconds)}}$$

The Impact of Environmental Change

Environmental change affects the number and distribution of species in an ecosystem. Change can be caused by seasonal or geographical factors or by human activity.

Temperature

Each species has a temperature range in which it can survive and a narrower range in which it will thrive.

Temperature changes caused by global warming will limit some species' ability to survive in their current habitats. This could be because:
- they cannot tolerate the warmer climate
- their habitat is damaged or destroyed
- other organisms which they rely on for food die out

For example, the Canada lynx is highly adapted to live in areas with snow cover for at least four months of the year. Increased temperatures would melt the snow, threatening the lynx's survival.

Water Availability

Some animals and plants are adapted to live in dry areas. However, if rainfall decreases and areas become significantly drier, some species living there will be unable to survive.

The migration patterns of some species coincide with seasonal rainfall patterns. Changes in rainfall patterns would disrupt migration patterns.

For example, wildebeest herds in Africa migrate to different areas as seasonal rainfall patterns shift.

The Composition of Environmental Gases

Species vary in their tolerance of air pollution. If the air in an area becomes more polluted, certain species will be unable to survive.

It is also possible that organisms that can survive air pollution will be unable to compete if the air becomes cleaner and new species arrive.

Some lichens can survive high levels of air pollution, but many cannot. The *Usnea* genus of lichen cannot adapt to air pollution and lives only in areas with clean air.

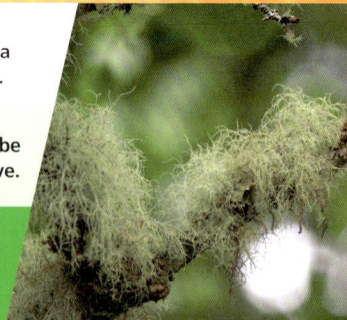

daydream

Biodiversity

Biodiversity is the variety of species in a given area. There are two aspects to biodiversity: the number of different species present and the number of individuals of each species.

Biodiversity makes ecosystems more stable. The more species there are, the less dependent each species is on another for food or shelter because there are always alternatives.

The future of humans relies on us maintaining a good level of biodiversity on the planet, yet many human activities are reducing it. As a result, many measures are now being taken to maintain biodiversity.

Waste Management

Waste causes different types of pollution, which damage ecosystems and seriously reduce biodiversity.

Increased life expectancies due to improved health care and medicine have caused the human population to grow. This, combined with an increase in people's standard of living, has meant that more resources are being used and more waste is being created.

Water Pollution

Water pollution can cause significant damage to marine ecosystems. Toxic chemicals, sewage and fertilisers from industry and agriculture all contribute to water pollution.

Air Pollution

Air pollution damages human health and can destroy whole ecosystems. The burning of fossil fuels for energy has increased the amount of greenhouse gases and chemicals in the atmosphere.

Land Pollution

Land pollution can damage ecosystems and contaminate water supplies. The disposal of waste in landfill sites and the use of toxic chemicals in farming are two of the main causes of land pollution.

Land Use

As the human population grows, more land is used for building, farming, quarrying and dumping waste. This destroys habitats and reduces the amount of land available for animals and plants.

Peat bogs are specialised habitats, and the species that live there are adapted to that environment. Peat is used for garden compost and as a fuel.

The removal of peat destroys the habitat of animals and plants, and burning it releases greenhouse gases such as carbon dioxide into the atmosphere.

Rate of Deforestation

Deforestation is the clearing of rainforests and wooded areas. It is estimated that 50% of the world's tropical rainforests have been lost to deforestation over the last 100 years.

Increased awareness of the importance of tropical rainforests has led many countries, such as Brazil, to reduce their deforestation rates.

Although the global rate is decreasing, it continues to increase in some areas. For example, in Indonesia, large areas of the rainforest are being cleared to make way for palm oil plantations. Indonesia is the world's biggest producer of palm oil, and its economy relies on its production.

Change in annual deforestation rate, 2000–2010

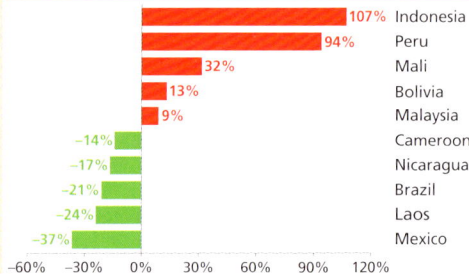

Country	Change
Indonesia	107%
Peru	94%
Mali	32%
Bolivia	13%
Malaysia	9%
Cameroon	−14%
Nicaragua	−17%
Brazil	−21%
Laos	−24%
Mexico	−37%

Causes of Deforestation

There are many reasons why rainforests are being destroyed.

Overpopulation

As population grows, trees are cleared to make room for settlements.

Mining

Trees and vegetation are cleared so that valuable metals and minerals can be mined.

Logging

Trees are felled to harvest timber for profit. Roads must also be built to access logging sites, requiring further deforestation.

Farming & Agriculture

Trees are cleared to create space for crops and grazing livestock.

Energy Development

Forests are flooded to build dams for hydroelectric power (HEP), and areas are razed to make way for biofuel crops.

Impacts of Deforestation

Indigenous peoples have long cleared small areas of forest with little damage. However, modern, large-scale deforestation has had huge environmental, economic and social impacts.

Trees remove CO_2 from the atmosphere. Therefore, deforestation leads to increased CO_2 levels, which contribute to the greenhouse effect and rising global temperatures. Fewer trees means fewer roots to soak up water from the soil, so more nutrients are leached. Deforestation also reduces biodiversity: plants and animals become extinct due to a lack of food and shelter.

In 1500, 6.9 million people were living in the Amazon rainforest. With homes having been destroyed by deforestation, only 200,000 remain there. Moreover, deforestation's effects make these areas less attractive to tourists, leading to lost income. However, more jobs are being created through logging, farming and mining. Also, selling timber can be very profitable.

daydream
EDUCATION

Maintaining Biodiversity

To preserve biodiversity, it is important to ensure the negative impacts of human interactions with ecosystems are kept to a minimum.

As the negative impacts of human interactions with ecosystems have become clearer, measures have been taken by scientists and concerned citizens to change these interactions and reduce their impacts on biodiversity.

Breeding Programmes

Breeding programmes for endangered species have been set up in zoos and wildlife parks. These aim to breed the animals in protected conditions and then release them back into the wild.

Protection & Regeneration

Rare and endangered habitats in nature reserves and national parks, for example, are protected by laws and regulations. Also, some habitats are being regenerated by careful management.

Reintroducing Hedgerows

Where farmers grow large areas of one type of crop (known as monoculture), hedgerows provide a haven of biodiversity. Many were removed in the past to make it easier to use large farm machinery, but they are now being reintroduced, sometimes with government grants.

Reducing CO_2 Emissions

Some governments are taking steps to reduce deforestation and CO_2 emissions. Many South American countries have laws that limit deforestation to preserve the Amazon rainforest. Many governments are also setting targets for lower CO_2 emissions.

Recycling

Efforts are being made to encourage people to recycle and reuse resources where possible to reduce the amount of waste being dumped in landfill sites.

Conflicting Pressures of Maintaining Biodiversity

Many of the measures aimed at maintaining biodiversity can conflict with the economic needs of a population. This is especially true in developing countries where ongoing economic development is vital for food, water and energy security.

For example, by implementing laws to prevent the deforestation of land that could be used for agriculture, mining and energy development, many countries risk damaging the economy and the livelihoods of local people.

daydream
EDUCATION

Global Warming: Causes & Effects

Human Factors

The greenhouse effect is a naturally occurring phenomenon that insulates the Earth and keeps it warm enough to sustain life. However, it is believed that human activity increases the greenhouse effect, resulting in higher global temperatures.

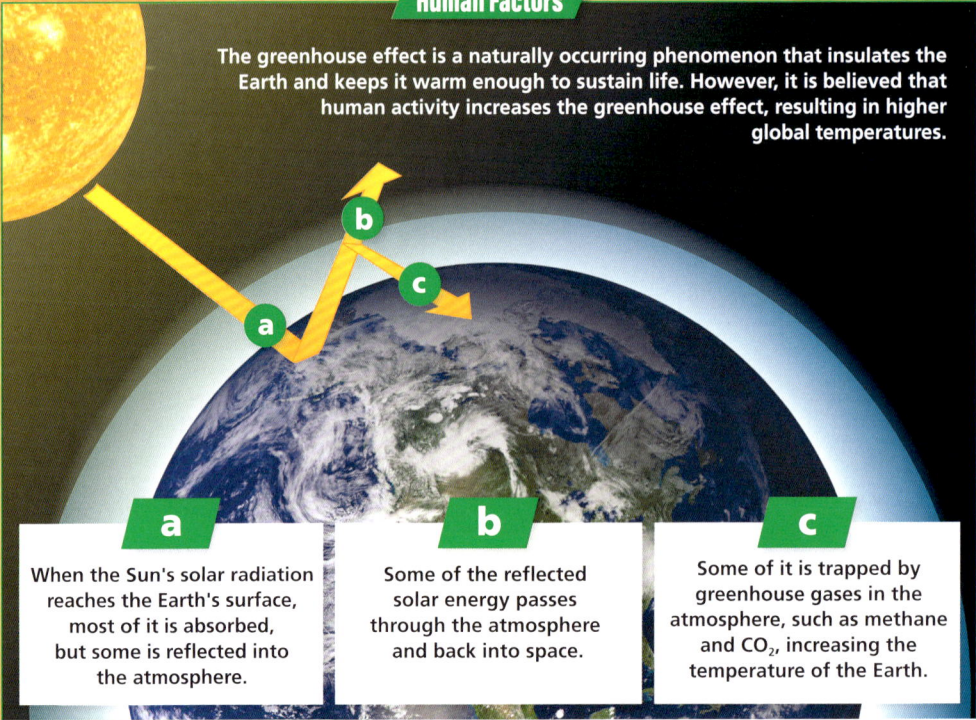

a
When the Sun's solar radiation reaches the Earth's surface, most of it is absorbed, but some is reflected into the atmosphere.

b
Some of the reflected solar energy passes through the atmosphere and back into space.

c
Some of it is trapped by greenhouse gases in the atmosphere, such as methane and CO_2, increasing the temperature of the Earth.

Several human activities increase the levels of greenhouse gases in the atmosphere, trapping more of the Sun's solar energy.

This graph shows the correlation between the average global temperature and the level of CO_2 in the atmosphere over time.

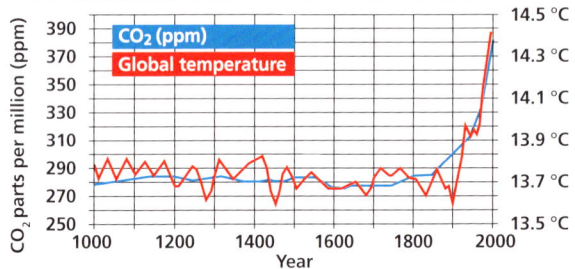

Graph:
- Y-axis (left): CO_2 parts per million (ppm) — 250, 270, 290, 310, 330, 350, 370, 390
- Y-axis (right): 13.5 °C, 13.7 °C, 13.9 °C, 14.1 °C, 14.3 °C, 14.5 °C
- X-axis: Year — 1000, 1200, 1400, 1600, 1800, 2000
- Legend: CO_2 (ppm), Global temperature

daydream EDUCATION

Fossil Fuels

Fossil fuels such as oil, gas and coal are burnt to generate energy for transportation, manufacturing and electricity production.

However, the process of burning fossil fuels releases CO_2 into the atmosphere and is the main source of greenhouse gas emissions.

Agriculture

Agriculture, especially livestock and rice farming, produces huge amounts of the greenhouse gas methane.

It is released by animals during digestion and by matter decomposed by microbes in flooded rice paddy fields.

Deforestation

Trees remove CO_2 from the atmosphere for photosynthesis. Therefore, clearing trees results in less CO_2 being removed from the atmosphere.

This is worsened by the burning of fossil fuels, which also releases greenhouse gases into the atmosphere.

Effects of Climate Change

Climate change has a significant effect on both the environment and people.

Effects on the Environment

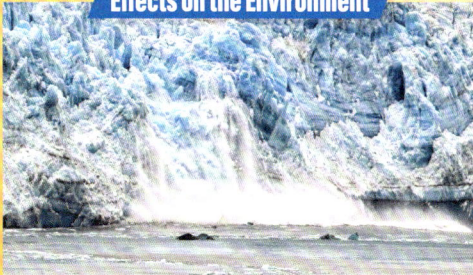

Warmer global temperatures will cause glaciers and ice sheets to melt, leading to rising sea levels and the loss of polar habitats.

Rising sea levels will result in low-lying coastal areas flooding more frequently or even becoming permanently submerged in water.

Many species of plants and animals are at risk of becoming extinct as their habitats are altered or damaged by climate change. For example, many of the world's coral reefs, which support a diverse range of marine life, are at risk of bleaching and destruction due to rising sea temperatures.

Warmer temperatures and higher sea levels will lead to more extreme weather events and a change in precipitation patterns.

Effects on People

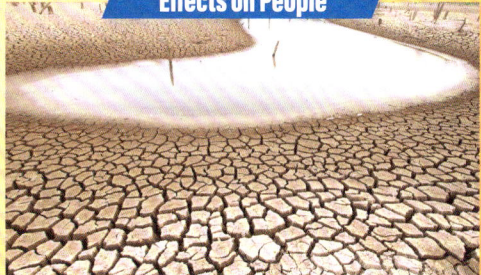

As global temperatures rise, people in already hot regions will be at increased risk of developing heat-related health problems.

Many coastal areas at risk of flooding and areas that experience extremely high temperatures may become uninhabitable. This could lead to mass migration and overcrowding in areas less at risk.

Although agriculture in some areas may benefit from warmer temperatures, many areas will become hotter and drier. This will result in drought, desertification and declining crop yields.

Drought and reduced crop yields will cause food and water shortages in many areas.

daydream
EDUCATION

Trophic Levels

In ecosystems, energy is transferred from one organism to another through food chains. The different levels within a food chain are known as **trophic levels**.

Trophic Levels in Food Chains

Each trophic level has a name which indicates its position in the food chain.

Trophic Level 4: Tertiary Consumers

Carnivores that eat other carnivores. Animals that have no predators are called apex predators and are at the top of the food chain.

Trophic Level 3: Secondary Consumers

Carnivores that eat primary consumers.

Trophic Level 2: Primary Consumers

Animals that eat plants (producers). Most are herbivores, but some are omnivores that eat both plants and animals.

Trophic Level 1: Producers

Plants and algae that use photosynthesis to produce the food chain's initial energy from light energy. Only about 1% of the incident energy from light is transferred for photosynthesis.

Plants are always producers, but some animals operate at different levels in different food chains. For example, humans are primary consumers when they eat plants but secondary consumers when they eat meat.

Decomposers

Decomposers, such as bacteria and fungi, feed on dead material, which may come from any level in the food chain. Therefore, they are not included in food chains.

Decomposers secrete enzymes to break down dead matter into small soluble molecules that can diffuse into microorganisms.

daydream
EDUCATION

Biomass Transfer

Energy is transferred from one trophic level to another as biomass when one organism eats another.

A **biomass pyramid** shows the flow of energy (biomass) through a food chain. Each block represents the biomass, not the number of organisms, present at each trophic level.

As energy moves up the pyramid, large amounts are lost at each level.

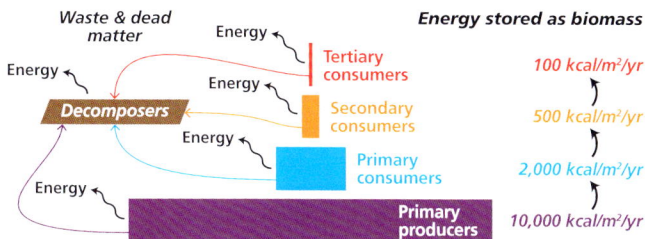

Waste & dead matter

Energy

Energy

Energy

Energy

Energy

Decomposers

Energy stored as biomass

Tertiary consumers — *100 kcal/m²/yr*

Secondary consumers — *500 kcal/m²/yr*

Primary consumers — *2,000 kcal/m²/yr*

Primary producers — *10,000 kcal/m²/yr*

Food chains usually have only four or five levels because energy (biomass) is always lost during transfer, eventually leaving an insufficient amount to support another level.

How Biomass Is Lost

Not All Material Is Eaten	Often an animal does not eat every bit of the organisms it feeds on. Herbivores rarely eat both the roots and shoots of a plant, and carnivores often leave the carcass of its prey.
Not All Biomass Is Digested	Some parts of an organism are difficult to digest. Cellulose in plants is rarely fully digested, as are the bones of vertebrates. This biomass is not absorbed and passes through the animal to emerge in faeces.
Some Biomass Is Used	Plants make glucose by photosynthesis and use some of it for respiration. In animals, not all food eaten is stored in the body. Some of it is used to provide energy for movement, for instance.
Some Biomass Is Converted to Waste	Some biomass leaves organisms as waste, such as urea (in animals) and carbon dioxide from respiration.

Biomass Calculations

Generally, only about 10% of an organism's energy intake passes to the next trophic level. The exact percentage can be calculated using the following equation:

$$\% \text{ efficiency} = \frac{\text{Biomass transferred to the next level}}{\text{Biomass taken in from previous level}} \times 100$$

The primary consumers in a habitat consume producers containing 2,400 kcal/m² in one year. In the same year, the secondary consumers consume primary consumers containing 200 kcal/m². What is the % efficiency of the energy transfer from the primary to secondary consumers?

$$\% \text{ efficiency} = \frac{200}{2,400} \times 100 = 8.3\%$$

Food Production

Food Security

According to the UN's Food and Agriculture Organisation:

" Food security is when all people, at all times, have...access to sufficient, safe and nutritious food that meets their dietary needs... for an active and healthy life. "

Threats to Food Security

| **Overpopulation** | The global population is growing rapidly due to increasing birth rates and life expectancies. As the population grows so will demand for food. |

| **Economic Development** | In countries undergoing economic growth, demand for food, and a greater variety of food, increases as people earn more income. |

| **Loss of Production** | Pests, disease and environmental changes (e.g. droughts and flooding) can reduce crop yields and, thus, food production. |

| **Conflict** | Wars can destroy farms, force people to flee their homes and prevent the transportation of water and food. |

| **Costs** | Increased prices of seeds, livestock and machinery can force farmers out of business, limiting the supply of food in some places. |

As the global population and demand for food continues to increase, new sustainable strategies to increase food supply are needed.

Factory Farming

Factory farming places limits on the movement of livestock and involves controlling the temperature of their surroundings to increase efficiency.

Advantages

- The animals spend less energy moving and keeping warm. As a result, more energy is used for growth, increasing food production but not input resources.

- Animals can be fed high protein diets to boost meat production.

Disadvantages

- The animals are close together, enabling diseases to spread easily.

- Many people view the cramped conditions as cruel and unethical.

- Controlling the temperature of farm buildings requires energy, often from fossil fuels.

Sustainable Fisheries

Fish stocks in the ocean are declining largely due to overfishing. If fish populations continue to shrink, some species may not be able to recover, greatly affecting marine ecosystems and food chains.

To try to maintain fish stocks at a sustainable level, the following strategies can be used:

Introducing Fishing Quotas

Laws can limit the number of fish that can be caught in certain areas and prohibit fishing at certain times of year.

Increasing the Mesh Size of Fishing Nets

Nets with small mesh can catch young fish before they get a chance to breed. This greatly affects future population size, more so than catching fish that have already bred. Therefore, nets with larger mesh should be used to prevent young fish from becoming caught.

Biotechnology

Biotechnology can be used to grow, or culture, large quantities of microorganisms for food.

Mycoprotein

Mycoprotein is the name given to proteins produced from fungi. It is a key ingredient in some meat substitutes, such as Quorn™. The fungus genus *Fusarium* is the main source of mycoprotein. It is cultured in large tanks called fermenters.

- Glucose syrup and minerals are provided to feed the fungi.

- Ammonia is added as a source of nitrogen for protein manufacture.

- Air is added to provide oxygen for respiration.

- Waste gases (mostly CO_2) are removed to release pressure.

- Cooling is necessary because fungal respiration generates heat.

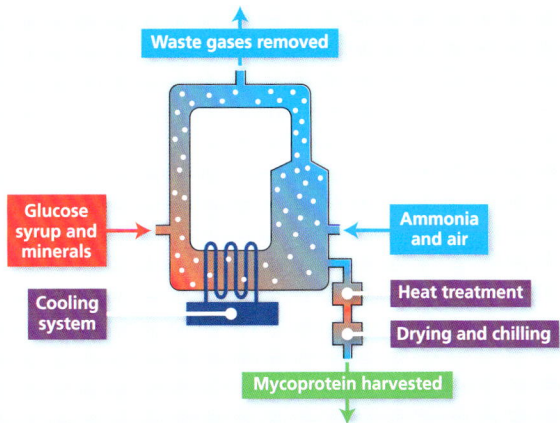

Waste gases removed

Glucose syrup and minerals

Ammonia and air

Cooling system

Heat treatment

Drying and chilling

Mycoprotein harvested

The harvested mycoprotein is heated to 65°C to kill any remaining fungi. It is then dried and chilled.

daydream

Genetically Modified (GM) Crops

GM crops can be used to improve yields and reduce food shortages.

Crops have been genetically modified to produce a variety of benefits, including:

- Improved nutritional value (e.g. rice with added vitamins)
- Longer shelf life
- Greater resistance to drought, pests and disease
- Reduced need for chemical pesticides
- Improved flavour

The effects of GM foods on the environment and human health are still relatively unknown. However, many people are worried about their effects on natural biodiversity and ecosystems. Because of this, the use of GM foods remains limited, with several countries banning them.

Additionally, the research to produce new GM crops is costly, potentially making the plants too expensive for poor countries to buy.

Human Insulin

Biotechnology can be used to produce substances that are useful for human health. One such substance is human insulin, for treating diabetes. Insulin is produced as follows:

1 The gene for insulin is removed from the human chromosome by using a restriction enzyme. This enzyme recognises the particular base sequence for insulin and cuts the DNA on either side of this sequence.

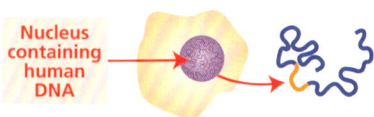

Nucleus containing human DNA

2 A loop of DNA (a plasmid) is removed from a bacterium and cut open using the same restriction enzyme. The insulin gene is inserted into the plasmid, and the ends are joined by using a ligase enzyme.

Bacterial cell

3 Copies of the plasmid are introduced into bacteria. The genetically modified bacteria will now use the gene to produce human insulin, which can be extracted from the growth medium and purified for use.

daydream
EDUCATION

Applications of Science

Scientific developments have led to remarkable discoveries and innovations. However, they have also created issues related to social, economic, environmental and ethical factors. Therefore, the evaluation of scientific applications should consider the advantages and disadvantages related to these issues.

Example: Evaluate the use of zoos to breed animals.

When evaluating something, always remember to consider the arguments for and against.

Social

How do zoos affect people?

- Zoos stimulate interest in animals and provide an opportunity to educate people and to promote animal protection.
- Animals can escape.

Economic

How do zoos affect the economy?

- Zoos create jobs and support local businesses.
- Some zoos donate money to animal charities.
- Zoos can be expensive to run and maintain.

Environmental

How do zoos affect the environment?

- Zoos provide a home for animals that have had their habitats destroyed.
- Removing animals from the wild can further endanger the wild population.

Ethical

Are zoos ethical?

- Zoos save endangered species and can help breed endangered species.
- It is cruel to keep animals in captivity.
- Surplus animals are sometimes killed.

Personal: How do zoos affect you? Do zoos affect your life in a positive or negative way?

? It is not always possible to answer questions relating to scientific developments, especially ethical questions. This is particularly difficult when there is little or no existing data. Sometimes it can take years of research for new data to come to light.

For example, for years, diesel was promoted as a way of reducing CO_2 emissions. However, in 2012, studies by the European Environment Agency found evidence that nitrogen dioxide (NO2) from diesel fumes were very harmful to human health, causing thousands of premature deaths each year. As a result, there has been a push to phase out diesel cars.

Risk

*A **hazard** is anything that can cause harm.*
Risk is the likelihood of a hazard causing harm.

Measuring Risk

The size of risk posed by something depends on how hazardous (harmful) it is and the likelihood of it happening. Look at the example below:

Lightning is **very hazardous** – it can kill.
But the **likelihood** of being hit by lightning is **very low**.
Therefore, the risk of being killed by lightning is low.

Hazards & Risk in Science

There are various hazards in practical science. It is important to identify these hazards and to try to reduce their risk and the likelihood of them occurring and causing harm.

Although scientific or technological developments frequently bring about many benefits, they can also often introduce new risks.

For example, the development of e-cigarettes has helped significantly increase the number of people giving up smoking. However, scientists are still unsure whether the chemicals used in the cigarettes are harmful to the body.

Look at the two examples below. Are the benefits of these technologies worth the risk?

Genetic Engineering

➕ **Benefit:** Genetic engineering can significantly increase food production.

➖ **Risk:** There are serious concerns about the effects of genetically modified foods on human health and biodiversity. Also, gene transfer between plants may lead to an uncontrollable 'escape' of genes into wild plants.

X-Rays

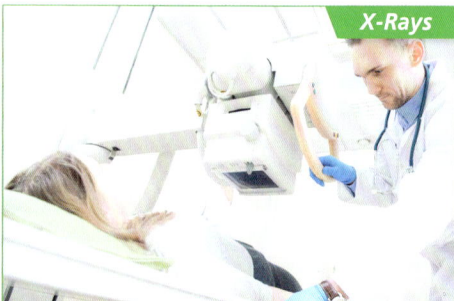

➕ **Benefit:** X-rays are used to check for bone fractures.

➖ **Risk:** Radiation exposure can cause cell mutations that may lead to cancer. However, this risk is thought to be very low.

daydream
EDUCATION

The size of risk posed by a hazard can be measured by looking at the number of times the hazard caused harm in a sample. Look at the example below:

Deaths per 1 billion passenger miles

Motorcycle	212.57
Car	7.28

The statistics above show that travelling by motorcycle is riskier than travelling by car.

Perceived Risk vs Measured Risk

The perception of risk is often very different from measured risk.

Familiar vs Unfamiliar

Which has the higher risk?

Running a marathon ←—— or ——→ Parachuting out of a plane

Although most people think parachuting out of a plane is riskier than running a marathon, the risk of dying in both activities is roughly the same: eight in one million. This is because familiar things feel less risky than unfamiliar things.

Visible vs Invisible

Some 3.8 million premature deaths are annually attributed to air pollution. However, because air pollution is invisible, people tend to underestimate its risk. This is the same for many other invisible hazards.

A similar perception applies to hazards that take a long time to take effect, such as an unhealthy diet.

Imposed vs Voluntary

Around 200 years ago, the leading cause of death was communicable diseases caused by poor sanitation and living conditions. People usually did not have a choice about this – the risks were imposed.

Now, the leading cause of death is non-communicable diseases like heart disease and cancer. Often, the risk of these is increased by lifestyle choices, or voluntary risks.

In general, people are more likely to accept the risks that are within their control than the risks over which they have no control.

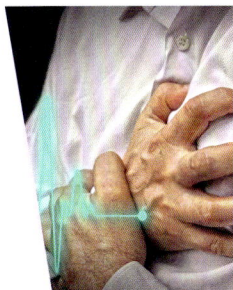

Peer Review

Peer review is a process that involves the evaluation of scientific, academic or professional work by others working in the same field.

Scientists publish their results in scientific journals. Before a work is published, its validity is checked by experts – this is peer review.

Scientific journals are print and online magazines that contain articles written by scientists about their research.

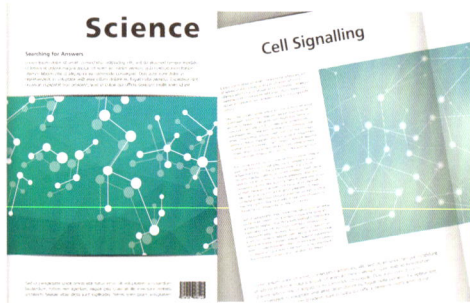

Science

Searching for Answers

Cell Signalling

Publication can lead to collaborations between scientists to develop ideas or inspire new ones.

It is important that experts review research in journals. Peer review lets readers know that they can be confident that the claims made are valid and believable. However, this does not mean the research findings are correct, just that they are not obviously wrong.

The Peer Review Process

- **Develop an idea or hypothesis to test**
- **Plan an investigation and carry out the research**
- **Write about research (methods, results, conclusions)**
- **Send to journal editor**
- **Reviewed by 3–5 experts in the field**
- **Article accepted, sent for revision or rejected**

Beware!

Scientific reports in the media do not go through peer review so they may be inaccurate or biased. If the report is based on a journal article, get more reliable information by reading the conclusions of the research.

daydream EDUCATION

Planning

A good plan is well designed for its purpose.

Reasons to Plan an Investigation

Make Observations

What structures can be seen in cells?

Produce a Substance

How can a salt be made using neutralisation?

Test a Hypothesis

Is the extension of a spring proportional to the weight added?

Explore Phenomenon

Wave Patterns Across the World

What are wave patterns like in oceans across the world?

What to Think About When Planning

What data or observations need to be collected? ▶ How many measurements need to be taken to see a pattern? ▶ What range of measurements is needed? ▶ How many repeats is enough?	I need to measure the extension of the spring as the mass on the end changes. I will increase the mass by 10 g (0.1 N) until 100 g (1 N) is reached. I will repeat the experiment twice.
What apparatus and techniques should be used?	I will use a spring held on a clamp stand, a 50-cm ruler and slotted masses. I will measure extension by viewing the spring at eye level and taking the reading from the bottom of the spring.
How is the apparatus used to record accurate measurements?	I will attach the ruler to the clamp stand to make sure it is measuring the length of the spring accurately.
What are the possible hazards? How can the risk of harm be reduced?	The clamp stand could fall over. Therefore, I will attach the clamp stand to the table with a clamp and make sure it is not placed over my feet.
What are the variables?	Independent variable = mass Dependent variable = length of extension

Variables

Investigations are often performed to identify if there are patterns or relationships between two variables. One variable is changed to see how it affects another variable.

Independent Variable

The independent variable is the one that is changed.

Dependent Variable

The dependent variable is the one that is measured for each change in the independent variable; it's what the investigator thinks will be affected during the experiment.

Control Variables

Control variables are all the other variables in an investigation that should be kept the same to ensure that it is the independent variable that is causing the dependent variable to change.

119

Presenting Data

Presenting data in an appropriate way makes it easy to spot patterns and draw conclusions from results.

Categorical Data

Includes non-numerical data (e.g. colour) and numerical data with definite values (e.g. number of cells)

Continuous Data

Numerical data that can take any value (e.g. height or time)

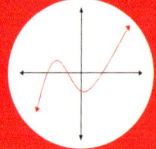

A population of plants is found growing in a field, including in a shady area under a tree.

There is lots of data that can be measured to answer the question:

How do light and shade affect plant growth?

Graphing Rules

- Label both axes.

- Give your charts and graphs a title.

- Include a key if you have more than one set of data.

- Usually, the dependent variable goes on the y-axis and the independent variable on the x-axis.

Bar Charts

Bar charts are used to present categorical data. Bar charts help to compare data.

Leave a gap between each bar.

Number of Plants Growing

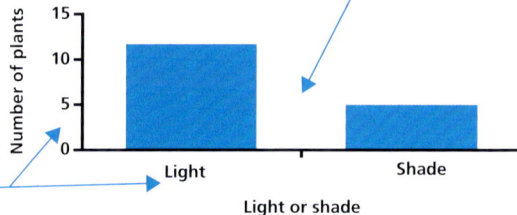

Use equal intervals on both axes.

daydream
EDUCATION

Line Graph

Line graphs are used to display continuous data. They can be used to show trends and change over time.

Change over Time

Plant Height over Time

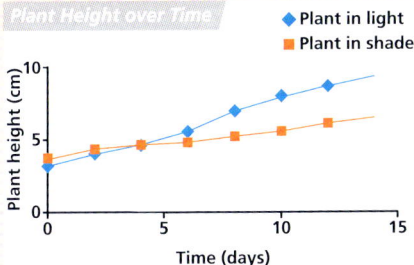

Data is plotted as a series of points that are joined by straight lines.

A Trend

How Light Intensity Affects Mean Leaf Area

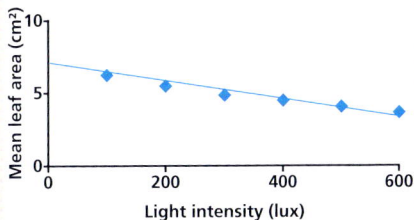

A line of best fit can be drawn to show an overall trend and that a proportional relationship exists between the two variables. In this example, as light intensity increases, mean leaf area decreases.

Frequency Tables and Charts

A frequency table is used to record how often a value (or set of values) occurs.

Length of Top Leaf (cm)	Frequency	
	Plants in Shade	Plants in Light
$3.0 \leq l < 3.5$	2	3
$3.5 \leq l < 4.0$	5	7
$4.0 \leq l < 4.5$	4	5
$4.5 \leq l < 5.0$	7	6
$5.0 \leq l < 5.5$	7	4
Total	**25**	**25**

Data from frequency tables is often displayed in frequency charts.

How Light Intensity Affects Leaf Length

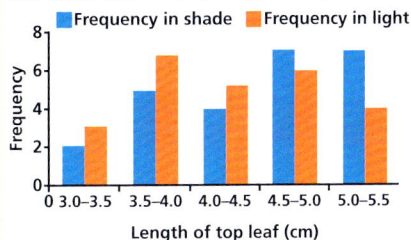

The groups (intervals) must be the same. Make sure to include units of measure in the column headings. A sample of 25 plants from each environment was used. The interval $5.0 \leq l < 5.5$ is equal to or greater than 5.0 and less than 5.5.

Evaluating Data

During data analysis, it is important to be objective and to evaluate data in terms of accuracy, precision, repeatability and reproducibility.

Students performed an experiment to determine how temperature affects reaction rate. They measured the time taken for a certain amount of sulfur to form when sodium thiosulfate solution reacts with acid at different temperatures.

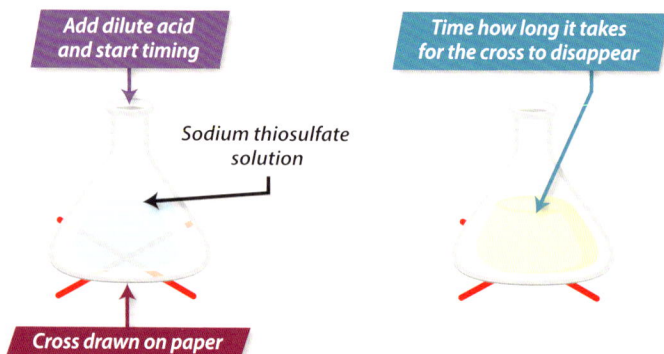

Add dilute acid and start timing

Time how long it takes for the cross to disappear

Sodium thiosulfate solution

Cross drawn on paper

This was measured by determining how long it took for the solution to become completely opaque at different temperatures.

Temperature (°C)	Time for Cross to Disappear (s)		
	1	2	3
10	196	194	196
20	95	88	96
30	53	53	53
40	28	24	26

Precision

Measurements are precise if they are similar and cluster around a single value.

How to Check for Precision: Look how close the repeated values are.

Evaluation: At 30°C, the repeats are all the same, which means these results are very precise. The results at 40°C are not as precise because they have a range of 4 seconds.

Range: the difference between the lowest and highest measurements

daydream EDUCATION

Accuracy

An accurate measurement is one that is close to the true value. There are few errors and little uncertainty.

How to Check for Accuracy:

Errors: Random errors are shown by anomalous (odd-looking) results, but they can be reduced by taking more measurements and finding the mean value.

Systematic errors are difficult to spot from results, so the equipment should be checked. Any anomalies should be investigated to try and find the cause and, if due to error, should be discarded.

Random error: results varying in unpredictable ways

Systematic error: measurements that differ from the true value by a consistent amount every time; usually caused by a problem with the measuring equipment

Mean

The sum of values divided by the number of values

Example for 40°C: $\dfrac{28 + 24 + 26}{3} = 26$

Percentage Uncertainty

$$\dfrac{range}{mean} \times 100$$

Example for 40°C: $\dfrac{4}{26} \times 100 = 15.38$

Uncertainty: The range of measurements around the mean. A low uncertainty is a sign of high accuracy.

Evaluation: The second recorded value at 20°C (88 s) is an anomaly (probably due to a mistake in measurement). The uncertainty is highest for 40°C because these show the most variation around the mean.

Repeatability

Measurements are considered repeatable if they produce similar results when performed by the same investigator under the same conditions.

How to Check for Repeatability:
Look how close the repeats are.
In the experiment above, the measurements show good repeatability because the overall measurements are around the same for each repeated value.

Reproducibility

Measurements are considered reproducible if they produce similar results when performed by a different investigator with different equipment.

How to Check for Reproducibility:
Get someone else to carry out the experiment using different equipment. If their experiment produces similar results to yours, the measurements can be considered reproducible.

Physical Units

International System of Units (SI Units)

Quantity Name	Unit Name	Unit Symbol
Length	metre	m
Mass	kilogram	kg
Time	second	s
Electric current	ampere	A
Thermodynamic temperature	kelvin	K
Amount of substance	mole	mol
Luminous intensity	candela	cd

Other Units

Quantity Name	Unit Name	Unit Symbol
Temperature	degree Celsius	°C
Energy	joule	J
Frequency	hertz	Hz
Force or weight	newton	N
Pressure	pascal	Pa
Power	watt	W
Voltage (potential difference)	volt	V
Resistance	ohm	Ω
Charge	coulomb	C
Capacitance	farad	F

SI Prefixes

These are added to unit names to produce multiples and sub-multiples, or fractions, of the original unit.

Multiples

Factor	Name	Symbol
10^{12}	tera	T
10^{9}	giga	G
10^{6}	mega	M
10^{3}	kilo	k
10^{2}	hecto	h
10^{1}	deca	da

Fractions

Factor	Name	Symbol
10^{-12}	pico	p
10^{-9}	nano	n
10^{-6}	micro	μ
10^{-3}	milli	m
10^{-2}	centi	c
10^{-1}	deci	d

Examples

You need to be able to convert from one unit to another.

10^{3} m (1,000 m) = 1 km 10^{3} g (1,000 g) = 1 kg 10^{-2} m (0.01 m) = 1 cm 10^{-3} g (0.001 g) = 1 mg

daydream

Standard Form

Standard form, or standard index form, is used when writing very small or very large numbers.

In standard form, a number is always written in the following format:

A is always a number between 1 and 10:
$1 \leq A < 10$

$$A \times 10^n$$

n tells you how many places you need to move the decimal point.

Converting Numbers into Standard Form

When writing large numbers in standard form, *n* is always positive.						
	8,000,000	=	$8 \times 1,000,000$	=	8×10^6
	45,000,000	=	$4.5 \times 10,000,000$	=	4.5×10^7
	160,000	=	$1.6 \times 100,000$	=	1.6×10^5

When writing small numbers in standard form, *n* is always negative.						
	0.000465	=	$4.65 \div 10,000$	=	4.65×10^{-4}
	0.009	=	$9 \div 1,000$	=	9.0×10^{-3}
	0.0000077	=	$7.7 \div 1,000,000$	=	7.7×10^{-6}

Examples

Example 1

There are around 87,000,000 species on the Earth. Convert this to standard form.

$$87,000,000 = 8.7 \times 10,000,000 = 8.7 \times 10^7$$

The decimal point has moved seven places to the left:

8.7000000
7 6 5 4 3 2 1

Example 2

The diameter of the DNA helix is 0.000000002 m. Convert this to standard form.

$$0.000000002 = 2.0 \div 1,000,000,000 = 2 \times 10^{-9}$$

The decimal point has moved nine places to the right:

0000000002.0
1 2 3 4 5 6 7 8 9

Sampling

It is not always possible to collect information on a whole population. In such instances, a proportion (sample) of the population is used.

Ecologists use a wide range of sampling methods to determine the abundance and distribution of species in an ecosystem.

A larger sample will more accurately reflect the population. A sample that is too small is likely to lead to statistical bias.

Quadrats

A quadrat is a square frame of a specific size (often 0.5 × 0.5 m). It is used to sample an area that is too big to completely survey. The number of one or more species in each quadrat is counted and then scaled up to estimate the number in the whole area.

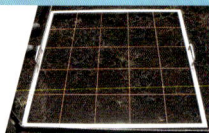

It would be nearly impossible to count the whole population of daisy plants in a field, but this can be estimated by using quadrats.

Quadrat Example

1	Measure the area of the field.	40 m × 30 m = 1,200 m²
2	Identify how many quadrats are required to provide a sufficient sample area, and calculate the total area.	20 quadrats: 20 × 0.25 m² = 5 m²
3	Place the quadrats in random locations, and count the total number of daisies in each quadrat.	In total, 86 daisies were found in the 20 quadrats.
4	Divide the total area of the field by the area surveyed to identify how much bigger the field is than the survey area.	1,200 ÷ 5 = 240
5	The field is 240 times bigger than the area surveyed. To find an estimate of the total number of daisies in the field, multiply the number of daisies found in all the quadrats by 240.	86 × 240 = 20,640

The accuracy of this estimate can be increased by taking more samples.

Transects

A transect is a line that is used to measure the distribution of organisms, not their numbers. It is usually marked by a rope or tape measure.

Samples are taken at regular intervals along the line, and the species seen at each point are recorded. The line is usually laid along some sort of gradient (e.g. low-tide mark to high-tide mark) to see its effect on distribution.

daydream EDUCATION

Notes

Index

Index

Thoughtweavers

Barry Maybury

OXFORD UNIVERSITY PRESS 1981

Oxford University Press, Walton Street, Oxford OX2 6DP

OXFORD   LONDON   GLASGOW
NEW YORK   TORONTO   MELBOURNE   WELLINGTON
KUALA LUMPUR   SINGAPORE   HONG KONG   TOKYO
DELHI   BOMBAY   CALCUTTA   MADRAS   KARACHI
NAIROBI   DAR ES SALAAM   CAPE TOWN

Selection and arrangement
© Barry Maybury 1981

ISBN 019 833159–2

Set in Great Britain by
Fakenham Press Limited, Fakenham, Norfolk
Printed in Hong Kong

Companion anthologies compiled by Barry Maybury:
Wordscapes   ISBN 0 19 833138 X
Thoughtshapes ISBN 0 19 833141 X
Wordspinners ISBN 0 19 833158 4

Contents

* written by a child at school

the power of poets

the man on the veranda
outside, giving coppers
to the old tramp and
feeling good isn't me.
I am the veranda.
I could have been
the tramp or even
the coppers. However
I choose to be the
veranda and it is
my poem. Such is
the power of poets.

ROGER MCGOUGH

Cataract

The cataract, whirling to the precipice,
   Elbows down rocks and, shouldering, thunders through.
Roars, howls, and stifled murmurs never cease;
   Hell and its agonies seem hid below.
Thick rolls the mist, that smokes and falls in dew;
   The trees and greenwood wear the deepest green.
Horrible mysteries in the gulf stare through,
   Roars of a million tongues, and none knows what they mean.

JOHN CLARE

The Laburnum top is silent, quite still
In the afternoon yellow September sunlight,
A few leaves yellowing, all its seeds fallen.

Till the goldfinch comes, with a twitching chirrup,
A suddenness, a startlement, at a branch-end.
Then sleek as a lizard, and alert, and abrupt
She enters the thickness, and a machine starts up
Of chitterings, and a tremor of wings, and trillings—
The whole tree trembles and thrills.
It is the engine of her family.
She stokes it full, then flirts out to a branch-end
Showing her barred face identity mask

Then with eerie delicate whistle-chirrup whisperings
She launches away, towards the infinite

And the laburnum subsides to empty.

from Autumn Nature Notes by TED HUGHES

The Docks

When I went to the docks
This is what I felt deep inside me,
Like a giant scalextric
The basins encircling the ships that dock there.
Like a huge Loch Ness Monster
A ship slowly, smoothly passed me.

Two buildings stuck together
Like a double-barrelled shot gun;
And down the slipway
A huge ship slides
Just been launched
By a champagne bottle
And named 'Fugitive'.

Like a massive elephant
A huge grain elevator
Feeds itself by sucking up grain;
A huge crab
Comes and picks up cargo.
I stare in wonder and think
What would happen if
The driver of the crane
Would suddenly stop at a dead halt.

Like a dirty black snake
The docks, wind on
Dirty, oily and horrid
It is hard to imagine
The docks are there
As I walk back home.

DAVID DEEN*

The Elm Decline

The crags crash to the tarn; slow-
motion corrosion of scree.
From scooped corries,
bare as slag,
black sykes ooze
through quarries of broken boulders.
The sump of the tarn
slumps into its mosses—bog
asphodel, sundew, sedges—
a perpetual
sour October
yellowing the moor.

        Seven
thousand years ago
trees grew
high as this tarn. The pikes
were stacks and skerries
spiking the green,
the tidal surge
of oak, birch, elm,
ebbing to ochre
and the wrackwood of backend.

        Then
round the year Three
Thousand B.C.,
the proportion of elm pollen
preserved in peat
declined from twenty
per cent to four.

                    Stone axes,
chipped clean from the crag-face,
ripped the hide off the fells.
Spade and plough
scriated the bared flesh,
skewered down to the bone.
The rake flaked into fragments
and kettlehole tarns
were shovelled chock-full
of a rubble of rotting rocks.

                    Today
electric landslips
crack the rock;
drills tunnel it;
valleys go under the tap.
Dynamited runnels
channel a poisoned rain,
and the fractured ledges
are scoured and emery'd
by wind-to-wind rubbings
of nuclear dust.

                    Soon
the pikes, the old
bottlestops of lava,
will stand scraped bare,
nothing but air round stone
and stone in air,
ground-down stumps
of a skeleton jaw—

                    Until
under the scree,
under the riddled rake,
beside the outflow of the reedless lake,
no human eye remains to see
a land-scape man
helped nature to make.

NORMAN NICHOLSON

skerries: shaley rocks

Giant Squid

We now gazed at the most wondrous phenomenon which the secret
seas have hitherto revealed to mankind. A vast pulpy mass, furlongs
in length and breadth, of a glancing cream-colour, lay floating on
the water, innumerable long arms radiating from its centre, and
curling and twisting like a nest of anacondas, as if blindly to clutch
at any hapless object within reach. No perceptible face or front did it
have; no conceivable token of either sensation or instinct; but undu-
lated there on the billows, an unearthly, formless, chance-like
apparition of life . . . with a low sucking sound it slowly disappeared
again.

from Moby Dick by HERMAN MELVILLE

Hare

The alert hare now sags from the hook
Its head in a polythene bag of blood
Drained.
It no longer twitches its nostrils
Nor suns its fur. Nor bounds
Across the meadow on tense legs.

DAVID MARNO

The Man-Eater

The author is stalking a tiger that, over several years, has killed a large number of people in a northern province of India. He thinks the tiger might be quite close.

Slipping my feet forward an inch at a time on the soft grass, I now started to approach the tree, and had covered about half the distance that separated me from it when I caught sight of a black-and-yellow object about three inches long on the rocky edge, which I now saw was a well-used game path. For a long minute I stared at this motionless object, until I was convinced that it was the tip of the tiger's tail. If the tail was pointing away from me the head must obviously be towards me, and as the ledge was only some two feet wide, the tiger could only be crouching down and waiting to spring the moment my head appeared over the bole of the tree. The tip of the tail was twenty feet from me, and allowing eight feet for the tiger's length while crouching, his head would be twelve feet away. But I should have to approach much nearer before I should be able to see enough of his body to get in a crippling shot, and a crippling shot it would have to be if I wanted to leave on my feet. And now, for the first time in my life, I regretted my habit of carrying an uncocked rifle. The safety-catch of my ·450/·400 makes a very distinct click when thrown off, and to make any sound now would either bring the tiger right on top of me or send him straight down the steep hillside without any possibility of my getting in a shot.

Inch by inch I again started to creep forward, until the whole of the tail, and after it the hind quarters, came into view. When I saw the hind quarters I could have shouted with delight, for they showed that the tiger was not crouching and ready to spring, but was lying down. As there was only room for his body on the two-foot ledge, he had stretched his hind legs out and was resting them on the upper branches of an oak sapling growing up the face of the almost perpendicular hillside. Another foot forward and his belly came into view, and from the regular way in which it was heaving up and down I knew that he was asleep. Less slowly now I moved forward, until his shoulder, and then his whole length, was exposed to my view. The back of his head was resting on the edge of the grass plot, which extended for three or four feet beyond the fallen tree; his eyes were fast shut, and his nose was pointing to heaven.

Aligning the sights of the rifle on his forehead I pressed the trigger and, while maintaining a steady pressure on it, pushed up the safety-catch. I had no idea how this reversal of the usual method of discharging a rifle would work, but it did work; and when the heavy bullet at that short range crashed into his forehead not so much as a quiver went through his body. His tail remained stretched straight out; his hind legs continued to rest on the upper branches of the sapling; and his nose still pointed to heaven. Nor did his position change in the slightest when I sent a second, and quite unnecessary, bullet to follow the first. The only change noticeable was that his stomach had stopped heaving up and down, and that blood was trickling down his forehead from two surprisingly small holes. . . .

My personal feelings in the matter are I know of little interest to others, but it occurs to me that possibly you also might think it was not cricket, and in that case I should like to put the arguments before you that I used on myself, in the hope that you will find them more satisfactory than I did. These arguments were (a) the tiger was a man-eater that was better dead than alive, (b) therefore it made no difference whether he was awake or asleep when killed, and (c) that had I walked away when I saw his belly heaving up and down I should have been morally responsible for the deaths of all the human beings he killed thereafter. All good and sound arguments, you will admit, for my having acted as I did; but the regret remains that through fear of the consequences to myself, or fear of losing the only chance I might ever get, or possibly a combination of the two, I did not awaken the sleeping animal and give him a sporting chance.

from The Man-Eaters of Kumaon by JIM CORBETT

Falcon Attack

Suddenly, and with a fierce scream of rage, the falcon swooped out from the ledge above, taking me completely by surprise. As she dipped slightly below me, I had a fleeting impression of a large grey-brown bird with a widely-fanned, wedge-shaped tail and powerful wings, very broad at the base. Out over the blue water she sailed, demonstrating her pent-up fury in a series of harsh and high-pitched cries. When about a quarter of a mile away, she rocketed upwards in a steep climb, then turned eastward, parallel to the cliff-face, careening over in a leisurely manner as a yacht will under press of sail. Her wing-beat had a winnowing rather than a flapping action, and the tips of the primaries reached far above and below the streaked and barred body at the limits of each stroke. Once more she turned, this time into the teeth of the wind. For a moment, the falcon appeared as if poised on fully-extended wings. Then she tilted forwards and, with wings almost closed, sped downwards and straight at me like an arrow from a bow. I was expecting her stoop but was a little disconcerted by the amazing speed of the attack. At one moment, she was several hundred yards away at an angle of about sixty degrees from the horizontal; at the next, whoosh! and she was within three or four feet of my head. Instinctively, I ducked, but the falcon pulled out of her power-dive immediately before reaching me. Once more she gained height and I saw her turn her head to watch me as she climbed. Again she tilted over in a steep bank as she turned righthanded along the cliffs. The beat of those magnificent wings as she gained her air-station was strong, purposeful and quite rapid. Another steep, careening turn, a moment to gather herself and whoosh! down she came again—a murderous, feathered fury.

I had no idea whether she would press home any of her assaults. I watched her, fascinated, utterly entranced by her complete mastery of the air, by her terrifying speed, her effortless grace, her lazy, disdainful confidence. It was an amazing experience being the target of those attacks which were diverted only in the final split-second of her breakneck career. The rush of air under the taut pinions made a queer, throbbing sound as the falcon checked her stoop on fully-extended wings—a sound which mingled un-pleasantly with the threatening cry 'hyaarr' hoarsely uttered at the climax of her attack. As I awaited that succession of hair-raising and vicious assaults, I realized what it felt like to be a knife-thrower's assistant at a circus.

Despite the fact that the falcon was directing her fury upon me, or perhaps indeed because of it, I was able fully to appreciate and to admire her skill in the air. The incredible velocity of the stoop itself was matched by her wonderful powers of steering. A falcon's expanded tail appears large in proportion to the size of the bird. As she swooped upwards after her dives, the long tail-feathers, of which there are twelve, appeared to be fully extended, thus ensuring the maximum control over the direction of flight. It is the efficiency of this delicately-adjusted steering mechanism which enables the gyr falcon to follow with ease at high speed the most abrupt twists and turns of its prey. The determined, gliding pursuit of a bird by a falcon is called by falconers 'raking'. The procedure at the conclu-sion of each dive-bombing attack was always the same: the falcon would hurtle upward in characteristic fashion and, after climbing a few hundred feet, she would wheel lazily round. Next, she would beat along to a flank, presumably because my proximity to the foot of the cliff made a frontal attack impossible. Momentarily, the wing action would cease as she banked once more in order to align herself on the aiming-point. A brief pause; then whoosh! and the violent switch-back dive of that winged thunderbolt would have been completed. In the thrill of those few minutes, and in my determination to miss nothing of the spectacle which I had come over twelve hundred miles to see, I had temporarily forgotten my companions; but they had seen what was happening, and hastened to join me at the top of the scree beneath the cliff. This seemed to discourage the falcon, which left us alone for a while and disappeared.

from The Gyr Falcon Adventure by STANLEY CERELY

A raven, orbiting elm-high, lazily,
Two cronks to each circuit.
Sky sprinkled with forked martins
Swallows glittering their voices.

from Autumn Nature Notes by TED HUGHES

Raven

Ghastly grim the ancient Raven
  wandering from the nightly shore—

A nomadic, black-plumed bird, the raven accompanied many heroes and gods onto the field of battle. It fed on the flesh of the dead and flew high on the Danish standard of Odin, hanging its wings at defeat and soaring if victory was imminent. Two ravens sat also on the shoulders of the god Odin, one called Mind and the other Memory, whispering oracular words and wisdom into his ears. Bran the Blessed had a raven as his prophet and when he lay dying of battle wounds, he asked for his head to be buried on the White Hill of London. The raven must have followed him there for the presence of the tame birds protecting the British crown at the Tower of London is otherwise unexplained.

In classical times the raven had all the characteristics of Saturn, the evil and sombre bearer of disaster. The day Cicero was murdered by his enemies, a raven entered the great orator's chamber and woke him with his ominous croaking. But in other cultures it was a bird associated with wider cosmic powers and less drastic acts. Its colour was symbolic of the blackness of a fertile soil and the primal darkness from which life appeared. So, for many Indians of the North American continent, the raven was the winged creator of the visible world.

Two legends claim that originally the raven was a white bird. It seems that it became a messenger of Noah during the time of the Great Flood, but when sent out of the ark to look for land, the raven never returned. Since then, in Jewish mythology, the raven's feathers were tarred and its image likened to Satan. According to Ovid, a raven was responsible for telling Apollo that his beloved nymph, Coronis, was faithless. In great anger, the god shot Coronis with an arrow and, despising the bearer of the tale,

'He blackened the raven o'er,

And bid him prate in his white plumes no more.'

The raven is also a symbol of solitude. The fugitive prophet, Elijah, was fed by a raven at the brook Cherith and for the hermit, St Paul, the bird was a daily bearer of a loaf of bread. One of the Chinese imperial emblems is a curious, three-legged, raven-like bird, its legs contained within the solar circle. This image represents the life of the Emperor and each of the three legs correspond to the sun's position at dawn, at noon and at dusk. The emblem also suggests the isolation and solitude of a great man.

from The Book of Symbols *by* JANA GARAI

Autumn Poem

litter

    is

        turning

           brown

              and

                 the

                    road

                       above

                    is

                 filled

              with

           hitch

        hikers

      heading

south

ROGER McGOUGH

November Night

All day the wind had wept in corners—
Could not rest at night
But set the trees to sobbing with it,
Wailed in drainpipes—rained its tears
Down roof and fence and streaming gutter;
Beat its petulant fists on bin lids,
Cried out so like a ghost to come in
It provoked the dog to madness.
Quiet usually as bitches go
She bit and scrawled the door to escape
And woke me, whimpering at my bedside.
What had she seen—what heard?
We shivered together and listened,
While something—
Something outside—some soul in the wind
Screamed its grief and went about slamming
All the doors of eternity.

PEGGY JONES

Carol Singing

And I remember that we went singing carols once, a night or two
before Christmas Eve, when there wasn't the shaving of a moon to
light the secret, white-flying streets. At the end of a long road was a
drive that led to a large house, and we stumbled up the darkness of
the drive that night, each one of us afraid, each one holding a stone
in his hand in case, and all of us too brave to say a word. The wind

made through the drive-trees noises as of old and unpleasant and maybe web-footed men wheezing in caves. We reached the black bulk of the house.

'What shall we give them?' Dan whispered.

'"Hark the Herald"? "Christmas comes but Once a Year"?'

'No,' Jack said: 'We'll sing "Good King Wenceslas". I'll count three.'

One, two, three, and we began to sing, our voices high and seemingly distant in the snow-felted darkness round the house that was occupied by nobody we knew. We stood close together, near the dark door.

> Good King Wenceslas looked out
> On the Feast of Stephen.

And then a small, dry voice, like the voice of someone who has not spoken for a long time, suddenly joined our singing: a small, dry voice from the other side of the door: a small, dry voice through the keyhole. And when we stopped running we were outside *our* house; the front room was lovely and bright; the gramophone was playing; we saw the red and white balloons hanging from the gas-bracket; uncles and aunts sat by the fire; I thought I smelt our supper being fried in the kitchen. Everything was good again, and Christmas shone through all the familiar town.

'Perhaps it was a ghost,' Jim said.

'Perhaps it was trolls,' Dan said, who was always reading.

'Let's go in and see if there's any jelly left,' Jack said. And we did that.

DYLAN THOMAS

Winter Morning

The morning wakens with the lumping flails,
Chilly and cold; the early-rising clown
Hurkles along and blows his finger nails;
Icicles from the cottage eaves hang down,
Which peeping children wish for in their play.
The field, once clad in autumn's russet brown,
Spreads from the eye its circle far away
In one huge sheet of snow; from the white wood
The crows all silent seek the dreary fens,
And starnels blacken through the air in crowds;
The sheep stand bleating in their turnip pen
And loathe their frozen food; while labouring men
Button their coats more close from angry clouds
And wish for night and its snug fire agen.

JOHN CLARE

clown: countryman
hurkles: crouching, shivering, drawing himself in

Mist

Like a stream of smoke flowing by,
The mist is like a blindfold to your eyes,
Damp and cold,
The condensation running down the windows like a cold sweat.
The mist of February and the damp air makes a shiver
Run like a string
Through your body.

YASMEEN THOMPSON*

Into the Cathedral

He blinked for a moment. There had been sun before, but not like this. . . . It smashed through the rows of windows in the south aisle, so that they exploded with colour, it slanted before him from right to left in an exact formation, to hit the bottom yard of the pillars on the north side of the nave. Everywhere, fine dust gave these rods and trunks of light the importance of a dimension. He blinked at them again, seeing, near at hand, how the individual grains of dust turned over each other, or bounced all together, like mayfly in a breath of wind. He saw how further away they drifted cloudily, coiled, or hung in a moment of pause, becoming, in the most distant rods and trunks, nothing but colour, honey-colour slashed across the body of the cathedral.

from The Spire by WILLIAM GOLDING

When Candle Light

When candle light singes the wings
of moths,

When candle light spreads withered
shadows across the room,

When the luminous flame
burns hot at the tip of a finger,

When all is quiet except for
the fire side crackling.

HEATHER DOCKERAY*

Clouds and Light

Over the roof-tops race the shadows of clouds;
Like horses the shadows of clouds charge down the street.

Whirlpools of purple and gold,
Winds from the mountains of cinnabar,
Lacquered mandarin moments, palanquins swaying and balancing
Amid the vermilion pavilions, against the jade balustrades.
Glint of the glittering wings of dragon-flies in the light:
Silver filaments, gold flakes settling downwards,
Rippling, quivering flutters, repulse and surrender,
The sun broidered upon the rain,
The rain rustling with the sun.

Over the roof-tops race the shadows of clouds;
Like horses the shadows of clouds charge down the street.

from Irradiations by JOHN GOULD FLETCHER

The City in the Sea

No rays from the holy Heaven come down
On the long night-time of that town;
But light from out the lurid sea
Streams up the turrets silently—
Gleams up the pinnacles far and free—
Up domes—up spires—up kingly halls—
Up fanes—up Babylon-like walls—
Up shadowy long-forgotten bowers
Of sculptured ivy and stone flowers—
Up many and many a marvellous shrine
Whose wreathed friezes intertwine
The viol, the violet, and the vine.
Resignedly beneath the sky
The melancholy waters lie.
So blend the turrets and shadows there
That all seem pendulous in air.

EDGAR ALLEN POE

fanes: temples

Storm

Poseidon ... gathered the clouds together, and disturbed the waters. He stirred up the blasts of all the winds, and he covered land and sea with thick cloud, throwing out the darkness of night. The east and south winds, and the squalling west, rushed together; the north wind came from the heights of heaven and raised a mighty wave. This wave crashed down on Odysseus, and whirled the raft round. He fell overboard, and the rudder left his grasp. The terrible blast of the fighting winds snapped the middle of the mast, and the sail and the yard-arm dropped far off in the sea. Odysseus was sucked under water, unable to raise himself from the swelling waves—he was weighed down by the clothes Calypso had given him. But at last he rose to the surface, and spat out the bitter salt water which poured down his face. Even then, although he was exhausted, he remembered his raft: he swam in pursuit, gripped hold of it, and sat in the middle of it. The raft was carried here and there by the strong current; the winds blew it from side to side. Sometimes the south wind tossed it across for the north wind to carry; sometimes the east wind yielded it up for the west to chase.

But now a friendly sea-nymph took pity on him—the slim-footed Ino. She advised him to rid himself of his heavy clothes, to leave the raft and to swim for the coast of Phaeacia. And she lent him an immortal veil to wind around him, to protect him from death. He took the veil from her hands, and a moment later Poseidon sent a monstrous wave against him, which broke up the raft and shattered its timbers. So now Odysseus mounted on one of the timbers, like a rider mounting a horse, and stripped off his clothes, and wound the veil around him. Then he stretched out his hands, and dropped into the sea, putting all his strength into swimming.

After this, Poseidon departed and left him to his fate. And then at once the goddess Athene smoothed Odysseus' way. She ordered the winds to cease, and put them all to rest except for a fresh north wind, which helped to carry him on towards Phaeacia. For two days and two nights he wandered among the waves, often seeing death before him. But when the third day dawned, a great wave lifted him up and he saw land in the distance. It was a joyful sight, and he swam eagerly for the shore.

from The Odyssey, translated from Greek by DAVID RAVEN

The Sea

White are the horses that crash on the beach
Golden the sand that the white horses reach.
Grey are the cliffs that tower over all,
Blue of the sea, and white of the fall.
Green of the grass, that covers the cliffs.
Brown is the house where the old man lives.
Grey is his hair, that matches the waves.
Wrinkled his skin, as the old man says:
'Mild was the sea, and blue was the sky,
Those were the days when the boats sailed by.
Now, wild is the sea and grey is the sky,
Stormy the sea as the years race by.'

SUSAN GIBSON*

Sea Fever

I must go down to the seas again, to the lonely sea and the sky,
And all I ask is a tall ship and a star to steer her by,
And the wheel's kick and the wind's song and the white sails
   shaking,
And a grey mist on the sea's face, and a grey dawn breaking.

I must go down to the seas again, for the call of the running tide
Is a wild call and a clear call that may not be denied;
And all I ask is a windy day with the white clouds flying,
And the flung spray and the blown spume, and the seagulls crying.

I must go down to the seas again, to the vagrant gipsy life,
To the gull's way and the whale's way where the wind's like a
   whetted knife;
And all I ask is a merry yarn from a laughing fellow-rover,
And quiet sleep and a sweet dream when the long trick's over.

JOHN MASEFIELD

Mutiny on the Bounty

April 28th, 1789. *HMS Bounty* is on the return trip from Tahiti and
sailing towards the island of Tonga. The crew are in an ugly mood,
angry and dissatisfied; some are mutinous. Captain Bligh, the
master, every day grows more tyrranical, punishing one or other for
petty offences. The men grow more miserable as they reflect on the
paradise island and the many friends they have had to leave behind
there. Some have thought of jumping ship and staying there forever.

The situation gets worse; there are violent quarrels, and fights

break out. Fletcher Christian, the first mate, is finding it increasingly difficult to bear the captain's insults and is now more in sympathy with the men than with the master. Returning below decks after yet another row, he is at breaking point. Then, as argument develops, the situation explodes and the men mutiny, Christian reluctantly leading them. He forces Bligh at gunpoint to hand over the ship. A longboat is made ready, fitted out with provisions and the captain is put aboard it, despite the opinion of several of the mutineers that the best thing to do with him is to throw him overboard for the sharks. The first mate won't hear of this. Others in the crew, uneasy about joining in the mutiny, are given the option of getting into the longboat with Bligh. Fourteen men join him, and the ship pulls away, leaving the captain threatening to hang every last one of the men who have taken his ship.

Christian turns the ship back and sails to Tahiti where the men are greeted by their friends.

During the next few days Christian debates whether to stay on the island or to sail out into the Pacific and look for another island—somewhere uninhabited where they can found a colony, grow things, live a life of freedom and peace, and where they will be safe from discovery.

Eight seamen and their women friends elect to go with Christian. They set off heading eastwards until they reach the Pitcairn Island, 1,300 miles south-east of Tahiti. It is exactly what they have been looking for—a beautiful coastline, sand, rivulets, plentiful supplies of fish, coconuts, fruits, and a fertile soil where they can farm. The place is the paradise island of their dreams. They set up huts, burn the ship for fear that some passing mariners might sight it, and settle down to an idyllic life.

Meanwhile Bligh, who though he might well have been a harsh master is a brilliant navigator, sails four thousand miles to reach Timor in the East Indies, eventually leaving for England where he is given command of another ship. Again he has trouble and faces another mutiny. After some years he accepts the governorship of New South Wales where his ruthless behaviour creates more trouble, and in 1847, after being promoted rear admiral, he dies.

For eighteen years the mutineers live on their island undisturbed by the outside world, until one day in 1808, an American whaling ship puts into shore for fresh water. The crew quickly discover that the men on the island are not Polynesians, and, sailors being what they are, it is not long after that the news is spread that the mutineers of the *Bounty* have survived and have settled in the Pitcairns. An English ship sets out to find them. Nevertheless, of the men who threw in their lot with Fletcher Christian in taking over the *Bounty*, only five are ever caught. They are taken back to England and tried. Three of them are hanged and the other two reprieved.

The descendants of the mutineers still live in the islands to this very day.

Galley-Slaves

The spectacle was to me new and strange, to see so many hundreds of miserably naked persons, having their heads shaven close and having only high red bonnets, a pair of coarse canvas drawers, their whole backs and legs naked, doubly chained about their middle and legs, in couples, and made fast to their seats, and all commanded in a trice by an imperious and cruel seaman. One Turk he much favoured, who waited on him in his cabin, but with no other dress than the rest, and a chain locked about his leg but not coupled. This galley was richly carved and gilded, and most of the rest were very beautiful. After bestowing something on the slaves, the captain sent a band of them to give us music at dinner where we lodged. I was amazed to contemplate how these miserable caitiffs live in their galley crowded together, yet there was hardly one but had some occupation by which, as leisure and calms permitted, they get some little money, insomuch as some of them have, after many years of cruel servitude, been able to purchase their liberty. Their rising forward and falling back at their oar is a miserable spectacle, and the noise of their chains with the roaring of the beaten waters has something of strange and fearful to one unaccustomed to it. They are ruled and chastised by strokes on their backs and soles of their feet on the least disorder, and without the least humanity; yet are they cheerful and full of knavery.

7 October 1644
from The Diary of John Evelyn

caitiff: old word for 'captive'; now means 'poor wretch'

The Seafarer

I can sing a true song about myself,
Tell of my travels, of many hard times
Toiling day after day; I can describe
How I have harboured bitter sorrow in my heart
And often learned that ships are homes of sadness.

Wild were the waves when I took my turn,
The arduous night-watch, standing at the prow
While the boat tossed near the rocks. My feet
Were tortured by frost, fettered
In frozen chains; fierce anguish clutched
At my heart; passionate longings maddened
The mind of the sea-weary man. Prosperous men,
Living on land, do not begin to understand
How I, careworn and cut off from my kinsmen,
Have as an exile endured the winter
On the icy sea....
Icicles hung round me; hail showers flew.
The only sound there, was of the sea booming—
The ice-cold wave—and at times the song of the swan.
The cry of the gannet was all my gladness,
The call of the curlew, not the laughter of men,
The mewing gull, not the sweetness of mead.
There, storms echoed off the rocky cliffs; the icy-feathered tern
Answered them; and often the eagle,
Dewy-winged, screeched overhead. No protector
Could console the cheerless man.

He who is accustomed to the comforts of life
And, proud and flushed with wine, suffers

Little hardship living in the city,
Will never know how I, heavy with weariness,
Have often had to make the ocean paths my home.
The night-shadow grew long, it snowed from the north,
Frost fettered the earth; hail, coldest of grain,
Battered the ground. But now my blood
Is stirred that I should make trial
Of the mountainous streams, the tossing salt waves;
My heart's longings always urge me
To undertake a journey, to visit the country
Of a foreign people far across the sea.

The seafarer will always feel longings.
The groves burst with blossom, towns become fair,
Meadows are beautiful once more, the whole world revives;
All these things urge the eager man
To set out on a journey over the salt streams.
And the cuckoo, too, harbinger of summer, sings
A mournful song, boding bitter sorrow
To the heart. Prosperous men know not
What hardship is endured by those
Who tread the paths of exile to the ends of the world.

Wherefore my heart leaps within me,
My mind roves with the waves
Over the whale's domain, it wanders far and wide
Across the face of the earth, returns again to me
Eager and unsatisfied; the solitary bird screams,
Irresistible, urging my heart to the whale's way
Over the stretch of the sea.

from The Seafarer
translated from Old English by KEVIN CROSSLEY-HOLLAND

The Old Man of the Sea

The vessel sank immediately and I found myself struggling in the water. By great good fortune I managed to grasp hold of a piece of driftwood to which I clung, paddling with my feet, until more dead than alive I was washed ashore on an island.

For a while I lay exhausted on the beach, but at last I felt sufficiently recovered to set off and explore my surroundings. Imagine my delight when I found that I had been cast up on an island paradise: the trees were weighed down with delicious fruit, there were fragrantly scented flowers everywhere, birds sang sweetly on all sides and there were clear streams of fresh water. Giving thanks to Allah I ate my fill of fruit and slaked my thirst, then I lay down and slept an untroubled sleep.

The next morning, as I was walking through the woods I suddenly came upon a very old man sitting by the side of a stream. He wore nothing but a waist-cloth made of palm leaves. Thinking he must be another survivor from the wreck I approached and greeted him. He acknowledged my greeting but said nothing. I asked him how he came to be there but still he did not reply but shook his head and moaned and made signs that he wanted me to carry him across the stream. Thinking that perhaps his legs were paralysed I agreed and lifted him on my back and so carried him to the other bank. But instead of getting down he wound his legs tightly round my neck and refused to budge. I was frightened and tried to throw him off but he clung still tighter gripping my neck with his legs until I nearly choked to death and fell to the ground gasping for breath.

At this the old man stood up and drummed with his feet on my back and shoulders so hard that it felt as if I were being beaten with canes. The pain was so great that it forced me to my feet again, but as soon as I rose he resumed his seat on my shoulders and made signs to me that I was to carry him to the trees that bore the best fruit. If I stopped for a moment or walked too slowly for his liking he beat me so cruelly with his feet that it felt as though I had been scourged, so that I was forced to carry him about the island like a slave. My back and shoulders were rubbed raw for he never dismounted, night and day, not even to sleep; but when he wished to rest he wound his legs about my neck and leaned back and slept awhile. As soon as he was awake again he beat me so hard that I sprang up in haste to do his bidding.

I cursed the day that I had taken pity on the old wretch and resolved never to make the same mistake a second time if I should escape his clutches. But there seemed no end to my misery until one day we stopped at a tree under which lay a number of dry gourds. I took one of them and cutting off the top scooped out the inside and cleaned it. Then I gathered some grapes from a nearby vine and squeezed them into the gourd until it was full of juice. I stopped up the mouth of the gourd and left it standing in the sun for some days until the juice had turned to wine.

Every day after that I used to drink some wine to help me endure the torment of carrying that old devil. The more I drank the lighter seemed my odious burden until one day I had drunk so much that I forgot about him altogether and began to dance with joy, singing and shouting at the top of my voice. Seeing this my tormentor became curious and snatching the gourd from my hands clapped it to his lips and drained it to the dregs. Soon he too grew merry. He began to clap his hands and jig to and fro on my shoulders. Before long he was hopelessly drunk, his legs released their hold and he began to sway backwards and forwards. This was my chance. I managed to loosen his grip from my shoulders and dash the old monster to the ground where he lay motionless.

Without stopping to find out if he were alive or dead I ran leaping and bounding down to the shore where to my delight I met a party who had just landed for water and provisions.

They were horrified at my wretched state and amazed to hear my story. I was taken aboard their ship where their captain treated me kindly. He congratulated me on a lucky escape for he said I had fallen into the hands of the 'Old Man of the Sea' whose victims were doomed to a slow but certain death. The island was well known as his haunt and sailors who landed there took good care not to be separated from their companions.

The next day the ship set sail and I left behind for ever that accursed island and the 'Old Man of the Sea'.

from The Fifth Voyage of Sindbad the Sailor,
translated from Arabic by SIR RICHARD BURTON

The Alice Jean

One moonlight night a ship drove in,
   A ghost ship from the west,
Drifting with bare mast and lone tiller;
   Like a mermaid drest
In long green weed and barnacles
   She beached and came to rest.

All the watchers of the coast
   Flocked to view the sight;
Men and women, streaming down
   Through the summer night,
Found her standing tall and ragged
   Beached in the moonlight.

Then one old woman stared aghast:
    'The *Alice Jean*? But no!
The ship that took my Ned from me
    Sixty years ago—
Drifted back from the utmost west
    With the ocean's flow?

'Caught and caged in the weedy pool
    Beyond the western brink,
Where crewless vessels lie and rot
    In waters black as ink,
Torn out at last by a sudden gale—
    Is it the *Jean*, you think?'

A hundred women gaped at her,
    The menfolk nudged and laughed,
But none could find a likelier story
    For the strange craft
With fear and death and desolation
    Rigged fore and aft.

ROBERT GRAVES

The Old Ships

I have seen old ships sail like swans asleep
Beyond the village which men still call Tyre,
With leaden age o'ercargoed, dipping deep
For Famagusta and the hidden sun
That rings black Cyprus with a lake of fire;

And all those ships were certainly so old
Who knows how oft with squat and noisy gun,
Questing brown slaves or Syrian oranges,
The pirate Genoese
Hell-raked them till they rolled
Blood, water, fruit and corpses up the hold.
But now through friendly seas they softly run,
Painted the mid-sea blue or shore-sea green,
Still patterned with the vine and grapes in gold.

But I have seen,
Pointing her shapely shadows from the dawn
An image tumbled on a rose-swept bay,
A drowsy ship of some yet older day;
And, wonder's breath indrawn,
Thought I—who knows—who knows—but in that same
(Fished up beyond Aeæa, patched up new
—Stern painted brighter blue—)
That talkative, bald-headed seaman came
(Twelve patient comrades sweating at the oar)
From Troy's doom-crimson shore,
And with great lies about his wooden horse
Set the crew laughing and forgot his course.

It was so old a ship—who knows, who knows?
—And yet so beautiful, I watched in vain
To see the mast burst open with a rose,
And the whole deck put on its leaves again.

JAMES ELROY FLECKER

hell-raked: volleyed gunshot the length of the ships from stem to stern
bald-headed seaman: Odysseus

Troy was sacked by the Greeks in the Trojan wars

Nautical Words

compartments

bunker
cabin
caboose, camboose
galley
head
hold, hole

sails

fore-topmast
  staysail
fore-topmast
  studding sail
fore-topsail
inner jib
jib
jimbo [cant]
jolly jumper
kites
lateen sail
lower studding sail
lug
lugsail
main gaff-topsail
main royal
moonraker
moonsail
outer jib
reef
royal
skysail
skyscraper [coll.]
spanker
spritsail
square sail
standing lug
staysail
stern staysail
studding sail
topgallant sail
topsail
trysail

ropes, rigging

backropes
backstay
boat line
bobstay
boltrope

bow fast
bowline
bowsprit shroud
brace
quarter fast
ratline, ratlin
reef earing
roband, raband,
  robbin
ropeband
sea gasket
sheet
shroud
span
spanker peak
  halyard
spanker sheet
spanker vang
spring
starboard or port
  tack
stay
stern fast
stirrup
swifter
tack
timenoguy
vang
weather sheet
whisker jumper

galleys

bireme
foist
galiot
galleass
galley foist
half galley
hepteris
hexeris
penteconter

parts of ships

back
balance rudder
beak, beakhead
beam
bilge keel
bilge keelson
bitt

board
bollard
bow
bridge
bull's-eye
bulwarks
casemate
centerboard
companion
companion ladder
companionway
conning tower
conning tower
  hatch
counter
crow's-nest
cutwater
davit
entrance
false keel
forefoot
foresheets
foretop
freeboard
futtock
gangplank
gangway
garboard strake
gunwale, gunnel
hatch
hatchway
hawse, hawsehole
hawsepiece
hawsepipe
hawse timber
head
heel
island
keel
keel and keelson
keelson
kevel
larboard
lee, leeside,
  leeward
leeboard
limber board
limber hole
maintop
mizzentop
monkey rail

nose
paddle wheel
poop
port, portside
porthole
post
propeller
prow
rail
rudder
rudderpost
rudderstock
run
scuttle
scuttlebutt
sheave hole
sheets
shelf, shelfpiece
sister or side
  keelson
snorkel, schnorkel
spirketing
stanchion
starboard
stem
stern
sternpost
stern sheets

anchors

Baldt anchor
bower
center anchor
drag anchor
Dunn anchor
floating anchor
grapnel
kedge, kedge
  anchor
killick
Martin's anchor
mushroom anchor
port anchor
sacred anchor. [Gr.
  & Rom. antiq.]
sea anchor
sheet anchor
starboard anchor
stern anchor
stream anchor
Trotman's anchor

The Sargasso Sea

The Sargasso Sea is characterized not only by its omnipresent seaweed but by its deadly calms, a fact that may have started the picturesque but unnerving legend of 'Sea of Lost Ships', the 'Graveyard of Lost Ships', and the 'Sea of Fear'. This sailors' legend told of a great Atlantic surface graveyard containing ships from all the ages of seafaring man, caught and immobilized in fields of seaweed, slowly decaying but still manned by skeleton crews, or rather crews of skeletons, comprised of the unfortunates who could not escape and shared the doom of their ships. In this area of death were to be found tramp steamers, yachts, whalers, clippers, packets, brigantines, pirate vessels, and, to make the story better, Spanish treasure galleons. In enthusiastic retelling of the stories, the tellers included other ships that should certainly have rotted away and disappeared by the time of the telling, such as the dragon ships of the Vikings, with skeletons still at their oars, Arab sailing galleys, Roman triremes with their great banks of oars, Phoenician trading ships with silver anchors, and even the great ships of the lost Atlantis, their bows covered with fitted gold plate—all doomed to rot for centuries in a motionless sea.

The first legends about the Sargasso Sea may stem from the Phoenicians and Carthaginians who possibly crossed it thousands of years ago and made landfalls in the Americas. . . . The following report from the Carthaginian admiral Himilco, made in 500 B.C., strikes a familiar if somewhat sensational chord:

> . . . No breeze drives the ship, so dead is the
> sluggish wind of this idle sea . . . there is much
> seaweed among the waves, it holds back the ship
> like bushes . . . the sea has no great depth, the
> surface of the earth is barely covered by a little

water ... the monsters of the sea move continuously
to and fro and fierce monsters swim among the sluggish
and slowly creeping ships. ...

from The Bermuda Triangle by CHARLES BERLITZ

Bermuda Triangle

*The Bermuda Triangle is an area in the North Atlantic in which a large
number of aeroplanes and ships have mysteriously disappeared.*

MAJOR SHIPS DISAPPEARED OR FOUND
DERELICT IN TRIANGLE AREA

1. 1840: *Rosalie*, a large French vessel; found on course to Havana
    from Europe, in Triangle area, with sails set, cargo intact, all
    hands missing.

2. January 1880: British frigate *Atalanta*: left Bermuda for
    England with 290 aboard; vanished presumably not far from
    Bermuda.

3. October 1902: German bark *Freya*: found soon after leaving
    Manzanillo, Cuba, listing badly, partly dismasted, anchor
    dangling; calendar in captain's cabin read October 4—day
    after sailing.

4. March 4, 1918: U.S. Navy supply ship U.S.S. *Cyclops*. 500 feet,
    19,000 tons displacement; sailed March 4 from Barbados to
    Norfolk with 309 aboard; no bad weather; no radio messages;
    no wreckage ever found.

5. 1925: S.S. *Cotopaxi*: vanished en route from Charleston to Havana.

6. April 1932: two masted *John and Mary*: New York registry; found floating but abandoned fifty miles south of Bermuda; sails furled, hull freshly painted.

7. February 1940: Yacht *Gloria Colite* from St. Vincent, B.W.I.: found abandoned; everything in order; 200 miles south of Mobile, Alabama.

8. October 22, 1944: Cuban freighter *Rubicon*: found by Coast Guard in Gulf Stream off Florida coast; deserted, except for a dog.

9. June 1950: S.S. *Sandra*, 350-foot freighter; sailed from Savannah, Georgia, bound for Puerto Cabello, Venezuela; cargo 300 tons insecticide; passed St. Augustine, Florida, then disappeared without leaving a trace.

10. September 1955: Yacht *Connemara IV*: mysteriously abandoned 400 miles south-west of Bermuda.

11. February 2, 1963: *Marine Sulphur Queen*, 425-foot freighter; vanished without message, clues, or debris; en route to Norfolk, Virginia, from Beaumont, Texas, with all hands; last heard from near Dry Tortugas.

12. July 1, 1963: *Sno' Boy*, sixty-three-foot fishing boat; forty aboard; sailed from Kingston, Jamaica, to Northeast Cay, eighty miles south; disappeared with all hands.

13. 1924: *Raifuku Maru*, Japanese freighter; radioed for help between Bahamas and Cuba, then disappeared.

14. 1931: *Stavenger*, freighter with crew of forty-three; last heard from near Cat Island, Bahamas.

15. March 1938: *Anglo-Australian*, freighter with crew of thirty-nine; last message received west of Azores: 'All well.'

16. December 1967: *Revonoc*, all-weather forty-six-foot racing yacht; disappeared within sight of land.

17. December 24, 1967: *Witchcraft*, cabin cruiser; passenger and owner, disappeared while craft was at harbour buoy one mile from Miami.

18. April 1970: *Milton Iatrides*, freighter en route from New Orleans to Capetown.

19. March 1973: *Anita*, 20,000-ton freighter with crew of thirty-two, sailing from Newport News to Germany.

Voyage

In twenty days the silver ship
Had passed the Isle of Serendip,
And made the flat Araunian coasts
Inhabited, at noon, by Ghosts.

In thirty days the ship was far
Beyond the land of Calcobar,
Where men drink Dead Men's Blood for wine,
And dye their beards alizarine.

But on the hundredth day there came
Storm with his windy wings aflame,
And drave them out to that Lone Sea
Whose shores are near Eternity.

For seven years and seven years
Sailed those forgotten mariners,
Nor could they spy on either hand
The faintest level of good red land.

Bird or fish they saw not one;
There swam no ship beside their own,
And day-night long the lilied Deep
Lay round them, with its flowers asleep.

The beams began to warp and crack,
The silver plates turned filthy black,
And drooping down on the carven rails
Hung those once lovely silken sails.

And all the great ship's crew who were
Such noble lads to do and dare
Grew old and tired of the changeless sky
And laid them down on the deck to die.

. . . . .

When thrice the seven years had passed
They saw a ship, a ship at last!
Untarnished glowed its silver mail,
Windless bellied its silken sail.

With a shout the grizzled sailors rose
Cursing the years of sick repose,
And they who spake in tongues unknown
Gladly reverted to their own.

The Captain leapt and left his prayers
And hastened down the dust-dark stairs,
And taking to hand a brazen Whip
He woke to life the long dead ship.

. . . . .

Nearer and nearer the new boat came,
Till the hands cried out on the old ship's shame—
'Silken sail to a silver boat,
We too shone when we first set float!'

Swifter and swifter the bright boat sped,
But the hands spake thin like men long dead—
'How striking like that boat were we
In the days, sweet days, when we put to sea.'

The ship all black and the ship all white
Met like the meeting of day and night,
Met, and there lay serene dark green
A twilight yard of the sea between.

And twenty masters of foreign speech
Of every tongue they knew tried each;
Smiling, the silver Captain heard,
But shook his head and said no word.

   • • • • •

Said Aristu to Aflatun—
'Surely our King, despondent soon,
Has sent this second ship to find
Unconquered tracts of humankind.'

But Aflatun turned round on him
Laughing a bitter laugh and grim.
'Alas,' he said, 'O Aristu,
A white weak thin old fool are you.

'And does yon silver Ship appear
As she had journeyed twenty year?
And has that silver Captain's face
A mortal or Immortal grace?

Theirs is the land (as well I know)
Where live the Shapes of Things Below:
Theirs is the country where they keep
The Images men see in sleep.

'Theirs is the Land beyond the Door,
And theirs the old ideal shore.
They steer our ship: behold our crew
Ideal, and our Captain too.

'And lo! beside that mainmast tree
Two tall and shining forms I see,
And they are what we ought to be,
Yet we are they, and they are we.'

He spake and some young Zephyr stirred,
The two ships touched: no sound was heard;
The Black Ship crumbled into air;
Only the Phantom Ship was there.

And a great cry rang round the sky
Of glorious singers sweeping by,
And calm and fair on waves that shone
The Silver Ship sailed on and on.

from The Ballad of Iskander by JAMES ELROY FLECKER

Serendip: old name for Sri Lanka (Ceylon)
Calcobar: remote mythic land
alizarine: reddish dye

Boy on a Dolphin

During the reign of Augustus Caesar a dolphin came into the Bay of Naples where it entered the lake known as Lucrinus. A young boy, the son of a poor man, used to walk every day to school round the lake and at noon time he would sit by the side of the lake and call to the dolphin. As the days passed the dolphin got used to the boy and would readily come to the boy's call, sometimes scudding across the water or leaping and diving until he came up to where the boy was sitting. The boy would carry bread to give to the dolphin, and so the creature and the boy became very much attached to each other. In the course of time the dolphin was so trusting of the boy that he would stay steady in the water for the boy to climb onto his back, and then, very gently he would swim across the lake, keeping on the surface so as not to let the boy go under water. And this happened day in and day out, the dolphin carrying the boy across the lake to and from school, and so it continued for many years. But then the boy fell sick, languished and at last died. Each day the dolphin came to look for the boy and for many days afterwards. And it seemed to those who saw it that the dolphin was mourning for the boy, until at last he was found dead upon the shore.

from A History of the World by PLINY
freely translated from Latin

62

Arion on the Dolphin's Back

According to the local inhabitants, and those of Lesbos too, the most amazing thing that ever happened while Periander was tyrant of Corinth, was the trip taken by Arion to Taenarum on a dolphin.

Arion was the world's leading singer at the time, and also one of the earliest known composers. He spent most of his time at Periander's court, but the story goes that on one occasion he decided to make an overseas tour in Italy and Sicily. There he made a great deal of money and had decided to return to Corinth from the port of Tarentum in South Italy.

He always felt at home among the Corinthians, so he chartered a Corinthian ship for the passage. But once they were out at sea, the crew started scheming to throw Arion overboard and keep his money. When he discovered their intentions, he tried desperately to dissuade them, even offering to let them have the money if they would let him go. But it was no use: they told him either to kill himself, so that he could have a decent burial ashore, or jump overboard at once. Seeing no way out of it, Arion asked them, as a last favour, to let him put on all his robes and sing them a farewell song on deck. When that was over, he assured them, he would kill himself.

The crew were delighted at the chance to hear the best singer in the world, so they agreed, and came back from the bows to the middle of the ship, while Arion put on his gear and got out his instrument. Then he went up on the afterdeck and sang them a religious piece. After that, dressed just as he was, he threw himself into the sea. The ship went on its way home to Corinth, but Arion, so they say, was picked up by a dolphin, which took him to Taenarum. After landing there, he made his way, still in the same clothes, to Corinth, and told the whole story. Periander did not believe him and put him under close arrest. But in the meantime he kept a sharp

64

look-out for the ship's crew, and when they turned up he sent for them. 'Have you any news of Arion?' he asked. 'Oh, yes,' they said; 'he's all right. He's in Italy; in fact, he was making a fortune in Tarentum when we left.'

At this point Arion suddenly appeared wearing just the same things as when he had jumped overboard, and they were so badly shaken by this that they broke down under further questioning and admitted everything.

Well, that is the story they tell in Corinth and Lesbos. And at Cape Taenarum there is a monument to Arion: a bronze statue, not very large, of a man riding on the back of a dolphin.

from Stories from Herodotus
translated from Greek by BRIAN WILSON and DAVID MILLER

Androcles and the Lion

According to the ancient legend, Androcles was a runaway slave who was noted for his understanding of creatures of all kinds. During his escape he hid in a cave, hoping to avoid recapture. While he was inside the cave a huge lion entered. Androcles, regretting his foolhardiness in trying to escape, expected the lion to leap at him and tear him to shreds. The lion approached slowly and held out its paw. Amazed, Androcles looked at the paw and saw that there was a large thorn embedded in it. Timorously Androcles approached the beast and with great care removed the thorn. The lion responded by licking his hand.

Later on Androcles was recaptured and along with the Christians was put into the arena in Rome to fight the lions. Fortune favoured Androcles for instead of eating him one of the lions approached him docilely and he saw that it was the very one he had encountered in the cave. Androcles and the lion trotted happily round the arena, earning the respect of the crowd, the emperor's favour and their freedom.

This is how the playwright Bernard Shaw deals with the encounter between Androcles, his wife Megaera and the lion.

MEGAERA. How is any woman to keep her house clean when you bring in every stray cat and lost cur and lame duck in the whole countryside? You took the bread out of my mouth to feed them: you know you did: dont attempt to deny it.

ANDROCLES. Only when they were hungry and you were getting too stout, dearie.

MEGAERA. Yes: insult me, do. [*Rising*] Oh! I wont bear it another moment. You used to sit and talk to those dumb brute beasts for hours, when you hadnt a word for me.

ANDROCLES. They never answered back, darling. [*He rises and again shoulders the bundle.*]

MEGAERA. Well, if youre fonder of animals than of your own wife, you can live with them here in the jungle. Ive had enough of them and enough of you. I'm going back. I'm going home.

ANDROCLES [*barring the way back*] No, dearie: dont take on like that. We cant go back. Weve sold everything: we should starve; and I should be sent to Rome and thrown to the lions—

MEGAERA. Serve you right! I wish the lions joy of you. [*Screaming*] Are you going to get out of my way and let me go home?

ANDROCLES. No, dear—

MEGAERA. Then I'll make my way through the forest; and when I'm eaten by the wild beasts youll know what a wife youve lost. [*She dashes into the jungle and nearly falls over the sleeping lion.*] Oh! Oh! Andy! Andy! [*She totters back and collapses into the arms of Androcles, who, crushed by her weight, falls on his bundle.*]

ANDROCLES [*extracting himself from beneath her and slapping her hands in great anxiety*] What is it, my precious, my pet? Whats the matter? [*He raises her head. Speechless with terror, she points in the direction of the sleeping lion. He steals cautiously towards the spot indicated by Megaera. She rises with an effort and totters after him.*]

MEGAERA. No, Andy: youll be killed. Come back.

The lion utters a long snoring sigh. Androcles sees the lion, and recoils fainting into the arms of Megaera, who falls back on the bundle. They roll apart and lie staring in terror at one another. The lion is heard groaning heavily in the jungle.

ANDROCLES [*whispering*] Did you see? A lion.

MEGAERA [*despairing*] The gods have sent him to punish us because youre a Christian. Take me away, Andy. Save me.

ANDROCLES [*rising*] Meggy: theres one chance for you. Itll take him pretty nigh twenty minutes to eat me (I'm rather stringy and tough) and you can escape in less time than that.

MEGAERA. Oh, dont talk about eating. [*The lion rises with a great groan and limps towards them.*] Oh! [*She faints.*]

ANDROCLES [*quaking, but keeping between the lion and Megaera*] Dont you come near my wife, do you hear? [*The lion groans. Androcles can hardly stand for trembling.*] Meggy: run. Run for your life. If I take my eye off him, it's all up. [*The lion holds up his wounded paw and flaps it piteously before Androcles.*] Oh, he's lame, poor old chap! He's got a thorn in his paw. A frightfully big thorn. [*Full of sympathy*] Oh, poor old man! Did um get an awful thorn into um's tootsums wootsums? Has it made um too sick to eat a nice little Christian man for um's breakfast? Oh, a nice little Christian man will get um's thorn out for um; and then um shall eat the nice Christian man and the nice Christian man's nice big tender wifey pifey. [*The lion responds by moans of self-pity.*] Yes, yes, yes, yes, yes. Now, now [*taking the paw in his hand*], um is not to bite and not to scratch, not even if it hurts a very very little. Now make velvet paws. Thats right. [*He pulls gingerly at the thorn. The lion, with an angry yell of pain, jerks back his paw so abruptly that Androcles is thrown on his back.*] Steadeee! Oh, did the nasty cruel little Christian man hurt the sore paw? [*The lion moans assentingly but apologetically.*] Well, one more little pull and it will be all over. Just one little, little, leetle pull; and then um will live happily ever after. [*He gives the thorn another pull. The lion roars and snaps his jaws with a terrifying clash.*] Oh, mustnt frighten um's good kind doctor, um's affectionate nursey. That didnt hurt at all: not a bit. Just one more. Just to shew how the brave big lion can bear pain, not like the little crybaby Christian man. Oopsh! [*The thorn comes out. The lion yells with pain, and shakes his paw wildly.*] Thats it! [*Holding up the thorn.*] Now it's out. Now lick um's paw to take away the nasty inflammation, See? [*He licks his own hand. The lion nods intelligently and licks his paw industriously.*] Clever little liony-piony! Understands um's dear old friend Andy Wandy. [*The lion licks his face.*] Yes, kissums Andy Wandy. [*The lion wagging his tail violently, rises on his hind legs, and embraces Androcles, who makes a wry face and cries*] Velvet paws! Velvet paws! [*The lion draws in his claws.*] Thats right. [*He embraces the lion, who finally takes the end of his tail in one paw, places that tight round Androcles' waist, resting it on his hip. Androcles takes the other paw in his hand, stretches out his arm, and the two waltz rapturously round and round and finally away through the jungle.*]

MEGAERA [*who has revived during the waltz*] Oh, you coward, you havnt danced with me for years; and now you go off dancing with a great brute beast that you havnt known for ten minutes and that wants to eat your own wife. Coward. Coward! Coward! [*She rushes off after them into the jungle.*]

from Androcles and the Lion by GEORGE BERNARD SHAW

Dragon

The dragon is as long as a date-palm, with glistening eyes which are as red as blood. It has a huge mouth and inner cavity, and it swallows many animals, so that the beasts of the sea and of the land are in dread of it. When it moves, the sea is agitated with waves on account of its great strength.

In its first stage it is a malignant serpent and devours all the terrestrial animals it sees; but when its mischief waxes great an angel lifts it up, throws it into the sea, where it preys upon the creatures of the sea in a like manner. Then it grows to an enormous size, whereupon God sends an angel who carries it away and throws it to Gog and Magog.

It is related on the authority of a certain person that he had seen a dragon nearly two leagues in length, having the colour of a leopard, scales like those of a fish, a head like that of a man in shape but as large as a large hill, enormous ears, and eyes excessively large and round.

AL-DAMÍRÍ
translated from Arabic by A. S. G. Jayaker

The Magpie and the Eel

I woll tell you an ensaumple of a woman that ete the good moresell in the absence of her husbonde.

There was a woman that had a pie in a cage, that spake and wolde tell tayls that she saw do. And so it happed that her husbonde made kepe a grete ele in a litell ponde in his gardin, to that entent to yeve it sum of his frendes that wolde come to see hym; but the wyff, whanne her husbonde was oute, saide to her maide, 'late us ete the gret ele, and y will saie to my husbond that the otour hathe eten hym'; and so it was done. And whan the good man was come, the pye began to tell hym how her mistresse had eten the ele. And he yode to the ponde, and fonde not the ele. And he asked his wyff wher the ele was become. And she wende to have excused her, but he saide her, 'excuse you not, for y wote well ye have eten yt, for the pye hathe told me.' And so ther was gret noyse betwene the man hys wiff for etinge of the ele. But whanne the good man was gone, the maistresse and the maide come to the pye, and plucked off all the fedres on the pyes hede, saieng, 'thou hast discovered us of the ele': and thus was the poor pie plucked. But ever after, what the pie sawe a balled or a pilled man, or a woman with an high forhede, the pie saide to hem, 'ye spake of the ele'. And therfor here is an ensaumpe that no woman shulde ete no lycorous morcelles in the absens and withoute weting of her husbond, but yet it so were that it be with folk of worshipp, to make hem chere; for this woman was afterward mocked for the pye and the ele.

anonymous; written about 1400 A.D.

pie: magpie
y: I
otour: otter
yode: went
wende: thought

fedres: feathers
balled: bald
pilled: shaven
lycorous: delicious
weting: knowledge

A Cure

Mugwort, plantain which is open eastward, lamb's cress, cock's-spur grass, mayweed, nettle, crab-apple, thyme and fennel, old soap; crush the herbs to dust, mix with the soap and with the apple's juice. Make a paste of water and of ashes; take fennel, boil it in the paste and bathe with egg-mixture, either before or after he puts on the salve. Sing that charm on each of the herbs: thrice before he works them together and on the apple likewise; and sing that same charm into the man's mouth and into both his ears and into the wound before he puts on the salve.

translated from Anglo-Saxon by R. K. GORDON

Football

We can gain some faint idea of what early football was like from the annual Shrovetide games still played at Atherstone, Chester-le-Street, Ashbourne, and elsewhere. Here, as in the past, there are no obvious rules and no referees; in a local handbook published at Workington we are told that the game there has only one rule which is 'to get the ball into the opponent's goal by any means short of murder'. Teams may be of any size, the more the merrier. The only qualifications for players are strength, enthusiasm, and a complete indifference to mud and dripping clothes. This last is certainly necessary, for the goals are usually widely separated, and the ground covers the whole of the parish, regardless of any rivers, ditches, or other obstacles that may lie across it. At Atherstone the traffic on the main London–Holyhead road has to be diverted for the afternoon, since that road is also the village street, and is quite impassable for as long as the game lasts. At Ashbourne the goals are three miles apart and separated from each other by several good-sized streams which have to be crossed in the course of the match. At Chester-le-Street the 'upstreeters' and 'downstreeters' wage their war from one end of the town to the other, between houses and shops prudently barricaded for the occasion. All these games are played with the utmost vigour and enthusiasm but, even so, they are only pale shadows of the lively fights which once raged in these townships and also in Derby, Kirkwall, Dorking, and several other places.

from English Sports and Pastimes by CHRISTINA HOLE

The Gambler

Of all the high players this country ever sees, there is no doubt but that the guy they call The Sky is the highest. In fact, the reason he is called The Sky is because he goes so high when it comes to betting on any proposition whatever. He will bet all he has and nobody can bet any more than this.

His right name is Obadiah Masterson, and he is originally out of a little town in southern Colorado where he learns to shoot craps,

and play cards, and one thing and another, and where his old man is a very well-known citizen, and something of a sport himself. In fact, The Sky tells me that when he finally cleans up all the loose scratch around his home town and decides he needs more room, his old man has a little private talk with him and says to him like this:

'Son,' the old guy says, 'you are now going into the wide, wide world to make your own way, and it is a very good thing to do, as there are no more opportunities for you in this burg. I am only sorry,' he says, 'that I am not able to bank-roll you to a very large start, but,' he says, 'not having any potatoes to give to you, I am now going to stake you to some very valuable advice, which I personally collect in my years of experience around and about, and I hope and trust you will always bear this advice in mind.

'Son,' the old guy says, 'no matter how far you travel, or how smart you get, always remember this: some day, somewhere,' he says, 'a guy is going to come to you and show you a nice brand-new deck of cards on which the seal is never broken, and this guy is going to offer to bet you that the jack of spades will jump out of this deck and squirt cider in your ear. But, son,' the old guy says, 'do not bet this man, for as sure as you do you are going to get an ear full of cider.'

from Guys and Dolls by DAMON RUNYON

Dad Crow and Foxy Boy

An old fable retold in heptalk

Dad Crow was living it up in the green leaves,
A piece of mouse-eat latched on to his candy crushers.
Foxy Boy really goes for the goodies,
And wings over to him this hot message:
'Man, like hiya cool crow!
Dig that crazy allover look—
You sure is a hot chick.
No kidding, it's that hifi chirping.
Like that smooth outside.
You're the coolest in all these green leaves.'

At these sending beats Dad Crow flips his lid
And tries to dig that stere-O.
He gives full volume, goes square, and loses his eats!
Foxy Boy grabs at the falling goodies
And blows out a new sound;
'OK, Daddy-O, let me clue you in to all that
Big eyes; life buggs hard so tune in to my wavelength.
This jive's been well worth the mouse-eat, no kidding.'
Dad Crow all riled and not in the groove
Lays it on his label but way out,
That he won't dig mugsville
Until he's in the wooden pad.

PAUL DAVY*

Lily Smalls looks in the glass

Oh there's a face!
Where you get that hair from?
Got it from a old tom cat.
Give it back then, love.
Oh there's a perm!

Where you get that nose from, Lily?
Got it from my father, silly.
You've got it on upside down!
Oh there's a conk!

Look at your complexion!
Oh no, *you* look.
Needs a bit of make-up.
Needs a veil.
Oh there's glamour!

Where you get that smile, Lil?
Never you mind, girl.
Nobody loves you.
That's what *you* think.

Who is it loves you?
Shan't tell.
Come on, Lily.
Cross your heart then?
Cross my heart.

And very softly, her lips almost touching her reflection, she breathes
the name and clouds the shaving-glass.

from Under Milk Wood by DYLAN THOMAS

80

Growing

Frankie went again to the kitchen mirror and stared at her own face. 'The big mistake I made was to get this close crew-cut. For the wedding I ought to have long bright yellow hair. Don't you think so?'

She stood before the mirror and she was afraid. It was the summer of fear, for Frankie, and there was one fear that could be figured in arithmetic with paper and a pencil at the table. This August she was twelve and five-sixths years old. She was five feet five and three-quarter inches tall, and she wore a number seven shoe. In the past year she had grown four inches, or at least that was what she judged. Already the hateful little summer children hollered to her: 'Is it cold up there?' And the comments of grown people made Frankie shrivel on her heels. If she reached her height on her eighteenth birthday, she had five and one-sixth growing years ahead of her. Therefore, according to mathematics and unless she could somehow stop herself, she would grow up to be over nine feet tall? And what would be a lady who is over nine feet high? She would be a Freak.

from The Member of the Wedding by CARSON McCULLERS

Childhood

When did my childhood go?
Was it the day I ceased to be eleven,
Was it the time I realized that Hell and Heaven,
Could not be found in Geography,
And therefore could not be,
Was that the day!

When did my childhood go?
Was it the time I realized that adults were not all they seemed to be,
They talked of love and preached of love,
But did not act so lovingly,
Was that the day!

When did my childhood go?
Was it when I found my mind was really mine,
To use whichever way I choose,
Producing thoughts that were not those of other people,
But my own, and mine alone,
Was that the day!

Where did my childhood go?
It went to some forgotten place,
That's hidden in an infant's face,
That's all I know.

MARKUS NATTEN*

My Hat

Mother said if I wore this hat
I should be certain to get off with the right sort of chap
Well look where I am now, on a desert island
With so far as I can see no one at all on hand
I know what has happened though I suppose Mother wouldn't see
This hat being so strong has completely run away with me
I had the feeling it was beginning to happen the moment I put it on
What a moment that was as I rose up, I rose up like a flying swan
As strong as a swan too, why see how far my hat has flown me away
It took us a night to come and then a night and a day
And all the time the swan wing in my hat waved beautifully
Ah, I thought, How this hat becomes me.
First the sea was dark but then it was pale blue
And still the wing beat and we flew and we flew
A night and a day and a night, and by the old right way
Between the sun and the moon we flew until morning day.
It is always early morning here on this peculiar island

The green grass grows into the sea on the dipping land
Am I glad I am here? Yes, well, I am,
It's nice to be rid of Father, Mother and the young man
There's just one thing causes me a twinge of pain,
If I take my hat off, shall I find myself home again?
So in this early morning land I always wear my hat
Go home, you see, well I wouldn't run a risk like that.

STEVIE SMITH

Lazy Man's Song

I could have a job, but am too lazy to choose it;
I have got land, but am too lazy to farm it.
My house leaks; I am too lazy to mend it.
My clothes are torn; I am too lazy to darn them.
I have got wine, but I am too lazy to drink;
So it's just the same as if my cup were empty.
I have got a lute, but am too lazy to play;
So it's just the same as if it had no strings.
My family tells me there is no more steamed rice;
I want to cook, but am too lazy to grind.
My friends and relatives write me long letters;
I should like to read them, but they're such a bother to open.
I have always been told that Hsi Shu-yeh
Passed his whole life in absolute idleness.
But he played his lute and sometimes worked at his forge;
So even *he* was not so lazy as I.

anonymous, written 811 A.D.
translated from Chinese by ARTHUR WALEY

89

An Old Jamaican Woman Thinks about the Hereafter

What would I do forever in a big place, who
have lived all my life in a small island?
The same parish holds the cottage I was born in, all
my family, and the cool churchyard.
                        I have looked
up at the stars from my front verandah and have been afraid
of their pathless distances. I have never flown
in the loud aircraft nor have I seen palaces,
so I would prefer not to be taken up high nor
rewarded with a large mansion.
                        I would like
to remain half-drowsing through an evening light
watching bamboo trees sway and ruffle for a valley-wind,
to remember old times but not to live them again;
occasionally to have a good meal with no milk
nor honey for I don't like them, and now and then to walk
by the grey sea-beach with two old dogs and watch
men bring up their boats from the water.

                        For all this,
for my hope of heaven, I am willing to forgive my debtors
and to love my neighbour ...
                        although the wretch throws stones
at my white rooster and makes too much noise in her damn
    backyard.

                                        A. L. HENDRIKS

Leaving Home

At the age of nineteen, Laurie Lee set out from home with a small tent, a change of clothes and a violin wrapped in a blanket, to find his fortune.

When I judged it to be tea-time I sat on an old stone wall and opened my tin of treacle biscuits. As I ate them I could hear mother banging the kettle on the hob and my brothers rattling their tea-cups. The biscuits tasted sweetly of the honeyed squalor of home—still only a dozen miles away.

I might have turned back then if it hadn't been for my brothers, but I couldn't have borne the look on their faces. So I got off the wall and went on my way. The long evening shadows pointed to folded villages, homing cows, and after-church walkers. I tramped the edge of the road, watching my dusty feet, not stopping again for a couple of hours.

When darkness came, full of moths and beetles, I was too weary to put up the tent. So I lay myself down in the middle of a field and stared up at the brilliant stars. I was oppressed by the velvety emptiness of the world and the swathes of soft grass I lay on. Then the fumes of the night finally put me to sleep—my first night without a roof or bed.

I was woken soon after midnight by drizzling rain on my face, the sky black and the stars all gone. Two cows stood over me, windily sighing, and the wretchedness of that moment haunts me still. I crawled into a ditch and lay awake till dawn, soaking alone in that nameless field. But when the sun rose in the morning the feeling of desolation was over. Birds sang, and the grass steamed warmly. I got up and shook myself, ate a piece of cheese, and turned again to the south.

from As I walked out one Midsummer Morning by LAURIE LEE

First Man

A cart drove between the two big stringybarks and stopped. These were the dominant trees in that part of the bush, rising above the involved scrub with the simplicity of true grandeur. So the cart stopped, grazing the hairy side of a tree, and the horse, shaggy and stolid as the tree, sighed and took root.

The man who sat in the cart got down. He rubbed his hands together, because already it was cold, a curdle of cold cloud in a pale sky, and copper in the west. On the air you could smell the frost. As the man rubbed his hands, the friction of cold skin intensified the coldness of the air and the solitude of that place. Birds looked from twigs, and the eyes of animals were drawn to what was happening. The man lifting a bundle from a cart. A dog lifting his leg on an anthill. The lip drooping on the sweaty horse.

Then the man took an axe and struck at the side of a hairy tree, more to hear the sound than for any other reason. And the sound was cold and loud. The man struck at the tree, and struck, till several white chips had fallen. He looked at the scar in the side of the tree. The silence was immense. It was the first time anything like this had happened in that part of the bush.

More quickly then, as if deliberately breaking with a dream, he took the harness from the horse, leaving a black pattern of sweat. He hobbled the strong fetlocks of the cobby little horse and stuck the nosebag on his bald face. The man made a lean-to with bags and a few saplings. He built a fire. He sighed at last, because the lighting of his small fire had kindled in him the first warmth of content. Of being somewhere. That particular part of the bush had been made his by the entwining fire. It licked at and swallowed the loneliness.

By this time also the red dog had come and sat at the fire, near, though not beside the man, who was not intimate with his animals. He did not touch or address them. It was enough for them to be there, at a decent distance. So the dog sat. His face had grown sharp with attention, and with a longing for food, for the tucker box that had not yet been lifted from the cart. So the sharp dog looked. Hunger had caused him to place his paws delicately. His yellow eyes consumed the man in the interval before meat.

·   ·   ·   ·   ·

The man got up. He dusted his hands. He began to take down the tucker box.

How the dog trembled then.

There was the sound of tin plate, tea on tin, the dead thump of flour. Somewhere water ran. Birds babbled, settling themselves on a roost. The young horse, bright amongst his forelock, and the young and hungry dog were there, watching the young man. There was a unity of eyes and firelight.

The gilded man was cutting from a lump of meat. It made the dog cavort like a mad, reddish horse. The man was throwing to the dog, while pretending, according to his nature, not to do so. The dog gulped at the chunks of fatty meat, the collar working forward on his neck, the eyes popping in his head. The man ate, swallowing with some ugliness, swallowing to get it down, he was alone, and after-wards swilling the hot, metallic tea, almost to get it finished with. But warmth came. Now he felt good. He smelled the long, slow scent of chaff slavered in the nosebag by the munching horse. He smelled the smell of green wood burning. He propped his head against the damp collar discarded by the horse. And the cavern of fire was enormous, labyrinthine, that received the man. He branched and flamed, glowed and increased, and was suddenly extinguished in the little puffs of smoke and tired thoughts.

from The Tree of Man by PATRICK WHITE

Portrait of an Elizabethan Lady

In the great hall of Bisham Abbey there hangs a portrait of Dame Elizabeth Hoby, a learned lady who was an adviser and friend of Queen Elizabeth I. It is said that Dame Hoby had a son who was a great disappointment to her because he was very poor at his lessons and, irritated and angered by the boy's slowness, she would beat him about the head in order to make him learn. But the boy only became worse and eventually he died of a seizure brought on, people thought, by the persistent beatings he had to endure.

Since that time down the years many people claim to have seen the ghost of Dame Elizabeth gliding down corridors or walking along the paths in the gardens, sometimes washing bloodstained hands in a bowl. Her face is dark, her clothes white like the negative of a photograph.

Towards the end of the last century the house was owned by Admiral Vansittart, a practical man who was also sceptical of the stories of the ghost of Lady Elizabeth. One day, however, he was standing in the great hall with his back to the portrait when he had the distinct impression that he was being watched. Turning round he saw a figure in Elizabethan dress moving away from him. Astonished, the admiral looked up at the portrait of Dame Elizabeth. For a moment he could not believe his eyes, for what he saw on the walls shook all the confidence of this tough old sailor. Where the portrait of the lady should have been was nothing but empty space.

Lost City

In the year 1753 Raposo (a Portuguese explorer) and a few hardy companions set off into the trackless hinterland in search of the lost mines of Muribeca ... For years they wandered deep in this unknown country in untiring search for the fabulous Muribeca treasure, surviving many dangers and hardships. Eventually they had to admit failure and the disheartened party started to make their way eastwards towards the coast settlements.

They travelled through swamps and bush, and then came across some jagged mountains, the rocks of which were made of crystal quartz, not unusual in that part of Brazil. The mountains glittered in the sun, and to Raposo and his men it looked as though they were studded with gems. They thought they had found the Muribeca treasure at last, and they pressed forward eagerly. When they reached the foot of the mountains they saw precipices rising sheer and unclimbable above them. They spent hours trying to find a way up. The place abounded with deadly rattlesnakes, against whose bite they knew no remedy.

Not until evening, when they had decided to camp for the night, did they discover the chink in the mountain's armour, and this quite by accident when two of the party were looking for firewood and came across a cleft in the face of the precipice which was fairly easily climbable. The party clambered up the crevice, which seemed in places to be artificially made, and emerged at the top on to a ledge high above the plain below, and stood there gazing in stupefied amazement at a large city stretched before them beyond the lip of the plateau.

Their first reaction was one of fear, for they thought the place was inhabited. They thought it might be the last stronghold of an ancient civilization, such as the Incas in Peru, still holding out in this impregnable fortress against the European who had invaded the continent. As they gazed from behind the crest they could see no sign of life, no wisp of tell-tale smoke. The city lay wrapped in complete silence. It was all very frightening and unnerving, and night fell quickly with them lying huddled together, talking in whispers, afraid to light a fire, unable to sleep, each a prey to his superstitious fears. The Indians in the party were no less afraid, and could throw no light on this strange place. To them it was just taboo.

The next morning Raposo sent an Indian to make a reconnaissance, and the man returned in a state of fear, saying that the city was one of the dead, uninhabited at least by the denizens of this world. And so Raposo and his men cautiously entered the deserted city. As they reached it they saw it was in a state of ruin, but the ruins were massive—huge arches, megalithic temples, tumbled columns, all belonging to an age so long past that their minds reeled. They came to a great square, in the middle of which was a huge column of black stone upon which stood a majestic statue of a man with one hand pointing towards the north. They went into a vast ruined temple where millions of bats winged in circles among the eroded frescoes and carvings.

They walked through streets of two-storeyed houses, the stone walls of which were made of blocks which fitted together with great accuracy, and in the building of which no kind of mortar had been used. One part of the city was in complete ruin, just mounds of stone and masonry, in some cases half buried by earth. Here they found great chasms and openings in the earth as though made by an earthquake.

The Portuguese explorers spent some time in this ruined city, exploring it, although their superstitions would not allow them to sleep in the place at night. They found gold coins and the sealed-up entrances of what looked like mines. They decided to return to civilization and then come back with a properly equipped expedition to remove all the treasure from the city and open and examine the mines.

Raposo and his party eventually got back to Bahia on the coast, where Raposo wrote a report and gave it to the Viceroy. It was pigeon-holed and forgotten. What happened to Raposo, whether he returned to the lost city or not, is unknown. The document eventually found its way into a government archive in Rio de Janeiro. In the nineteenth century a half-hearted and unsuccessful attempt was made to investigate the story, after which the document was again forgotten until Colonel Fawcett dug it out when he was at Rio.

He was convinced of its authenticity. What impressed him was Raposo's remarkable description of the city, particularly such details as the statue of the man pointing north and the mortarless joins of the great stone buildings. Raposo could not have known about any of the ancient cities of old Peru, thought Fawcett, which had not been discovered in his century. The fact that he was able to describe the city as he did showed that he could not have invented it . . .

However, convinced that the 1753 lost city existed, Fawcett set out to find it early in 1925. A letter was received from him dated 20 May, 1925, and was sent from Baciary Post, Matto Grosso, in which he said he expected to be at his main objective in August. 'Thereafter our fate is in the lap of the gods.' The last message came back with returning natives from Dead Horse Camp (Lat. 11 43° S. and 54 35° W.) saying that he, Fawcett, and his son Jack were well, but that he was worried about Raleigh Rimell, who was having trouble with his leg, but refused to go back. Fawcett added: 'You need have no fear of any failure.'

Since then nothing has been heard of them, and their fate remains a mystery to this day.

from Fifty Great Journeys by FRANK USHER

The Song of the Witch's Cat

I am nothing, me, nothing.
Think what I could be, poor cat,
if I didn't rot my life away in slavery.
I sit, I wait, till I'm told what to do.
Witch spells it out, I have to obey.

I am cat, me, cat.
I am born for that, to hunt,
play, scratch, lick fur, have my own way.
And if witch would set me free ...
but she won't.

Want to hunt, me, hunt,
but I can't without she says so.
Want to laze in the sun
but there's always her cursing work to be done.
Want to play, me, play.
Please may I, my lady?

In dreams I escape her
or rip her to pieces. I serve her
poison dishes, glasses
of deadly drink. I sink her
in the river's deep places.
But her cold laughter wakes me,
she spits in my face.

Who will help me? Who will?
Whipwind, will you?
Ragerain? Sharpsteel? Flashfire? Slowsoil?
Creatures: you all carry her burden?
Wiseword? Strongsong? All silent?
Not a sound heard.
The world is afraid.

GORDON HODGEON

A Night at a Cottage

On the evening that I am considering I passed by some ten or twenty cosy barns and sheds without finding one to my liking: for Worcestershire lanes are devious and muddy, and it was nearly dark when I found an empty cottage set back from the road in a little bedraggled garden. There had been heavy rain earlier in the day, and the straggling fruit trees still wept over it.

But the roof looked sound, there seemed no reason why it should not be fairly dry inside—as dry, at any rate, as I was likely to find anywhere.

I decided: and with a long look up the road and a long look down the road, I drew an iron bar from the lining of my coat and forced the door, which was only held by a padlock and two staples. Inside, the darkness was damp and heavy: I struck a match, and with its haloed light I saw the black mouth of a passage somewhere ahead of me: and then it spluttered out. So I closed the door carefully, though I had little reason to fear passers-by at such a dismal hour in so remote a lane: and lighting another match, I crept down this passage to a little room at the far end, where the air was a bit clearer, for all that the window was boarded across. Moreover, there was a little rusted stove in this room: and thinking it too dark for any to see the smoke, I ripped up part of the wainscot with my knife, and soon was boiling my tea over a bright, small fire, and drying some of the day's rain out of my steamy clothes. Presently I piled the stove with wood to its top bar, and setting my boots where they would best dry, I stretched my body out to sleep.

I cannot have slept very long, for when I woke the fire was still burning brightly. It is not easy to sleep for long together on the level boards of a floor, for the limbs grow numb, and any movement wakes. I turned over, and was about to go again to sleep when I was startled to hear steps in the passage. As I have said, the window was boarded, and there was no other door from the little room—no cupboard even—in which to hide. It occurred to me rather grimly that there was nothing to do but to sit up and face the music, and that would probably mean being haled back to Worcester Jail, which I had left two bare days before, and where, for various reasons, I had no anxiety to be seen again.

The stranger did not hurry himself, but presently walked slowly down the passage, attracted by the light of the fire: and when he came in he did not seem to notice me where I lay huddled in a corner, but walked straight over to the stove and warmed his hands at it. He was dripping wet; wetter than I should have thought it possible for a man to get, even on such a rainy night: and his clothes were old and worn. The water dripped from him on to the floor: he wore no hat, and the straight hair over his eyes dripped water that sizzled spitefully on the embers.

It occurred to me at once that he was no lawful citizen, but another wanderer like myself; a gentleman of the Road; so I gave him some sort of greeting, and we were presently in conversation. He complained much of the cold and wet, and huddled himself over the fire, his teeth chattering and his face an ill white.

'No,' I said, 'it is no decent weather for the Road, this. But I wonder this cottage isn't more frequented, for it's a tidy little bit of a cottage.'

Outside the pale dead sunflowers and giant weeds stirred in the rain.

'Time was,' he answered, 'there wasn't a tighter little cot in the co-anty, nor a purtier garden. A regular little parlour, she was. But now no folk'll live in it, and there's very few tramps will stop here either.'

There were none of the rags and tins and broken food about that you find in a place where many beggars are used to stay.

'Why's that?' I asked.

He gave a very troubled sigh before answering.

'Gho-asts,' he said; 'gho-asts. Him that lived here. It is a mighty sad tale, and I'll not tell it you: but the upshot of it was that he drowned himself, down to the mill-pond. All slimy, he was, and floating, when they pulled him out of it. There are fo-aks have seen un floating on the pond, and fo-aks have seen un round the corner of the school, waiting for his childer. Seems as if he had forgotten, like, how they were all gone dead, and the why he drowned hisself. But there are some say he walks up and down this cottage, up and down; like when the small-pox had 'em, and they couldn't sleep but if they heard his feet going up and down by their do-ars. Drownded hisself down to the pond, he did: and now he Walks.'

The stranger sighed again, and I could hear the water squelch in his boots as he moved himself.

'But it doesn't do for the like of us to get superstitious,' I answered. 'It wouldn't do for us to get seeing ghosts, or many's the wet night we'd be lying in the roadway.'

'No,' he said; 'no, it wouldn't do at all. I never had belief in Walks myself.'

I laughed.

'Nor I that,' I said. 'I never see ghosts, whoever may.'

He looked at me again in his queer melancholy fashion.

'No,' he said. ''Spect you don't ever. Some folk do-an't. It's hard enough for poor fellows to have no money to their lodging, apart from gho-asts sceering them.'

'It's the coppers, not spooks, make me sleep uneasy,' said I. 'What with coppers, and meddlesome-minded folk, it isn't easy to get a night's rest nowadays.'

The water was still oozing from his clothes all about the floor, and a dank smell went up from him.

'God! man,' I cried, 'can't you *never* get dry?'

'Dry?' He made a little coughing laughter. 'Dry? I shan't never be dry . . . 'tisn't the like of us that ever get dry, be it wet *or* fine, winter *or* summer. See that.'

He thrust his muddy hands up to the wrist in the fire, glowering over it fiercely and madly. But I caught up my two boots and ran crying out into the night.

from A Moment in Time by RICHARD HUGHES

The Nightmare

Once, as in the darkness I lay asleep by night,
Strange things suddenly saw I in my dream;

All my dream was of monsters that came about me while I slept,
Devils and demons, four-horned, serpent-necked,
Fishes with bird-tails, three-legged bogies
From six eyes staring; dragons hideous,
Yet three-part human.
On rushed the foul flocks, grisly legions,
Stood round me, stretched out their arms,
Danced their hands about me, and sought to snatch me from
my bed.
Then cried I (and in my dream
My voice was thick with anger and my words all awry),
'Ill-spawned elves, how dare you
Beset with your dire shapes Creation's cleanest
Shapeliest creature, Man?' Then straightway I struck out,

Flashed my fists like lightning among them, thumped like thunder,
Here slit Jack-o'-Lantern,
Here smashed fierce Hog-Face,
Battered wights and goblins,
Smote venturous vampires, pounded in the dust
Imps, gnomes and lobs,
Kobolds and kelpies;
Swiped bulge-eyed bogies, oafs and elves;
Clove Tough-head's triple skull, threw down
Clutching Night-hag, flogged the gawky Ear-wig Fiend
That floundered toward me on its tail.

I struck at staring eyes,
Stamped on upturned faces; through close ranks
Of hoofs I cut my way, buried my fingers deep
In half-formed flesh;
Ghouls tore at my touch; I slit sharp noses,
Trod on red tongues, seized shaggy manes,
Shook bald-heads by the beard.
Then was a scuffling. Arms and legs together
Chasing, crashing and sliding; a helter-skelter
Of feet lost and found in the tugging and toppling,
Cuffing, cudgelling, frenzied flogging....

So fought I, till terror and dismay
Shook those foul flocks; panic spread like a flame
Down mutinous ranks; they stand, they falter,
Those ghastly legions; but fleeing, suddenly turn
Glazed eyes upon me, to see how now I fare.
At last, to end their treachery
Again I rushed upon them, braved their slaver and snares,
Stood on a high place, and lashed down among them,

Shrieking and cursing as my blows crashed.
Then three by three and four by four
One after another hop-a-trot they fled,
Bellowing and bawling till the air was full of their breath—
Grumbling and snarling,
Those vanquished ogres, demons discomfited,
Some that would fain have run
Lolling and lurching, some that for cramped limbs
Could not stir from where they stood. Some over belly-wounds
Bent double; some in agony gasping and groaning.
Suddenly the clouds broke and (I knew not why)
A thin light filtered the darkness; then, while again
I sighed in wonder that those disastrous creatures,
Dire monstrosities, should dare assail
A clean and comely man, ... there sounded in my ears
A twittering and crowing. And outdoors it was light.
The noisy cock, mindful that dawn was in the sky,
Had crowed his warning, and the startled ghosts,
Because they heard dawn heralded, had fled
In terror and tribulation from the rising day.

Wang Yen-Shou translated from Chinese
by ARTHUR WALEY

The Wealth and Splendour of Solomon

Now the weight of gold that came to Solomon in one year was six hundred three-score and six talents of gold, beside that he had of the merchantmen, and of the traffick of the spice merchants, and of all the kings of Arabia, and of the governors of the country. And king Solomon made two hundred targets of beaten gold: six hundred shekels of gold went to one target. And he made three hundred shields of beaten gold; three pound of gold went to one shield: and the king put them in the house of the forest of Lebanon. Moreover the king made a greater throne of ivory, and overlaid it with the best gold. The throne had six steps, and the top of the throne was round behind: and there were stays on either side on the place of the seat, and two lions stood beside the stays. And twelve lions stood there on the one side and on the other upon the six steps: there was not the like made in any kingdom. And all king Solomon's drinking vessels were of gold, and all the vessels of the house of the forest of Lebanon were of pure gold; none were of silver: it was nothing accounted of in the days of Solomon. For the king had at sea a navy of Tharshish with the navy of Hiram: once in three years came the navy of Tharshish, bringing gold, and silver, ivory, and apes, and peacocks.

So king Solomon exceeded all the kings of the earth for riches and for wisdom. And all the earth sought to Solomon, to hear his wisdom, which God had put in his heart. And they brought every man his present, vessels of silver, and vessels of gold, and garments, and armour, and spices, horses, and mules, a rate year by year.

And Solomon gathered together chariots and horsemen: and he had a thousand and four hundred chariots, and twelve thousand horsemen, whom he bestowed in the cities for chariots, and with the king at Jerusalem. And the king made silver to be in Jerusalem as stones, and cedars made he to be as the sycamore trees that are in the vale, for abundance. And Solomon had horses brought out of Egypt, and linen yarn: the king's merchants received the linen yarn at a price. And a chariot came up and went out of Egypt for six hundred shekels of silver, and an horse for an hundred and fifty: and so for all the kings of the Hittites, and for the kings of Syria, did they bring them out by their means.

from the Book of Kings, chapter 10, verses 14-30
Authorized version of the Bible

Circe's Palace

Around her fountain which flows
With the voice of men in pain,
Are flowers that no man knows.
Their petals are fanged and red
With hideous streak and stain;
They sprang from the limbs of the dead.
We shall not come here again.

Panthers rise from their lairs
In the forest which thickens below,
Along the garden stairs
The sluggish python lies;
The peacocks walk, stately and slow,
And they look at us with the eyes
Of men whom we knew long ago.

T. S. ELIOT

The Fortress at Loches

Ludovico Sforza, Duke of Milan, was captured by the French
armies in April 1500. He was a small dark man, cunning and
unscrupulous in politics but a great patron of the arts and employed
at his court many artists and musicians, among them Leonardo da
Vinci.

After his capture he was taken as a prisoner to the sombre fortress
at Loches in France where he was put into a large bare room in the
heart of the castle and allowed only his jester for company and

occasional visits from his doctor. The room was dark and forbidding and as the days passed into weeks and months and eventually into years Ludovico went through stages of hope and despair as the possibility of his release diminished. But he managed to persuade his captors to let him have paints and brushes and with these he decorated the bare walls of his room.

Eleven years passed by and at last Ludovico was allowed his freedom. As he reached the courtyard from the steps which led up from the dungeons he staggered and fell in the bright sunlight. Within minutes he was dead. According to his doctor, after being shut away for so long the intensity of the sunlight was too much for him and he was overcome by it.

Visitors to the fortress can still see Ludovico's paintings on the walls of his gloomy prison cell.

The Prisoner

Tartars led in chains,
Tartars led in chains!
Their ears pierced, their faces bruised—they are driven into the land of Ch'in.
The Son of Heaven took pity on them and would not have them slain.
He sent them away to the south-east, to the lands of Wu and Yüeh.
A petty officer in a yellow coat took down their names and surnames;
They were led from the city of Ch'ang-an by relays of armed guards.
Their bodies were covered with the wounds of arrows, their bones stood out from their cheeks.

They had grown so weak they could only march a single stage a day.

In the morning they must satisfy hunger and thirst with neither
  plate nor cup;

At night they must lie in their dirt and rags on beds that stank with
  filth.

Suddenly they came to the Yangtze River and remembered the
  waters of Chiao.

With lowered hands and levelled voices they sobbed a muffled song.

Then one Tartar lifted up his voice and spoke to the other Tartars,

'Your sorrows are none at all compared with my sorrows.'

Those that were with him in the same band asked to hear his tale;

As he tried to speak the words were choked by anger.

He told them, 'I was born and bred in the plain of Liang-chou;

In the frontier wars of Ta-li I fell into the Tartars' hands.

Since the days the Tartars took me alive, forty years ago,

I have had to wear a coat of skins tied with a fur belt.

Only on the first of the first month might I wear my Chinese dress.

As I put on my coat and arranged my cap, how fast the tears flowed!

I made in my heart a secret vow I would find a way home;

I hid my plan from my Tartar wife and the children she had borne
  me in the land.

I thought to myself, 'It is well for me that my limbs are still strong,'

And yet, being old, in my heart I feared I should never live to return.

The Tartar chieftains shoot so well that the birds are afraid to fly;

From the risk of their arrows I escaped alive and fled swiftly home.

Hiding all day and walking all night, I crossed the Great Desert,

Where clouds are dark and the moon black and the sands eddy in
  the wind.

Frightened, I sheltered at the Green Grave, where the frozen grasses
  are few;

Stealthily I crossed the Yellow River, at night, on the thin ice,

Suddenly I heard Han drums and the sound of soldiers coming;

I went to meet them at the road-side, bowing to them as they came.

But the moving horsemen did not hear that I spoke the Han tongue;

Their captain took me for a Tartar born and had me bound in chains.

They are sending me away to the south-east, to a low and swampy land

Provided with hardly any kit and no protective drugs.

Thinking of this my voice chokes and I ask of Heaven above,

Was I spared from death only to spend the rest of my years in sorrow?

My native village in Liang plain I shall not see again;

My wife and children in the Tartars' land I have fruitlessly deserted.

When I fell among Tartars and was taken prisoner, I pined for the land of Han;

Now that I am back in the land of Han, they have turned me into a Tartar.

Po Chu-I translated from Chinese by ARTHUR WALEY

Green Grave: the grave of Choa-chun, a Chinese girl who in 33BC was 'bestowed upon the Khan of the Hsiung-nu as a mark of Imperial regard'. Hers was the only grave in this desolate district on which grass would grow
Han: Chinese

Old Idea of Choan by Rosoriu

The narrow streets cut into the wide highway at Choan,
Dark oxen, white horses,
       drag on the seven coaches with outriders
The coaches are perfumed wood,
The jewelled chair is held up at the crossway,
Before the royal lodge:
A glitter of golden saddles, awaiting the princess;
They eddy before the gate of the barons.
The canopy embroidered with dragons
       drinks in and casts back the sun.
Evening comes.
       The trappings are bordered with mist.
The hundred cords of mist are spread through
       and double the trees,
Night birds, and night women,
Spread out their sounds through the gardens.

Birds with flowery wing, hovering butterflies
       crowd over the thousand gates,
Trees that glitter like jade,
       terraces tinged with silver,
The seed of a myriad hues,
A network of arbours and passages and covered ways,
Double towers, winged roofs,
       border the network of ways:
A place of felicitous meeting.

EZRA POUND

The Wall

It was our third job that night.

Until this thing happened, work had been without incident. There had been shrapnel, a few enquiring bombs, and some huge fires; but these were unremarkable and have since merged without identity into the neutral maze of fire and noise and water and night, without date and without hour, with neither time nor form, that lowers mistily at the back of my mind as a picture of the air-raid season.

I suppose we were worn down and shivering. Three a.m. is a meanspirited hour. I suppose we were drenched, with the cold hose water trickling in at our collars and settling down at the tails of our shirts. Without doubt the heavy brass couplings felt moulded from metal-ice. Probably the open roar of the pumps drowned the petulant buzz of the raiders above, and certainly the ubiquitous fire-glow made an orange stage-set of the streets. Black water would have puddled the City alleys and I suppose our hands and our faces were black as the water. Black with hacking about among the burnt up rafters. These things were an every-night nonentity. They happened and they were not forgotten because they were never even remembered.

But I do remember it was our third job. And there we were—Len, Lofty, Verno and myself, playing a fifty-foot jet up the face of a tall city warehouse and thinking of nothing at all. You don't think of anything after the first few hours. You just watch the white pole of water lose itself in the fire and you think of nothing. Sometimes you move the jet over to another window. Sometimes the orange dims to black—but you only ease your grip on the ice-cold nozzle and continue pouring careless gallons through the window. You know the fire will fester for hours yet. However, that night the blank, indefinite hours of waiting were sharply interrupted—by an unusual sound. Very suddenly a long rattling crack of bursting brick and mortar perforated the moment. And then the upper half of that five-storey building heaved over towards us. It hung there, poised for a timeless second before rumbling down at us. I was thinking of nothing at all and then I was thinking of everything in the world.

In that simple second my brain digested every detail of the scene. New eyes opened at the sides of my head so that, from within, I photographed a hemispherical panorama bounded by the huge length of the building in front of me and the narrow lane on either side.

Blocking us on the left was the squat trailer pump, roaring and quivering with effort. Water throbbed from its overflow valves and from leakages in the hose and couplings. A ceaseless stream spewed down its grey sides into the gutter. But nevertheless a fat iron exhaust pipe glowed red-hot in the middle of the wet engine. I had to look past Lofty's face. Lofty was staring at the controls, hands tucked into his armpits for warmth. Lofty was thinking of nothing. He had a black diamond of soot over one eye, like the White-eyed Kaffir in negative.

To the other side of me was a free run up the alley. Overhead swung a sign—'Catto and Henley'. I wondered what in hell they sold. Old stamps? The alley was quite free. A couple of lengths of dead, deflated hose wound over the darkly glistening pavement. Charred flotsam dammed up one of the gutters. A needle of water fountained from a hole in a live hose-length. Beneath a blue shelter light lay a shattered coping stone. The next shop along was a tobacconist's, windowless, with fake display cartons torn open for anybody to see. The alley was quite free.

Behind me, Len and Verno shared the weight of the hose. They heaved up against the strong backward drag of waterpressure. All I had to do was yell 'Drop it'—and then run. We could risk the live hose snaking up at us. We could run to the right down the free alley—Len, Verno and me. But I never moved. I never said 'Drop it' or anything else. That long second held me hypnotized, rubber boots cemented to the pavement. Ton upon ton of red-hot brick hovering in the air above us numbed all initiative. I could only think. I couldn't move.

Six yards in front stood the blazing building. A minute before I would never have distinguished it from any other drab Victorian atrocity happily on fire. Now I was immediately certain of every minute detail. The building was five storeys high. The top four storeys were fiercely alight. The rooms inside were alive with red fire. The black outside walls remained untouched. And thus, like the lighted carriages of a night express, there appeared alternating rectangles of black and red that emphasized vividly the extreme symmetry of the window spacing: each oblong window shape posed as a vermilion panel set in perfect order upon the dark face of the wall. There were ten windows to each floor, making forty windows in all. In rigid rows of ten, one row placed precisely above the other, with strong contrasts of black and red, the blazing windows stood to attention in strict formation. The oblong building, the oblong windows, the oblong spacing. Orange-red colour seemed to *bulge* from the black frame-work, assumed tactile values, like boiling jelly that expanded inside a thick black squared grill.

Three of the storeys, thirty blazing windows and their huge frame of black brick, a hundred solid tons of hard, deep Victorian wall, pivoted over towards us and hung flatly over the alley. Whether the descending wall actually paused in its fall I can never know. Probably it never did. Probably it only seemed to hang there. Probably my eyes only digested its action at an early period of momentum, so that I saw it 'off true' but before it had gathered speed.

The night grew darker as the great mass hung over us. Through smoke-fogged fireglow the moonlight had hitherto penetrated to the pit of our alley through declivities in the skyline. Now some of the moonlight was being shut out as the wall hung ever further over us. The wall shaded the moonlight like an inverted awning. Now the pathway of light above had been squeezed to a thin line. That was the only silver lining I ever believed in. It shone out—a ray of hope. But it was a declining hope, for although at this time the entire hemispherical scene appeared static, an imminence of movement could be sensed throughout—presumably because the scene was actually moving. Even the speed of the shutter which closed the photograph on my mind was powerless to exclude this motion from a deeper consciousness. The picture appeared static to the limited surface sense, the eyes and the material brain, but beyond that there was hidden movement.

The second was timeless. I had leisure to remark many things. For instance, that an iron derrick, slightly to the left, would not hit me. This derrick stuck out from the building and I could feel its sharpness and hardness as clearly as if I had run my body intimately over its contour. I had time to notice that it carried a foot-long hook, a chain with three-inch rings, two girder supports and a wheel more than twice as large as my head.

A wall will fall in many ways. It may sway over to the one side or the other. It may crumble at the very beginning of its fall. It may remain intact and fall flat. This wall fell as flat as a pancake. It clung to its shape through ninety degrees to the horizontal. Then it detached itself from the pivot and slammed down on top of us.

The last resistance of bricks and mortar at the pivot point cracked off like automatic gunfire. The violent sound both deafened us and brought us to our senses. We dropped the hose and crouched. Afterwards Verno said that I knelt slowly on one knee with bowed head, like a man about to be knighted. Well, I got my knighting. There was an incredible noise—a thunderclap condensed into the space of an eardrum—and then the bricks and the mortar came tearing and burning into the flesh of my face.

Lofty, away by the pump, was killed. Len, Verno and myself they dug out. There was very little brick on top of us. We had been lucky. We had been framed by one of those symmetrical, oblong window spaces.

WILLIAM SAMSOM

Hit by a Bullet

The whole experience of being hit by a bullet is very interesting and I think it is worth describing in detail.

It was at the corner of the parapet, at five o'clock in the morning. This was always a dangerous time, because we had the dawn at our backs, and if you stuck your head above the parapet it was clearly

outlined against the sky. I was talking to the sentries preparatory to changing the guard. Suddenly, in the very middle of saying something, I felt—it is very hard to describe what I felt, though I remember it with the utmost vividness.

Roughly speaking it was the sensation of being *at the centre* of an explosion. There seemed to be a loud bang and a blinding flash of light all round me, and I felt a tremendous shock—no pain, only a violent shock, such as you get from an electric terminal; with it a sense of utter weakness, a feeling of being stricken and shrivelled up to nothing. The sand-bags in front of me receded into immense distance. I fancy you would feel much the same if you were struck by lightning. I knew immediately that I was hit, but because of the seeming bang and flash I thought it was a rifle nearby that had gone off accidentally and shot me. All this happened in a space of time much less than a second. The next moment my knees crumpled up and I was falling, my head hitting the ground with a violent bang which, to my relief, did not hurt. I had a numb, dazed feeling, a consciousness of being very badly hurt, but no pain in the ordinary sense.

The American sentry I had been talking to had started forward. 'Gosh! Are you hit?' People gathered round. There was the usual fuss—'Lift him up! Where's he hit? Get his shirt open!' etc., etc. The American called for a knife to cut my shirt open. I knew that there was one in my pocket and tried to get it out, but discovered that my right arm was paralysed. Not being in pain, I felt a vague satisfaction. This ought to please my wife, I thought; she had always wanted me to be wounded, which would save me from being killed when the great battle came. It was only now that it occurred to me to wonder where I was hit, and how badly; I could feel nothing, but I was conscious that the bullet had struck me somewhere in the front of the body. When I tried to speak I found that I had no voice, only a faint squeak, but at the second attempt I managed to ask where I was hit. In the throat, they said. Harry Webb, our stretcher-bearer, had brought a bandage and one of the little bottles of alcohol they gave us for field-dressings. As they lifted me up a lot of blood poured out of my mouth, and I heard a Spaniard behind me say that the bullet had gone clean through my neck. I felt the alcohol, which at ordinary times would sting like the devil, splash on to the wound as a pleasant coolness.

They laid me down again while somebody fetched a stretcher. As soon as I knew that the bullet had gone clean through my neck I took it for granted that I was done for. I had never heard of a man or an animal getting a bullet through the middle of the neck and surviving it. The blood was dribbling out of the corner of my mouth. 'The artery's gone,' I thought. I wondered how long you last when your carotid artery is cut; not many minutes, presumably. Every-thing was very blurry. There must have been about two minutes during which I assumed that I was killed. And that too was interesting—I mean it is interesting to know what your thoughts would be at such a time. My first thought, conventionally enough, was for my wife. My second was a violent resentment at having to leave this world which, when all is said and done, suits me so well. I had time to feel this very vividly. The stupid mischance infuriated me. The meaninglessness of it! To be bumped off, not even in battle, but in this stale corner of the trenches, thanks to a moment's carelessness! I thought, too, of the man who had shot me—won-dered what he was like, whether he was a Spaniard or a foreigner, whether he knew he had got me, and so forth. I could not feel any resentment against him. I reflected that as he was a Fascist I would have killed him if I could, but that if he had been taken prisoner and brought before me at this moment I would merely have congratu-lated him on his good shooting. It may be, though, that if you were really dying your thoughts would be quite different.

They had just got me on to the stretcher when my paralysed right arm came to life and began hurting damnably. At the time I imagined that I must have broken it in falling; but the pain reassured me, for I knew that your sensations do not become more acute when you are dying. I began to feel more normal and to be sorry for the four poor devils who were sweating and slithering with the stretcher on their shoulders. It was a mile and a half to the ambulance, and vile going, over lumpy, slippery tracks. I knew what a sweat it was, having helped to carry a wounded man down a day or two earlier. The leaves of the silver poplars which, in places, fringed our trenches brushed against my face; I thought what a good thing it was to be alive in a world where silver poplars grow.

from Homage to Catalonia by GEORGE ORWELL

Parachute Jump

Then suddenly there was a hard tug at my shoulders, and the sensation of being a snowflake in a maelstrom ceased as abruptly as it had begun. The parachute had opened. I looked up and felt inside me a great surging gratitude. I seemed to be suspended snug and safe, as I had lain years before rocking gently in a garden hammock, and the contrast and the relief were so sudden and overwhelming that I still wish they had never ended. Craning back I could see the parachute swaying above me. My shoulder cords were twisted and I was spinning slowly round and round like someone with the ropes twisted on a swing.

The first thing to do was to get the ropes separated and straight over your shoulders. That you did by gripping them above your head and forcing them apart, and then after unspinning you held them as wide apart as possible to prevent overspinning in the other direction. The instructions worked nicely, and I had time to look down and found that the earth had suddenly got a great deal closer. This was most distressing. Drifting up there by oneself after the stresses and anguish of the jump was utterly delightful, and I wanted to go on and on floating through the sky ... floating there produced a satisfying airy feeling of isolation from the whole world, and all the time I was hugging myself at having got the jump over. Next time I should know much better what to expect....

Meanwhile the earth itself appeared to be behaving in the most remarkable manner. First it tilted itself on one side, and then it spun round slowly like a plate juggled on the end of a stick, presenting an entirely different aspect, until I was not at all sure if I was going to swing on to it sideways or face forwards or flat on my back.

There was hardly time to feel more than surprised, and then the earth which had appeared at first miles and miles away suddenly seemed to rush up at me, much too fast to allow me to remember the

landing drill. However, it was an easy day, with little or no wind, and I dropped without sufficient force to knock me over, although I somehow curled up and rolled, not being sure if it would be necessary, and wishing in any case to learn it as a habit.

A. M. RENDEL

Thoughts of Flight

Then I watched some birds on the other side of the ravine circling over the rocks, catching insects as they skimmed the air. It was a beautiful sight, and I thought as I watched them, *that* is what man had in mind when he first said, 'I want to fly.' And I thought about some old genius working up in a remote mountain valley actually making a little flying machine that he could strap on his back like a knapsack, and this old man would come down to a big air base and he would go out on the flight line and announce to everyone, 'Folks, I have invented a flying machine.' There would be a silence and then everyone would start laughing as if they would never stop, and finally the Captain would pause long enough to explain to the old man that flying machines had *already* been invented, that right over there—that big silver thing with the huge wings, *that* was a flying machine, and over there, those enormous bullet-shaped things, *those* were flying machines. 'Well,' the old man would say, shaking his head sadly, 'I won't waste no more of your time. I'll just head on home,' and he would press a button on his knapsack, and silently, easy as a bird, he would lift off the ground, and skimming the air, fly towards the hills. For a moment everyone would be too stunned to move, and then the General would cry, 'Come back, come back,' and everyone at the air base would run beneath the flying old man, crying, 'Wait, wait, come back, come back!' because that was the way every one of those men really wanted to fly, free and easy and silent as a bird. But the old man, who was a little hard of hearing, would not hear their cries and would fly off into the distance and never be seen again.

from The Midnight Fox by BETSY BYARS

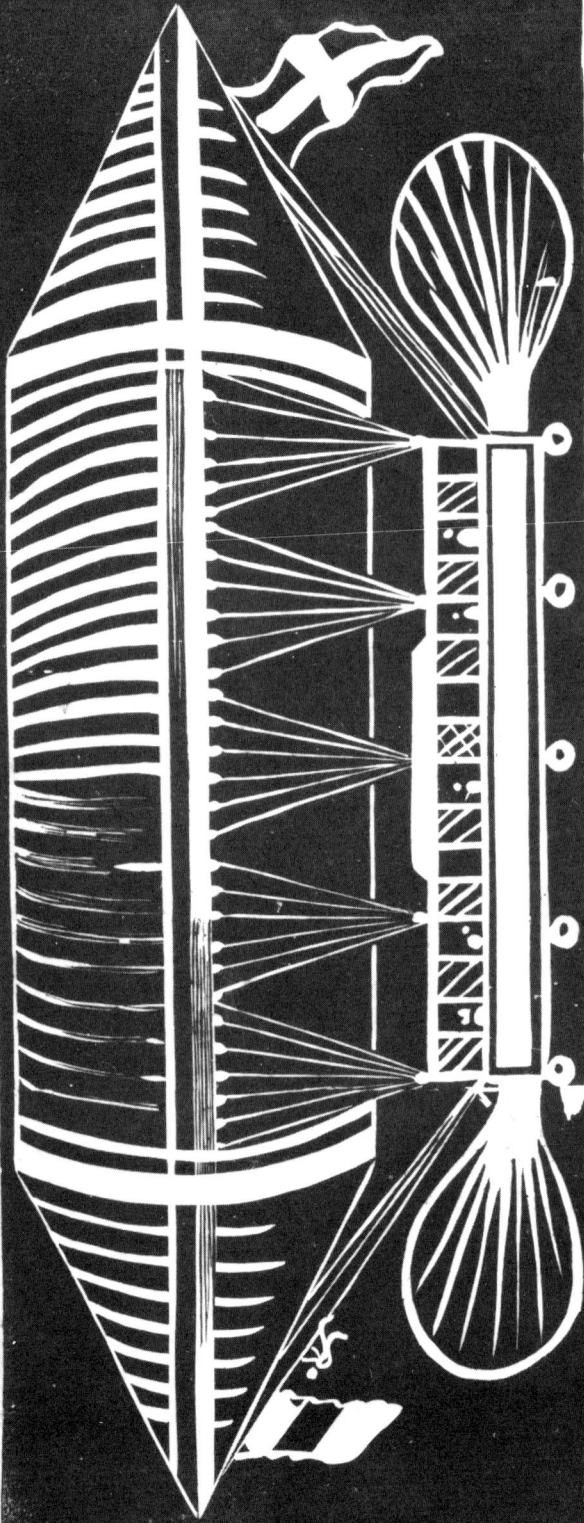

THE AERIAL SHIP

The EAGLE, 160 Feet in length and 50 Feet in height.

This stupendous and wonderful Machine is

REMOVED to VAUXHALL GARDENS,

From whence it will make its first Ascent in England during the present Month. *(September 1835)*

It is now exhibited daily from Nine in the Morning until dusk.

Admission, ONE SHILLING.

N.B. Gentlemen wishing to Ascend with the Ship, on its First Trip, may know the Terms on application at the Gardens.

BALNE, Printer, 38, Gracechurch Street.

Escape by Air

In ancient times Daedalus was regarded as the most gifted crafts-man who had ever lived. He is supposed to have invented, among other things, the axe and the saw. For King Minos of Crete he built the fabulous labyrinth which housed the minotaur, a ferocious creature half man and half bull. The maze was so complex that no one was able to find a way out until Theseus killed the minotaur and escaped by means of the thread which Ariadne, the king's daughter, left for him to follow.

But King Minos became displeased with Daedalus and, fearing that he would go back to his own country and perhaps offer others the benefit of his inventive skill, he locked him up together with his son, Icarus, in a high tower overlooking the sea. And everywhere about the island the king set guards to prevent them slipping away secretly.

As the weeks of captivity dragged on, Daedalus became more and more restless and his thoughts turned to escape. It would be hard enough to break out of the tower, but to steal unnoticed to the coast and lay hands on a boat would be well-nigh impossible. Everyone everywhere knew the famous inventor and his son. They would both be recognized as soon as they set foot in the street. Even if he made some kind of disguise it was unlikely to fool the king's guards who were themselves under threat of death should they allow the prisoners to get free. Very well, then, thought Daedalus, since it's impossible to escape by land and sea, what other ways are there? He considered for a while and then looked up into the sky and a smile dawned across his face. King Minos might keep close watch on the shores, but not even he could guard the air. Daedalus, who believed he could make anything, decided to make wings.

For several days he brooded on the problem, considering the movement of the air and the weight and extent of the wingspan that would be necessary to lift a human body. Watching the gulls as they took off or landed, doing calculations in the dust on the floor, slowly the plan took shape in his mind. Only then did he tell Icarus. The boy was thrilled with the idea, and the two of them put their heads together to find a way of getting hold of the necessary quantity of feathers. For a while the problem seemed hopeless and they began to despair, when the boy came up with an idea. The old woman who brought the milk from the farm—she kept chickens and geese didn't she? What did she do with the feathers? This was to be the solution.

And so, as the weeks went by, they gathered dozens and dozens of all kinds of feathers from the old farm woman, telling her they were making a pair of mattresses.

The feathers were laid out, from the smallest to the largest in the shape of wings, each group of feathers carefully arranged and overlapping like the reeds in a shepherd's pipe. The largest feathers were fixed together with the thicker threads from the string, others with finer threads from their clothing, and the smallest feathers

Daedalus welded together with wax from the candles.

Then Daedalus made a second pair of wings for Icarus, which of course the lad wanted to try out right away.

'No,' said his father. 'We must wait for favourable winds. We are not like birds, used to flying. We don't have enough strength in our muscles. We must rely on gliding and moving into warm currents of air to get the necessary lift. It would be foolish to venture out until the conditions are absolutely right.'

At last the right day came and Daedalus told his son to prepare the wings. Icarus couldn't wait.

'You must follow me closely at all times,' Daedalus said. 'Remember not to glide too low or the spray from the sea will clog the feathers of your wings. And if you soar too high in the heavens the sun will scorch the wax. The wings are well made, but they are only as good as the flier.' And then he leapt from the battlements and circled twice round the tower beckoning Icarus to follow him. Together they beat their wings faster and faster and rose high over the tower and above the morning mists.

No words can create the sense of delight the boy felt at this. During the last weeks he had dreamt many times of flying, but in his dreams he was always prevented from rising into the air. Always something held him back. But this was different. This was unrestrained, ecstatic flight. There was nothing holding him now. And Daedalus himself, careful though he was, could not resist the thrill of gliding high above the still sleeping world, twisting and banking and diving. The wind roared in their ears as they swooped down and the craftsman had to fight with his own nature to resist the skyriding acrobatics into which free movement in the air seemed to lure him. He yelled through the rushing wind for Icarus to come alongside him and keep a steady course. In his excitement he had almost forgotten that they were trusting their lives to nothing more than feathers, wax and string. With the powerful tensions on the wings as they plunged or pulled out of a dive, they were taking such risks as Daedalus feared to calculate. If a thread broke, if the wax gave, they would plummet not only back into captivity, but into certain death.

As the sun came up the mist began to clear. And now they could see the wonders of the island from the air. The fields, the green patches of vineyards, the grey olive trees so small as to look like tiny silver flowers and the day breaking into magnificence over streams and woods—these, let alone the wind, were enough to take the lad's breath away. For the first time, his joy in the activity of flying gave way to the thrill of what he saw beneath him. The town with its grey and creamy sun-drenched buildings, the massive palace of King Minos and the elaborate marble entrance to the labyrinth, and beyond that the circular arena where the bull contests took place, were all laid out like a model before him.

The two were silent in admiration as they flew over the sleeping city, but once above the countryside they could see shepherds and early workers in the fields who looked up amazed at what was taking place above their heads and, believing they were being visited by the gods, fell to their knees in astonished adoration.

Icarus swooped low, laughing at the shepherds and showing off his growing skill. But his father called out to him:

'Come back . . . it's dangerous to fly so low . . .' His words were lost on the wind and he had to swoop down himself to join the boy and insist that they maintained a safer level.

Soon they were over the coast and at last out at sea. For a while Daedalus breathed freely again. At least they had escaped from the island and the power of King Minos. The problem now was to prevent the boy from doing anything silly. The day was clear. There was enough wind, but not too much to make flying difficult, and if you were cautious and adroit in handling the wings and held your position in relation to the drifts of warm air, you could cruise into an upflowing current and glide holding the air beneath you. This made it possible to relax a little since the constant fluctuating of the wings was exhausting. Daedalus realized now how powerful must be those delicate muscles of a bird to sustain it on such long flights. He thought of the seabirds, the petrels, the albatrosses flying for hours on end, days even, if the sea were too rough to make it possible to settle on the water.

While these thoughts were turning over in the craftsman's head, his son was luxuriating in the thrill of his newfound mastery of the air, and despite his father's constant warnings he began to soar grandly, sometimes catching an upward drift and going to the very limit before letting himself plunge towards the green pellucid sea rushing up to meet him. But they were far out now, passing over small islands, some of which had mountains or hills and the changing surface made flying a more uncertain business since the air currents could be unpredictable. Icarus ignored the calls of his father; he was enjoying himself too much. He began to roam the sky higher and higher until he was way above Daedalus. Looking up, the craftsman knew it was impossible for him to reach the boy quickly enough should anything go wrong. Yet still he called desperately into the wind and beat his wings faster and faster.

'Icarus ... don't ... Icarus ... the sun ... the heat ...' But now Icarus had quite forgotten all that his father had told him and was soaring still higher on a warm airstream that was lifting him splendidly into the heavens. But too far. The intense heat of the glowing sun as it rose in the sky began to melt the wax. The smaller feathers were dislodged, the carefully constructed pattern of the wings was altered and the balance changed so that the boy began to detect a difference. He was falling, losing control. He was in conflict with the wind, now plunging faster, more dangerously, and then spiralling, twisting and turning headlong through the vortex of air which began to sear his face. And he felt his hair was being torn out by the roots and his arms pulled from their sockets.

From above, Daedalus watched helplessly as his son fell out of the sky. He tried to dive to rescue the boy but it was too late. He saw the white of the feathers, growing smaller and smaller until they were hardly visible, and finally a tiny burst of white foam against the bluey-green showed where the boy had hit the water. And then nothing.

Now Daedalus himself was falling towards the sea, his own eyes streaming to the point where he could no longer make out what was beneath him. As he came dangerously close to the water he pulled back out of the steep dive and drew level with the surface. The waves were calm but there was no trace of his son. Again and again he circled, searching the waters until at last a few feathers broke the surface, and finally the body itself was there, floating brokenly like a fallen bird.

Hovering above the waves, with infinite care Daedalus gathered up the body, and laboriously, painfully he flew to the nearest land where he buried the boy. It was then an unknown island and he named it Icaria after the lad. Heavy with grief, Daedalus made his way westwards to Cumae in Italy where he mourned for Icarus, building a temple there with a golden roof dedicated to Apollo, god of the air. And there he hung up the wings which had so miraculously enabled him to escape, and which, through the boy's reckless delight in their power, had caused the death of his son.

BARRY MAYBURY

The Aeronautics of Leonardo da Vinci

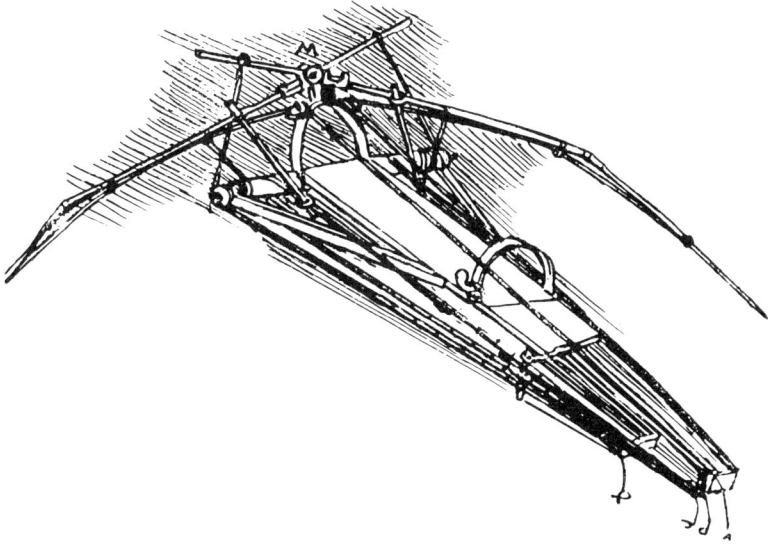

Type A, prone ornithopter, with alternate action of the legs to lower and raise the wings: 1486–90.

In most of Leonardo's developed ideas for ornithopter flight, each of his wings comprises the structure of a main spar, to which are added one or more articulated 'fingers', which hinge downwards from the end of the spar. In order to get the 'rowing' action of the wings—downwards and backwards—which he thought birds employed for propulsion, Leonardo generally arranged for the wing-spar and finger(s) to be collectively twisted, so that the down-beating fingers—operated by cables running out from pulleys on the central supporting member—in fact beat both downwards and backwards, thus simultaneously producing a lift component and a thrust component. He also provided for a bird-type tail-unit, and went on from there to a cruciform type.

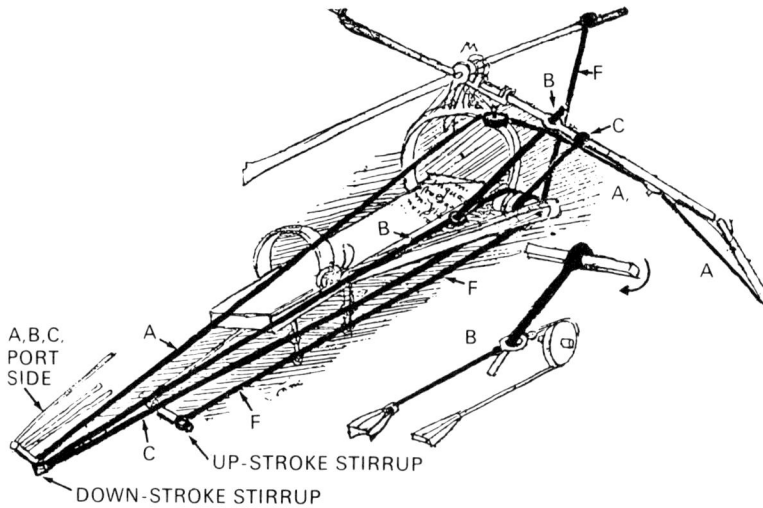

A,B,C,
PORT
SIDE

A

B

A₁

A

B

F

B

F

C

F

UP-STROKE STIRRUP

DOWN-STROKE STIRRUP

Type A, prone ornithopter, annotated and drawn over to show the cable runs: c. 1487.

Leonardo's typical wing-operation therefore involved three simultaneous movements, *i.e.* (a) beating down; (b) twisting; and (c) the added beating down of the finger(s), which—by virtue of the twisting—beat backwards as well. I have included one of Leonardo's drawings, which I have drawn-over and annotated. Here the stirrup effecting the downstroke simultaneously involves these three movements: cable C pulls down the spar; B twists the spar (Leonardo includes a separate sketch of this system, just below the main drawing); and A, *via* a pulley on the support, runs out to the finger, and pulls it down, which—owing to the twisting movement of B—beats both downwards and backwards. The stirrup in this drawing which effects the upstroke, operates the cables FF, which pull down the extensions of the two spars beyond their fulcrum, and hence raise the two wings, whilst twisting back the spars to their normal 'resting' position.

from The Aeronautics of Leonardo da Vinci
by CHARLES H. GIBBS-SMITH

24th August, Anno Domini 79

In the middle of August A.D. 79, there were signs that Vesuvius was again about to erupt, but since Vesuvius was often active, at first there was no alarm. On the forenoon of the 24th, however, it became clear that a disaster of unparalleled dimensions was in the making. The top of the mountain split apart with a thunderous explosion. Smoke mushroomed into the sky, darkening the sun. A rain of volcanic cinder and ashes began to sift down, amid terrific crashes and terrifying flashes of light. Birds tumbled dead out of the air, people ran about screaming, animals slunk into hiding. Meanwhile torrents of water rushed through the streets, and no one could tell whether they came from the sky or out of the earth.

This violence descended on the two cities of Pompeii and Herculaneum during the busy, sunny hours of early morning and worked their total destruction in two different ways. An avalanche of mud—a mixture of volcanic ash, rain, and lava—poured massively over Herculaneum, forcing its way into streets and alleys, rising higher and higher, and always increasing in pressure. The flow covered roofs, ran in through doors and windows, and eventually filled Herculaneum as water fills a sponge. Everything and everyone not immediately evacuated was buried deep.

At Pompeii it was different. Here there was no flood of slime; disaster began with a light fall of ash, so light that people were able to brush the powdery dust off their shoulders. Soon however, lapilli began to come down, then occasional bombs of pumice weighing many pounds. The extent of the danger was only gradually revealed, and only when it was too late. Clouds of sulphur fumes settled down on the city. They seeped through cracks and crevices and billowed up under the cloths that the suffocating townsfolk held up to their faces. If they ran outdoors seeking air and freedom, they were met by a thick hail of lapilli that drove them back in terror to the shelter of their homes. Roofs caved in, whole families were buried. Others were spared for a time. For a half-hour or so they crouched in fear and trembling under stairs and arched doors. The fumes reached them, and they choked to death.

The sun came out twenty-eight hours later, but by this time Pompeii and Herculaneum had ceased to exist. For a distance of eleven miles around, the landscape had been destroyed. Clouds of ash were borne by air currents as far as Africa, Syria, and Egypt. Yet now nothing but a thin column of smoke issued from Vesuvius, smudging the lovely blue dome of sky.

from Gods, Graves and Scholars by C. W. CERAM

lapilli: small fragments of volcanic rock

There will come soft rains

In the living-room the voice-clock sang, *Tick-tock, seven o'clock, time to get up, time to get up, seven o'clock!* as if it were afraid that nobody would. The morning house lay empty. The clock ticked on, repeating its sounds into the emptiness. *Seven-nine, breakfast time, seven-nine!*

In the kitchen the breakfast stove gave a hissing sigh and ejected from its warm interiors eight pieces of perfectly browned toast, eight eggs sunny-side up, sixteen slices of bacon, two coffees, and two cool glasses of milk.

'Today is August 4, 2026,' said a second voice from the kitchen ceiling, 'in the city of Allendale, California.' It repeated the date three times for memory's sake. 'Today is Mr Featherstone's birthday. Today is the anniversary of Tilita's marriage. Insurance is payable, as are the water, gas, and light bills.'

Somewhere in the walls, relays clicked, memory tapes glided under electric eyes.

Eight-one, tick-tock, eight-one o'clock, off to school, off to work, run, run, eight-one! but no doors slammed, no carpets took the soft tread of rubber heels. It was raining outside. The weather box on the front door sang quietly: 'Rain, rain, go away; rubbers, raincoats for today ...' And the rain tapped on the empty house, echoing.

Outside, the garage chimed and lifted its door to reveal the waiting car. After a long wait the door swung down again.

At eight-thirty the eggs were shrivelled and the toast was like stone. An aluminium wedge scraped them into the sink, where hot water whirled them down a metal throat which digested and flushed them away to the distant sea. The dirty dishes were dropped into a hot washer and emerged twinkling dry.

Nine-fifteen, sang the clock, *time to clean.*

Out of warrens in the wall, tiny robot mice darted. The rooms were a-crawl with the small cleaning animals, all rubber and metal.

They thudded against chairs, whirling their moustached runners, kneading the rug nap, sucking gently at hidden dust. Then, like mysterious invaders, they popped into their burrows. Their pink electric eyes faded. The house was clean.

Ten o'clock. The sun came out from behind the rain. The house stood alone in a city of rubble and ashes. This was the one house left standing. At night the ruined city gave off a radioactive glow which could be seen for miles.

Ten-fifteen. The garden sprinklers whirled up in golden founts, filling the soft morning air with scatterings of brightness. The water pelted window-panes, running down the charred west side where the house had been burned evenly free of its white paint. The entire west face of the house was black, save for five places. Here the silhouette in paint of a man mowing a lawn. Here, as in a photograph, a woman bent to pick flowers. Still farther over, their images burned on wood in one titanic instant, a small boy, hands flung into the air; higher up, the image of a thrown-ball, and opposite him a girl, hands raised to catch a ball which never came down.

The five spots of paint—the man, the woman, the children, the ball—remained. The rest was a thin charcoaled layer.

The gentle sprinkler rain filled the garden with falling light.

Until this day, how well the house had kept its peace! How carefully it had inquired, 'Who goes there? What's the password?' and, getting no answer from lonely foxes and whining cats, it had shut up its windows and drawn shades in an old-maidenly preoccupation with self-protection which bordered on a mechanical paranoia.

It quivered at each sound, the house did. If a sparrow brushed a window, the shade snapped up. The bird, startled, flew off! No, not even a bird must touch the house!

The house was an altar with ten thousand attendants, big, small, servicing, attending, in choirs. But the gods had gone away, and the ritual of the religion continued senselessly, uselessly.

Twelve noon.

A dog whined, shivering, on the front porch.

The front door recognized the dog voice and opened. The dog, once huge and fleshy, but now gone to bone and covered with sores, moved in and through the house, tracking mud. Behind it whirred angry mice, angry at having to pick up mud, angry at inconvenience.

For not a leaf fragment blew under the door but what the wall-panels flipped open and the copper scrap rats flashed swiftly out. The offending dust, hair, or paper, seized in miniature steel jaws, was raced back to the burrows. There, down tubes which fed into the cellar, it was dropped into the sighing vent of an incinerator which sat like evil Baal in a dark corner.

The dog ran upstairs, hysterically yelping to each door, at last realizing, as the house realized, that only silence was here.

It sniffed the air and scratched the kitchen door. Behind the door, the stove was making pancakes which filled the house with a rich baked odour and the scent of maple syrup.

The dog frothed at the mouth, lying at the door, sniffing, its eyes turned to fire. It ran wildly in circles, biting at its tail, spun in a frenzy, and died. It lay in the parlour for an hour.

Two o'clock, sang a voice.

Delicately sensing decay at last, the regiments of mice hummed out as softly as blown grey leaves in an electrical wind.

Two-fifteen.

The dog was gone.

In the cellar, the incinerator glowed suddenly and a whirl of sparks leaped up the chimney.

Two thirty-five.

Bridge tables sprouted from patio walls. Playing-cards fluttered on to pads in a shower of pips. Martinis manifested on an oaken bench with egg-salad sandwiches. Music played.

But the tables were silent and the cards untouched.

At four o'clock the tables folded like great butterflies back through the panelled walls.

Four-thirty.

The nursery walls glowed.

Animals took shape: yellow giraffes, blue lions, pink antelopes, lilac panthers cavorting in crystal substance. The walls were glass. They looked out upon colour and fantasy. Hidden films clocked through well-oiled sprockets, and the walls lived. The nursery floor was woven to resemble a crisp, cereal meadow. Over this ran aluminium roaches and iron crickets, and in the hot, still air butterflies of delicate red tissue wavered among the sharp aroma of animal spoors! There was the sound like a great matted yellow hive of bees within a dark bellows, the lazy bumble of a purring lion. And there was the patter of okapi feet and the murmur of a fresh jungle rain, like other hoofs, falling upon the summer-starched grass. Now the walls dissolved into distances of parched weed, mile on mile, and warm, endless sky. The animals drew away into thornbrakes and water-holes.

It was the children's hour.

Five o'clock. The bath filled with clear hot water.

Six, seven, eight o'clock. The dinner dishes manipulated like magic tricks, and in the study a *click*. In the metal stand opposite the hearth where a fire now blazed up warmly, a cigar popped out, half an inch of soft grey ash on it, smoking, waiting.

Nine o'clock. The beds warmed their hidden circuits, for nights were cool here.

Nine-five. A voice spoke from the study ceiling:

'Mrs McClellan, which poem would you like this evening?'

The house was silent.

The voice said at last, 'Since you express no preference, I shall select a poem at random.' Quiet music rose to back the voice. 'Sara Teasdale. As I recall, your favourite. . . .

'There will come soft rains and the smell of the ground,
The swallows circling with their shimmering sound;

And frogs in the pools singing at night,
And wild plum-trees in tremulous white;

Robins will wear their feathery fire,
Whistling their whims on a low fence-wire;

And not one will know of the war, not one
Will care at last when it is done.

Not one would mind, neither bird nor tree,
If mankind perished utterly;

And Spring herself, when she woke at dawn,
Would scarcely know that we were gone.'

The fire burned on the stone hearth and the cigar fell away into a mound of quiet ash on its tray. The empty chairs faced each other between the silent walls, and the music played.

At ten o'clock the house began to die.

The wind blew. A falling tree-bough crashed through the kitchen window. Cleaning solvent, bottled, shattered over the stove. The room was ablaze in an instant!

'Fire!' screamed a voice. The house-lights flashed, water-pumps shot water from the ceilings. But the solvent spread on the linoleum, licking, eating, under the kitchen door, while the voices took it up in chorus: 'Fire, fire, fire!'

The house tried to save itself. Doors sprang tightly shut, but the windows were broken by the heat, and the wind blew and sucked upon the fire.

146

The house gave ground as the fire in ten billion angry sparks moved with flaming ease from room to room and then up the stairs. While scurrying water-rats squeaked from the walls, pistolled their water, and ran for more. And the wall-sprays let down showers of mechanical rain.

But too late. Somewhere, sighing, a pump shrugged to a stop. The quenching rain ceased. The reserve water supply which had filled baths and washed dishes for many quiet days was gone.

The fire crackled up the stairs. It fed upon Picassos and Matisses in the upper halls, like delicacies, baking off the oily flesh, tenderly crisping the canvases into black shavings.

Now the fire lay in beds, stood in windows, changed the colours of drapes!

And then, reinforcements.

From attic trap-doors, blind robot faces peered down with faucet mouths gushing green chemical.

The fire backed off, as even an elephant must at the sight of a dead snake. Now there were twenty snakes whipping over the floor, killing the fire with a clear, cold venom of green froth.

But the fire was clever. It had sent flame outside the house, up through the attic to the pumps there. An explosion! The attic brain which directed the pumps was shattered into bronze shrapnel on the beams.

The fire rushed back into every closet and felt the clothes hung there.

The house shuddered, oak bone on bone, its bared skeleton cringing from the heat, its wire, its nerves revealed as if a surgeon had torn the skin off to let the red veins and capillaries quiver in the scalded air. Help, help! Fire! Run, run! Heat snapped mirrors like the first brittle winter ice. And the voices wailed Fire, fire, run, run, like a tragic nursery rhyme, a dozen voices, high, low, like children dying in a forest, alone, alone. And the voices fading as the wires popped their sheathings like hot chestnuts. One, two, three, four, five voices died.

In the nursery the jungle burned. Blue lions roared, purple giraffes bounded off. The panthers ran in circles, changing colour, and ten million animals, running before the fire, vanished off towards a distant steaming river....

Ten more voices died. In the last instant under the fire avalanche, other choruses, oblivious, could be heard announcing the time, playing music, cutting the lawn by remote-control mower, or setting an umbrella frantically out and in the slamming and opening front door, a thousand things happening, like a clock-shop when each clock strikes the hour insanely before or after the other, a scene of maniac confusion, yet unity; singing, screaming, a few last cleaning mice darting bravely out to carry the horrid ashes away! And one voice, with sublime disregard for the situation, read poetry aloud in the fiery study, until all the film-spools burned, until all the wires withered and the circuits cracked.

The fire burst the house and let it slam flat down, puffing out skirts of spark and smoke.

In the kitchen, an instant before the rain of fire and timber, the stove could be seen making breakfasts at a psychopathic rate, ten dozen eggs, six loaves of toast, twenty dozen bacon strips, which, eaten by fire, started the stove working again, hysterically hissing!

The crash. The attic smashing into kitchen and parlour. The parlour into cellar, cellar into sub-cellar. Deep freeze, arm-chair, film tapes, circuits, beds, and all like skeletons thrown in a cluttered mound deep under.

Smoke and silence. A great quantity of smoke.

Dawn showed faintly in the east. Among the ruins, one wall stood alone. Within the wall, a last voice said, over and over again and again, even as the sun rose to shine upon the heaped rubble and steam:

'Today is August 5, 2026, today is August 5, 2026, today is ...'

RAY BRADBURY

148

Saturn

The immense system of rings now spanned the sky, and already the ship was passing over its outermost edge. As he looked down upon them from a height of some ten thousand miles, Bowman could see through the telescope that the rings were made largely of ice, glittering and scintillating in the light of the Sun. He might have been flying over a snow-storm that occasionally cleared to reveal, where the ground should have been, baffling glimpses of night and stars.

As *Discovery* curved still closer towards Saturn, the Sun slowly descended towards the multiple arches of the rings. Now they had become a slim, silver bridge spanning the entire sky; though they were too tenuous to do more than dim the sunlight, their myriads of crystals refracted and scattered it in dazzling pyrotechnics. And as the Sun moved behind the thousand-mile-wide drifts of orbiting ice, pale ghosts of itself marched and merged across the sky, and the heavens were filled with shifting flares and flashes. Then the Sun sank below the rings, so that they framed it with their arches, and the celestial fireworks ceased.

A little later, the ship curved into the shadow of Saturn, as it made its closest approach over the night side of the planet. Above shone the stars and the rings; below lay a dimly visible sea of clouds. There were none of the mysterious patterns of luminosity that had glowed in the Jovian night; perhaps Saturn was too cold for such displays. The mottled cloudscape was revealed only by the ghostly radiance reflected back from the circling icebergs, still illuminated by the hidden Sun. But in the centre of the arch there was a wide, dark gap, like the missing span of an uncompleted bridge, where the shadow of the planet lay across its rings.

Radio contact with Earth had been broken, and could not be resumed until the ship had emerged from the eclipsing bulk of Saturn. It was perhaps as well that Bowman was too busy now to think of his suddenly enhanced loneliness; for the next few hours, every second would be occupied as he checked the braking manœuvres, already programmed by the computers on Earth.

After their months of idleness, the main thrusters began to blast out their miles-long cataracts, rivers of glowing plasma. Gravity returned, though briefly, to the weightless world of the Control Deck. And hundreds of miles below, the clouds of methane and frozen ammonia blazed with a light that they had never known before as *Discovery* swept, a fierce and tiny sun, through the Saturnian night.

At last, the pale dawn lay ahead; the ship, moving more and more slowly now, was emerging into day. It could no longer escape from the Sun, or even from Saturn—but it was still moving swiftly enough to rise away from the planet until it grazed the orbit of Japetus, two million miles out.

It would take *Discovery* fourteen days to make that climb, as she coasted once more, though in reverse order, across the paths of all the inner moons. One by one she would cut through the orbits of Mimas, Enceladus, Tethys, Dione, Rhea, Titan, Hyperion ...

worlds bearing the names of gods and goddesses who had vanished only yesterday, as time was counted here.

Then she would meet Japetus, and must make her rendezvous. If she failed, she would fall back towards Saturn, and repeat her twenty-eight-day ellipse indefinitely.

There would be no chance of a second rendezvous, if *Discovery* missed on this attempt. The next time round, Japetus would be far away, almost on the other side of Saturn.

It was true that they would meet again, when the orbits of ship and satellite meshed for a second time. But that appointment was so many years ahead that, whatever happened, Bowman knew he would not witness it.

from 2001: A Space Odyssey by ARTHUR C. CLARKE

Report Back

Galactic probe seven-thousand and four
Reports an uneventful journey, free
From any serious meteoric collisions.
Geological and radiation
Surveys are now being prepared, though our first
Instrumentation suggests little, if
Any, difficulty in setting up
The usual research apparatus.

        And looking into the void
        From the far edge of our empire
        We see the next galaxy
        A rapidly receding
        Thumb-smudge of light in a mid-
        Night violet sky pierced by the
        Dead-lights of a handful of planets,
        Red-tinged and steady like the
        Eyes of disappointed lovers,
        And our perspective's gone.

Gravity repulsion is now reduced
To a minimum, while preliminary
Spectroscopic analysis suggests
Possible vegetation, though we seem,
At present, on what is clearly a desert.

        Pock-marked with small craters
        To the edge of a ragged
        Horizon, and long-shadowed
        In what passes for a moon

On the galactic periphery,
Here is an austere beauty,
Barren, uncompromising,
Like that which must have been
Experienced by men
On the ice-caps and deserts
As they once existed on earth
Before their urbanization.
Harsh and unambiguous
It throws, as it were, a man
Into himself. Is this what
The early poets wrote about?

Our first extra-craft exploration has
Returned with specimens, one of which may
Be a new mineral. We are working
On the uranium breakdown now.
We have found, also, what appear to be
Pebbles, which suggest the action of seas,
Suggesting life, if not now, at some time.
With the spectroscopic analysis
This could prove most interesting. We will
Begin work radio-gravitation
Project immediate first light. Meanwhile,
We are now occupied with lab. work as
It is eighty hours until the next 'dawn'.
The darkness, as expected, is intense.

O the dark, the deep hard dark
Of these galactic nights!
Even the planets have set
Leaving it slab and impenetrable,

As dark and directionless
As those long nights of the soul
The ancient mystics spoke of.
Beyond there is nothing,
Nothing we have known or experienced.
It is such a dark
To be lost in which a man
Might, perhaps, find, himself.

Excessive hyperwarp has set up
A fault in our auxiliary booster,
Could you contact the depot-ship asking
To send a supply-cruiser with a spare?
And, while they are at it, some playing-cards
Or a set of Galaxtopoly with
A few of the latest girlie magazines.
Anything to kill the time.

If a man could stare out
Such a darkness and endure,
In such a darkness a man
Might, perhaps, find himself,
Scoured to the quick
In the timeless sands of the void.

Anything, as I said, to kill the time.

JOHN COTTON

Stars

A few stars are known which are hardly bigger than the earth, but the majority are so large that hundreds of thousands of earths could be packed inside each and leave room to spare; here and there we come upon a giant star large enough to contain millions of millions of earths. And the total number of stars in the universe is probably something like the total number of grains of sand on all the seashores of the world. Such is the littleness of our home in space when measured up against the total substance of the universe.

This vast multitude of stars are wandering about in space. A few form groups which journey in company, but the majority are solitary travellers. And they travel through a universe so spacious that it is an event of almost unimaginable rarity for a star to come anywhere near to another star. For the most part each voyages in splendid isolation, like a ship on an empty ocean. In a scale model in which the stars are ships, the average ship will be well over a million miles from its nearest neighbour, whence it is easy to understand why a ship seldom finds another within hailing distance.

We believe, nevertheless, that some two thousand million years ago this rare event took place, and that a second star, wandering blindly through space, happened to come within hailing distance of the earth, so this second star must have raised tides on the surface of the sun. But they would be very different from the puny tides which the small mass of the moon raises in our oceans; a huge tidal wave must have travelled over the surface of the sun, ultimately forming a mountain of prodigious height, which would rise ever higher and higher as the cause of the disturbance came nearer and nearer. And, before the second star began to recede, its tidal pull had become so powerful that this mountain was torn to pieces and threw off small fragments of itself, much as the crest of a wave throws off spray. These small fragments have been circulating around their parent sun ever since. They are the planets, great and small, of which our earth is one.

from The Mysterious Universe by Sir James Jeans

Destination Jupiter

A long silver spaceship floated around Earth ready for its giant nuclear engines to burst into life and hurl five men from their home planet into strange and unexplored regions of that endless frontier—space.

The interplanetary probe *Arcturus* was to carry the five men to their destination in this year: 2001.

The shape of the probe was a sphere joined by a long line of fuel tanks to a block at the rear which contained the reactors and three engines. It took plenty of brains to build this deep space probe and cost a thousand billion pounds.

The engines were to be fired at 0600 hours B.S.T. (British Standard Time), and result in bringing *Arcturus* to a speed of a hundred and ten thousand miles per hour. The crew of five were Neil Whittaker (mission command), Harry Scott (doctor), Jim Allen (geologist), Tom Wilson (engineer) and Fred Lancaster (electrician).

Morning came and the astronauts woke at 0100 hours B.S.T. on board the giant space station 'Orbit 5'.

The five men were debriefed and went through several medical check-ups before the small space taxi carried the five men to the *Arcturus*.

The time was 0.55955—just five seconds to go. Neil knew that in the next five seconds *Arcturus* could easily explode.

Five, four, three, two, one, zero. The three nuclear engines ignited and the giant ship drew away from the Earth and its swirling white clouds and blue sea which stretched far across the horizon and beyond.

This Earth had once been mankind's only home but now, thousands of years later, five intrepid men were making their way to another member of the solar system to spread the spirit of men's achievement of space exploration.

The *Arcturus* was now safely on its way with all parts functioning properly and the reactors shut down and though *Arcturus* would later on rely on its atomic batteries, at the moment they were using the probe's radar dish to pick up solar radiation and convert it into electricity to work the ship's computers, lights, heaters, radio, etc.

Neil spent most of his time playing a computerized game of chess with the master computer and half the time lost. One form of entertainment was, however, the colour television which was hardly ever switched on.

After twelve months, the *Arcturus* crew were farther from Earth than any other astronauts had been before and if anything went wrong there would be no hope for themselves unless they could repair whatever was wrong. The one and a half years of time to get to Jupiter were nearly over and the vast expanse of space nearly covered. The atmosphere aboard *Arcturus* was an isolated one and seemed to grow. However, one morning there was great excitement, as their destination came nearer.

Jupiter was a huge crescent with its slowly moving moons aligned in a row as if guarding the planet and millions of stars glittered in the black background.

This gigantic planet had been here millions of years, watching over the birth of our species and had waited all this time for us to visit it.

Arcturus approached Jupiter and Neil prepared for the crucial moment when he would fire the retro-rockets to bring *Arcturus* into the correct orbit around Jupiter.

The retro burn was successful and *Arcturus* was soon safely in orbit. Hours passed and Tom Wilson and Jim Allen prepared for the descent in the landing module to one of Jupiter's moons, Ganymede. Jupiter itself was not to be landed on as its gravitational pull was too strong.

The landing module began its descent after unlocking with *Arcturus*.

'Ten seconds to descent engine ignition,' were Tom's excited words as the moon's gravity began to increase the module's speed. It seemed fantastic that they were these thousands of millions of miles from Earth and landing on another planet's moon. Suddenly the two astronauts felt the descent engine start up and the module began to decelerate, and caused pressure on the astronauts.

Tom had to control the module manually as the main guidance computers had failed on him.

'It handles beautifully,' he said. Both the astronauts grew tense as the yellowish landscape came nearer and their heart-beats rose to a hundred and ten a minute.

Then the trouble began. The descent engine cut out far too early and would not re-start. Tom fumbled with switches and sweat was dripping off him. The two astronauts had not suspected this and grew more and more horrified as the module gathered speed. There was no hope for them. Ganymede had a small atmosphere with air and they were going to burn up. Soon the heat grew and reached the fuel cells and there was a large explosion which ended the lives of the two men.

When the three remaining astronauts knew that Tom and Jim had been killed they were very worried and they did not know that in that reactor housing at the rear of the *Arcturus*, radiation was finding its way along the ship to reach them and destroy their minds. Already the tiny atomic particles were slowly carrying out their evil work.

Neil's mind began to empty, the crew became ill and even Harry, a qualified doctor, lost knowledge of his past medical experience.

The astronauts were going to die a very painful and slow death.

Their vision was blurred and after many hours of pain they met their death.

Somehow *Arcturus*'s engines accidentally started up and sent it out of orbit and through a time span of millions of years. *Arcturus* found its way out of the solar system through millions of stars. Perhaps one day it will find its way to another planet far away with living beings on it who will realise that they are not alone in the universe.

NICHOLAS BRITTON*

Eternity

You have often seen the sand on the seashore. How fine are its tiny grains! And how many of those tiny little grains go to make up the small handful which a child grasps in its play. Now imagine a mountain of that sand, a million miles high, reaching from the earth to the farthest heavens, and a million miles broad, extending to remotest space, and a million miles in thickness: and imagine such an enormous mass of countless particles of sand multiplied as often as there are leaves in the forest, drops of water in the mighty ocean, feathers on birds, scales on fish, hairs on animals, atoms in the vast expanse of the air: and imagine that at the end of every million years a little bird came to that mountain and carried away in its beak a tiny grain of that sand. How many millions upon millions of centuries would pass before that bird had carried away even a square foot of that mountain, how many eons upon eons of ages before it had carried away all? Yet at the end of that immense stretch of time not even one instant of eternity could be said to have ended. At the end of all those billions and trillions of years eternity would have scarcely begun. And if that mountain rose again after it had been all carried away and if the bird came again and carried it all away again grain by grain: and if it rose and sank as many times as there are stars in the sky, atoms in the air, drops of water in the sea, leaves on the trees, feathers upon birds, scales upon fish, hairs upon animals, at the end of all those innumerable risings and sinkings of that immeasurably vast mountain not one single instant of eternity could be said to have ended; even then, at the end of such a period, after that eon of time the mere thought of which makes our very brain reel dizzily, eternity would scarcely have begun.

from Portrait of the Artist as a Young Man by JAMES JOYCE

160

The Future

The Future does not look like this...

you
are
here

PAST   FUTURE   END

PRESENT

The Future looks more like this...

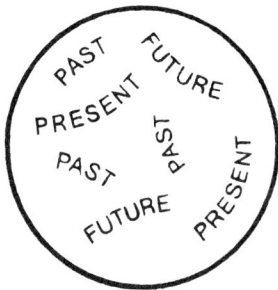

PAST FUTURE
PRESENT
PAST PAST
FUTURE PRESENT

or this...

PAST PRESENT FUTURE
PRESENT FUTURE PAST PRESENT
PAST PRESENT FUTURE PAST
FUTURE PRESENT FUTURE
PAST PRESENT

you
are
or this... here

ROGER McGOUGH

List of Illustrations

Acknowledgements

The editor wishes to thank the following for permission to include copyright material.

Charles Berlitz: Extract from *The Bermuda Triangle*. Reprinted by permission of Souvenir Press Ltd. **Ray Bradbury:** Extract from *The Silver Locusts*, copyright 1950 by Ray Bradbury, renewed 1977. Reprinted by permission of the Harold Matson Company, Inc; **Betsy Byars:** Extract from *The Midnight Fox*. Reprinted by permission of Faber & Faber Ltd; **C. W. Ceram:** Extract from *Gods, Graves and Scholars*. Reprinted by permission of Victor Gollancz Ltd. **Stanley Cerely:** Extract from *The Gyr Falcon Adventure*. Reprinted by permission of Collins, Publishers; **Arthur C. Clarke:** Extract from *2001: A Space Odyssey*. Reprinted by permission of the Hutchinson Publishing Group Ltd; **Jim Corbett:** Extract from *The Man Eaters of Kumaon* (1944). Reprinted by permission of Oxford University Press; **John Cotton:** From *Old Movies and other poems* (Chatto & Windus). Reprinted by permission of the author; **Kevin Crossley-Holland:** Extract from *The Battle of Malden and other Anglo-Saxon Poems* (Macmillan). Reprinted by permission of the author and Deborah Rogers Ltd; **T. S. Eliot:** From *Poems Written in Early Youth*. Reprinted by permission of Faber & Faber Ltd; **Jana Garai:** Extract from *The Book of Symbols*. Reprinted by permission of Lorrimer Publishing; **William Golding:** Extract from *The Spire*. Reprinted by permission of Faber & Faber Ltd; **Robert Graves:** From *Penny Fiddle*. Reprinted by permission of the author and A. P. Watt Ltd; **A. L. Hendricks:** From *On This Mountain*. Reprinted by permission of André Deutsch. **Gordon Hodgeon:** First appeared in *Platform Poets*,3 (editor, Geoff Tomlinson). Reprinted by permission of the author. **Christine Hole:** Extract from *English Sports and Pastimes*. Reprinted by permission of B. T. Batsford Ltd; **Richard Hughes:** Extract from *A Moment in Time* (Chatto). Reprinted by permission of David Higham Associates Ltd; **Ted Hughes:** From *Season Songs*. Reprinted by permission of Faber & Faber Ltd; **James Jeans:** Extract from *The Mysterious Universe*. Reprinted by permission of Cambridge University Press; **Peggy Loosemore Jones:** First appeared in *Platform Poets* (editor, Geoff Tomlinson). Reprinted by permission of the author; **James Joyce:** Extract from *A Portrait of the Artist as a Young Man*. Reprinted by permission of Jonathan Cape Ltd. on behalf of the Executors of the James Joyce Estate; **Laurie Lee:** Extract from *As I Walked Out One Midsummer Morning*. Reprinted by permission of André Deutsch; **Roger McGough:** 'Power of Poets' from *Gig* (Cape), copyright © 1973 by Roger McGough; 'Autumn Poem' and 'The Future' both from *In the Classroom* (Cape), copyright © 1976 by Roger McGough. Reprinted by permission of Hope Leresche and Sayle; **John Masefield:** From *Collected Poems* (Macmillan). Reprinted by permission of The Society of Authors as the literary representative of the Estate of John Masefield; **Markus Natten:** From *Children as Writers*, 6 (ed. W. H. Smith & Son). Reprinted by permission of Heinemann Educational Books Ltd; **Norman Nicholson:** Extract from *A Local Habitation* (Faber). Reprinted by permission of David Higham Associates Ltd; **George Orwell:** From *Homage to Catalonia* (1951). Reprinted by permission of A. M. Heath & Co Ltd. for Mrs Sonia Brownell Orwell, and Martin Secker & Warburg as publishers; **Ezra Pound:** From *Collected Shorter Poems*. Reprinted by permission of Faber & Faber Ltd; **David Raven:** Extract from *Stories from Homer* (1973). Reprinted by permission of Oxford University Press; **A. M. Rendel:** From *Appointment in Crete*. Reprinted by permission of the author; **Damon Runyan:** Extract from *Guys and Dolls*. Reprinted by permission of Constable Publishers; **William Sansom:** From *The Stories of William Sansom* (Hogarth Press), © William Sansom 1963. Reprinted by permission of Elaine Greene Ltd; **George Bernard Shaw:** Extracts from *Androcles and the Lion* (Constable). Reprinted by permission of The Society of Authors on behalf of the Bernard Shaw Estate; **Stevie Smith:** From *The Collected Poems of Stevie Smith* (Allen Lane). Reprinted by permission of James MacGibbon, Executor; **Dylan Thomas:** Extract from *Under Milk Wood* (Dent). Reprinted by permission of David Higham Associates Ltd. for The Trustees for the Copyrights of the late Dylan Thomas; **Frank Usher:** Extracts from *Fifty Great Journeys*. Reprinted by permission of the Hamlyn Publishing Group Limited; **Arthur Waley:** From *Chinese Poems*. Reprinted by permission of George Allen & Unwin (Publ.) Ltd; **Patrick White:** Extracts from *The Tree of Man* (Cape). Reprinted by permission of Curtis Brown (Aust.) Pty. Ltd; **B. W. G. Wilson** and **D. J. D. Miller:** Extracts from *Stories from Herodotus* (adapted & translated by B. W. J. G. Wilson and D. J. D. Miller, 1973). Reprinted by permission of Oxford University Press.

The editor would also like to thank the following for permission to reproduce poems:

The Headmaster, Hattersley Comprehensive School for 'When Candle Light' by Heather Dockery, from *Festival Writing*; Manchester Education Committee for 'Mist' by Yasmeen Thompson, and 'The Dock' by David Deen, both from *Early Lines*; J. Perrett, Headmaster, Upper Arley School, Worcs. for 'Destination Jupiter' by Nicholas Britton.

Although every effort has been made to trace all copyright owners, this has not always been possible; if they contact the Publisher, correct acknowledgement will be made in future editions.

163

Thematic Index